Praise for *Now We're*

'Having the right conversation is at
book shows how to do this, with]
adopt. This gives new ways to rel.
and board meetings.'

> Dr Andrew White, Senior Fellow in Management
> Practice, Saïd Business School, University of Oxford;
> CEO of Transcend.Space; 2050 Leadership Podcast Host

'Read this book if you want to expand you ability to have the important or difficult conversations - whether with yourself, in your private life or at work. A skill so important right now and none better to lead us to success than Sarah!'

> Alexander Hiller, Managing Director,
> Russell Reynolds Associates

'Cultivating the right mindset for engaging in authentic dialogue is essential for effective leadership in today's complex and dynamic world. In an age of profound "polycrisi"', *Now We're Talking* is a must-read for those truly focused on the power of purpose and what matters most.'

> David Hartman, Ambassador of Canada to the Philippines

'Much of my work consists of enabling conversation, often challenging conversation, among senior leaders in the church. This book is both inspiration and tonic – full of ideas which I hope to imitate and adapt, while at the same time nailing and calming the fears which could otherwise derail. Thank you, Sarah!'

> The Rt Revd Dr Jo Bailey Wells, Bishop for
> Episcopal Ministry in the Anglican Communion;
> Deputy Secretary General

'JFK once said "Leadership and learning are indispensable to each other". This book provides the ideal basis for those in leadership and management positions to reflect on what more they can to develop their skills, become an active listener and learn how to effect positive change.'

Professor Sir Anton Muscatelli, Principal and Vice-Chancellor, University of Glasgow

'*Now We're Talking* builds your understanding and grows your skillset with its step-by-step process to having richer, more connected conversations. A wonderful toolkit for tackling those difficult conversations – with your boss, employees, family or in your personal relationships – with confidence.'

Niamh Dowling, Principal and CEO, RADA

'Eminently practical, this beautifully researched, accessible book is an absolute must for any leader wanting to handle difficult conversations with greater care and skill. The tools shared here are easy to follow and have the potential to be real game changers for those wise enough to try them out.'

Paul Williamson, Group Head of Talent Development, Ambassador Theatre Group

'Sarah balances insight that prompts self-reflection and deep thinking with practical tools and suggestions that will help leaders with day-to-day situations. Highly readable and full of engaging exemplification from modern culture, familiar examples of leadership, and Sarah's own experience, *Now We're Talking* makes a compelling case for talking more and doing it better.'

Annie Crombie, Deputy CEO, BookTrust

'A wonderful, practical guide for taking a team or an organisation from struggling to good to great to excellent. *Now We're Talking* puts words to what I didn't realise I did to build a culture of trust by creating safe spaces to talk, share and learn.'

                      Paul Allen, CEO and Trustee, Vibrance

'This book will give you a step-by-step guide to mastering the magic of dialogue that transcends conflicts and dissolves problems with the power of your own authenticity.'

                      Dr. Harvey Z. Chen, Chairman of the board of advisors, Center for Creative Leadership, Greater China

'Sarah brings great wisdom to the vital topic of how to have the "difficult" conversations that really matter. Her wisdom is based on long experience in the field and is above all clear and immediately applicable, making this an essential handbook.'

                      Nicholas Janni, co-founder of Matrix Development; author of *Leader as Healer - a new paradigm for 21st century leadership*, Business Book Awards Business Book of the Year 2023

'The capacity for true dialogue is the key that unlocks the most pressing challenges in our personal lives, our organisations, and indeed for all of society. Having worked with senior leaders of corporates, governments, and civil society across the world, I have found that when magic and beauty are created, it is because true dialogue is enabled; when it is absent, pain, stress, broken relationships and indeed tragedy can follow. Sarah's powerful book will equip you with an extraordinary set of notions, tools, insights, and inspiration that will magnify your ability to live a joyful life and be an even stronger force for good for others, and the world.'

                      Mac McKenzie, CEO, Bridge Institute

'Having worked in many leadership roles, I cannot think of another book that has the potential for such major positive change and impact on the way leaders and employees, in every workplace, communicate. Mastering effective human dialogue sounds an easy task, yet, in practice, is possibly the most difficult challenge we face. *Now We're Talking* provides a wealth of learning in every chapter. The content is inciteful and provides the reader with clear actionable steps to improve communication in any organisation, large or small. If this had been essential reading for new leaders some years ago, the world of work would be a better place and business would be more successful and profitable.'

Gina Lodge, CEO World View Mentor, Association for Coaching UK, Africa and India Chair; member of 100 women at Davos.

'*Now We're Talking* provides invaluable advice on how to reframe and prepare for difficult conversations to get positive outcomes. A great guide using practical tools that will help navigate difficult conversations in business and in life.'

Sidone Thomas, former Chief Operating Officer at Sydney Airport

Now We're Talking

Pearson

At Pearson, we have a simple mission: to help people make more of their lives through learning.

We combine innovative learning technology with trusted content and educational expertise to provide engaging and effective learning experiences that serve people wherever and whenever they are learning.

From classroom to boardroom, our curriculum materials, digital learning tools and testing programmes help to educate millions of people worldwide – more than any other private enterprise.

Every day our work helps learning flourish, and wherever learning flourishes, so do people.

To learn more, please visit us at **www.pearson.com**

Now We're Talking

How to discuss what really matters

Sarah Rozenthuler

Harlow, England • London • New York • Boston • San Francisco • Toronto • Sydney
Dubai • Singapore • Hong Kong • Tokyo • Seoul • Taipei • New Delhi
Cape Town • São Paulo • Mexico City • Madrid • Amsterdam • Munich • Paris • Milan

PEARSON EDUCATION LIMITED
KAO Two
KAO Park
Harlow CM17 9NA
United Kingdom
Tel: +44 (0)1279 623623
Web: www.pearson.com

First edition published 2024 (print and electronic)

© Pearson Education Limited 2024 (print and electronic)

The right of Sarah Rozenthuler to be identified as author of this work has been asserted by her in accordance with the Copyright, Designs and Patents Act 1988.

The print publication is protected by copyright. Prior to any prohibited reproduction, storage in a retrieval system, distribution or transmission in any form or by any means, electronic, mechanical, recording or otherwise, permission should be obtained from the publisher or, where applicable, a licence permitting restricted copying in the United Kingdom should be obtained from the Copyright Licensing Agency Ltd, Barnard's Inn, 86 Fetter Lane, London EC4A1EN.

The ePublication is protected by copyright and must not be copied, reproduced, transferred, distributed, leased, licensed or publicly performed or used in any way except as specifically permitted in writing by the publishers, as allowed under the terms and conditions under which it was purchased, or as strictly permitted by applicable copyright law. Any unauthorised distribution or use of this text may be a direct infringement of the author's and the publisher's rights and those responsible may be liable in law accordingly.

All trademarks used herein are the property of their respective owners. The use of any trademark in this text does not vest in the author or publisher any trademark ownership rights in such trademarks, nor does the use of such trademarks imply any affiliation with or endorsement of this book by such owners.

Pearson Education is not responsible for the content of third-party internet sites.

ISBN: 978-1-292-72725-7 (print)
         978-1-292-72724-0 (ePub)

British Library Cataloguing-in-Publication Data
A catalogue record for the print edition is available from the British Library

Library of Congress Cataloging-in-Publication Data
A catalog record for the print edition is available from the Library of Congress

10 9 8 7 6 5 4 3 2 1
28 27 26 25 24

Cover design by Nick Redeyoff
Cover image Qvasimodo art/Shutterstock

Print edition typeset in 10/14 pt Charter ITC Pro regular by Straive
Printed by Ashford Colour Press Ltd, Gosport

NOTE THAT ANY PAGE CROSS REFERENCES REFER TO THE PRINT EDITION

'Between what is said and not meant,
and what is meant and not said,
most of love is lost.'[1]
Kahlil Gibran

'Come, be human. Sit down
and let's talk.'
William Stafford[2]

While we work hard to present unbiased, fully accessible content, we want to hear from you about any concerns or needs with this Pearson product so that we can investigate and address them:

- Please contact us with concerns about any potential bias at https://www.pearson.com/report-bias.html
- For accessibility-related issues, such as using assistive technology with Pearson products, alternative text requests, or accessibility documentation, email the Pearson Disability Support team at **disability.support@pearson.com**

Contents

About the author — xv
Author's acknowledgements — xvi
Publisher's acknowledgements — xix
What this book is about — xxiv

Part 1 The foundations — **1**
1. Why dialogue matters — 3
2. What stops us from talking — 21
3. What every conversation needs — 45
4. Turn down the heat — 65

Part 2 The four secrets — **85**
5. Find your ground — 87
6. Build a bridge — 103
7. Read the room — 129
8. Hold space — 151

Part 3 Dialogic leadership in action — 179
9. Lead change through dialogue — 181
10. Conversations about purpose — 209

Afterword — 239
Index — 243

List of exercises

Exercise 1	Conversation continuum	14
Exercise 2	What is a difficult conversation?	24
Exercise 3	Find time to talk	26
Exercise 4	Dealing with a difficult person	27
Exercise 5	Taking stock of obstacles	36
Exercise 6	Create a container	50
Exercise 7	Notice your triggers	70
Exercise 8	Shift from reactivity to creativity	79
Exercise 9	Left-hand column case	93
Exercise 10	Beginning a difficult conversation	99
Exercise 11	Deepening your listening	115
Exercise 12	Generate a great outcome	121
Exercise 13	Your conversational profile	139
Exercise 14	Intervening in your team	147

List of exercises

Exercise 15	Hold a 'check-in'	159
Exercise 16	Change the choreography	173
Exercise 17	Identify your most critical conversation	188
Exercise 18	Activate the four principles of dialogue	202
Exercise 19	Organisational purpose reality check	215
Exercise 20	Dialogue to unpack an organisation's purpose	224
Exercise 21	Explore alternative roles	227

About the author

Sarah Rozenthuler is a world-renowned speaker, leadership consultant and dialogue coach. As a chartered psychologist, she has over 20 years' experience working in organisations across the world in the public, private and not-for-profit sectors. With her expertise as an executive coach, team coach and facilitator of board meetings, Sarah supports leaders to catalyse positive change in their teams, organisations and wider communities. She is the author of two critically acclaimed books, *How to Have Meaningful Conversations* and *Powered by Purpose*.

At Saïd Business School, University of Oxford, Sarah is on the faculty of the Advanced Management and Leadership Programme. She teaches dialogue skills and supports leaders to have the conversations that matter most. Sarah founded Bridgework Consulting in 2007 to strengthen connections between leaders, enabling them to do great work together. She equips purpose-led leaders to inspire their people and take their organisation on a journey to become a force for good in the world.

Author's acknowledgements

Thank you to the many people in organisations with whom I've worked over the years. You are all woven into the writing here. I've had the great privilege of working with many courageous clients, inspiring leaders and dialogic practitioners who I thank for all the learning, insights and ideas. Without these experiences, this would be a book about theory only rather than the lived experience of making change happen through dialogue.

Deep gratitude to the many friends and colleagues who have supported and challenged me over the last 25 years. A particular thank you to Cliff Penwell for his soul-enriching friendship and generosity. Cliff, a wise and wonderful dialogue practitioner and editor, read an earlier version of this book and brought precision, intelligence and inspiration to what I'd written. I want to especially acknowledge Peter Owen for holding my feet to the fire and for reviewing every chapter, providing incisive insights to add bite, fluidity and dynamism. A heartfelt thank you to Tricia Grace-Norton for her eagle eye, which improved the book immeasurably. Our coaching conversations have been a bedrock and gave me the energy and encouragement to keep going while managing a full work schedule.

I also want to thank others who found the time to help shape my ideas, including for the title (which, in the end, came as a flash of intuition, aided by their input). Special thanks to Becky Hall, Emily Hunt, Michael Cahill, Mike Wilson and Tom Hunt. I'm truly grateful for the interest that Louise Davison showed from the very start and for her insights about making difficult conversations a success on the corporate pitch when the pressure is on.

Fellow writers have provided valuable feedback. I particularly appreciate novelist Ellie Porter's sensitive critique of Chapter 6, Build a bridge. It's been super to learn also from poet Michael Woods and young adult fiction writer Olivia Levez as well as the other students at the Inkwell writing retreats I've attended. I've been fortunate to benefit from Roger Cross and Tia Azulay reading my work with immense care over the years to ensure that what I was writing reflected 'me' to the best of my ability.

Several colleagues and clients have helped me enormously to extend my consulting practice. Dr Claus Springborg has been an amazing co-leader of the dialogue programmes we've co-created, including for participants in the China region. Sarah-Jane Menato has deepened my appreciation of how dialogue helps us to build good 'endings' muscle during these disruptive times. Paul Sandham, who has been a friend and colleague for over 20 years, has brought light, laughter and a love of making dialogue happen. Dawn Gosden, a fellow chartered psychologist, has brought many a smile and helped me to hone my coaching skills. Damion Wonfor has been a calming presence and generous co-pilot of the group caoching programmes we've led together.

Chris Blackwell and Alberto Gonzalez Otero, my co-founders at the Purpose Collective, have been terrific co-conspirators in building global connections, along with Adrian Pagdin, prime mover at Purpose into Action. These two communities of purpose pioneers have been a source of real inspiration. Dr Andrew White, Steve Mostyn and Simon Lau at Saïd Business School, University of Oxford, have trusted me with their clients, and probably don't know how much I appreciate them. Katy Lyne, a fellow psychologist at the Church of England, has been a beacon of light in our dialogue work. Jennie McLaughlin generously shared ideas about purpose and inspiring client stories. Anne Schulze gave great encouragement to widen the reach of the book. Meryem Belqziz generously checked out cultural references and made sure I wasn't going off track. Marko Rinck and Lisa Barrett, two of my excellent Diamond Approach teachers at the Ridhwan School, have brought clarity and calmness; pure gold for writing. Ruth Harvey-Regan has been a fantastic cheerleader who helped me across the finishing line for the manuscript.

I have been very fortunate to have Eloise Cook as my hands-on editor at Pearson Education who expertly honed the book at every stage. Without Eloise's spark of an idea to commission this book, it never would have been birthed. What joy to have a book come and find me instead of having to beat a path to a publisher's door (which I've done before). Thank you too to Amer Parikh, for his marketing magic. Yashmeena Bisht managed the production of the book with great care and consideration. It's been brilliant to work with the whole team at Pearson to produce this book.

Finally, a huge thank you to my dear parents and wider family for the loving and warm 'surround' they've given me over the years: Mum and Dad, Anna and Chris, Johnty and Lucie, Emily and Tom as well as the little ones who bring such delight, Orla and Esme, Miles and Nina. And most of all to Jan Rakowicz, a true companion of body, mind and soul, who has supported me with love, patience, humour and nourishment way beyond all the meals cooked and cups of tea brewed. I am truly grateful for him allowing me all the space I needed to write and for the richness of our conversations over the years.

Publisher's acknowledgements

Image credits

1 Shutterstock: Qvasimodo art / Shutterstock; 1 Clive Sherlock: Clive Sherlock.

Text credits

8 Penguin Random House: Gibran, K. (1923), The Prophet, Alfred A. Knopf, Inc.; 32 Leadership Circle: Anderson, R. J. (2021). The Spirit of Leadership, https://leadershipcircle.com/wp-content/uploads/2021/07/Spirit-of-Leadership-Whitepaper-2021-07.pdf.; 35 McGraw Hill: Boniwell, I. and Tunariu, A. (2019) Positive Psychology: Theory, research and applications, Second edition, Open University Press.; 35 Oxford University Press.: Seligman, M. E. P. (2002) Positive psychology, positive prevention, and positive therapy. In Snyder, C. R. & Lopez, S.J. (Eds.), Handbook of Positive Psychology. Oxford University Press.; 4 Atlantic Books: Seldon, A. and Newell, R. (2023) Johnson at 10, Atlantic.; 5 Gallup, Inc: GALLUP, State of the Global Workplace 2023 Report, THE VOICE OF THE WORLD'S EMPLOYEES.; 9 John Wiley & Sons, Inc: Palmer, P. (1998) The Courage to Teach,

Publisher's acknowledgements

John Wiley & Sons.; 9 Charing Cross Press: Sanfancon, G. (2015) The Council of Equals: A guide and handbook for shared governance, Charing Cross Press.; 10 The King's Fund: Keith Grint and Clare Holt, Followership in the NHS, 2011.; 13 Informa PLC: Bohm, D. (1996). On Dialogue, London: Routledge.; 15 SAGE Publications: Deal, T. E. and Kennedy, A. A. (1983) Culture: A new look through old lenses, The Journal of Applied Behavioural Science, 19(4), pp. 498–505.; 15 Podcast Republic LLC: The Rest is Politics podcast, 16 November 2022; 16 The New York Times Company: EZRA KLEIN, The Great Delusion Behind Twitter Dec. 11, 2022, https://www.nytimes.com/2022/12/11/opinion/what-twitter-can-learn-from-quakers.html; 16 The Oxford and Cambridge Magazine: Forster E. M. (1909) 'The Machine Stops', The Oxford and Cambridge Review.; 17 A Medium Corporation: Otto Scharmer, Sep 7, 2022, Protect the Flame Circles of Radical Presence in Times of Collapse Otto Scharmer.; 21 George Eliot: Quotes by George Eliot; 28 American Psychological Association: Rogers, C. (1957) 'The necessary and sufficient conditions of therapeutic personality change', Journal of Counseling Psychology, 21, pp. 95–103.; 29 Donald Factor: Bohm D., Factor, D. and Garrett, P. (1991) Dialogue – A proposal, https://aofpd.org/library/public-resources/dialogue-a-proposal/; 30 Collins: Dictionary definition of Permacrisis; 30–31 The Financial Times Limited: Anjli Raval, Science Museum's Ian Blatchford: 'If the arts world is not careful, it will be eaten alive by its own piety, Financial Times, 27 November 2022; 33 Bob Sutton: Bob Sutton, Nov 24, 2013. If Performance Evaluations Were a Drug, They Would Not Receive F.D.A. Approval," But They Aren't Always Bad; 34 John Wiley & Sons, Inc: Lencioni, P. (2002) The Five Dysfunctions of a Team: A leadership fable, John Wiley & Sons.; 37–38 The Financial Times Limited: Chris Flood, Corporate culture ETFs aim to gain from happier employees, The Financial Times Limited, MAY 5 2023.; 38 Penguin Random House: Isaacs, W. (1999) Dialogue and the Art of Thinking Together, Currency Doubleday.; 38 Taylor & Francis: Bohm, D. (1996) On Dialogue, Routledge.; 39 Penguin Random House: Zeldin, T. (1988) Conversation, Harvill.; 39 Bloomsbury Publishing: Freire, P. (2005) Pedagogy of the Oppressed, Continuum.; 45 Bill Isaacs: Quotes by

Publisher's acknowledgements

William Isaac; 48 The Spectator: Nelson, F. (2022) Lockdown: the inside story. The Spectator, 27 August; 48 New Statesman: Cunliffe, R. (2022) Encounter with Rory Stewart, The New Statesman, 22–28 July.; 49 New Statesman: Marr, A. (2022) Politics column, The New Statesman, 22–28 July.; 52 Strategy+business: Isaacs, W. (8 February 2017) Conversations that Change the World, Strategy+Business.; 61 Shambhala Publications: Le Guin, U. (2004) The Wave in the Mind: Talks and essays on the writer, the reader, and the imagination, Shambhala Publications Inc.; 65 Richie Norton: Quotes by Richie Norton; 68 The Financial Times Limited: Andrew Edgecliffe-Johnson JULY 16 2023, LinkedIn's Ryan Roslansky: 'You can only learn how to be a CEO by being a CEO, The Financial Times Limited; 73 Neale Donald Walsch: Quotes by Neale Donald Walsch; 77 Lexundria: Marcus Aurelius, Meditations, Book 5.20; 77–78 John Wiley & Sons, Inc: Anderson, R. J. and Adams, W. A. (2016) Mastering Leadership: An integrated framework for breakthrough performance and extraordinary business results, Wiley; 87 Mark Twain: Quotes by Mark Twain; 89 Dylan Thomas: Quotes by Dylan Thomas; 90 Penguin Random House: Kross, E. (2021) Chatter: The voice in our head and how to harness it, Vermilion.; 98 O'Reilly Media, Inc: Rozenthuler, S. (2020) Powered by Purpose: Energise your people to do great work, Pearson.; 103 Margaret Wheatley: Quotes by Margaret Wheatley; 117 Penguin Random House: Isaacs, W. (1999) Dialogue and the Art of Thinking Together, Currency Doubleday.; 124 Maya Angelou: Quotes by Maya Angelou; 129 Neale Donald Walsch: Quotes by Neale Donald Walsch; 132 Kaz Nejatian: Quotes by Kaz Nejatian; 133 John Wiley & Sons, Inc.: Kantor, D. (2012) Reading the Room: Group dynamics for coaches and leaders, Jossey-Bass.; 134 LID Publishing: Janni, N. (2022) Leader as Healer: A new paradigm for 21st century leadership, LID Publishing.; 135 John Wiley & Sons, Inc.: Kantor, D. (2012) Reading the Room: Group dynamics for coaches and leaders, Jossey-Bass.; 135 John Wiley & Sons, Inc.: Adapted from David Kantor (2011) Reading the Room: Group Dynamics for Coaches and Leaders; 136 John Wiley & Sons, Inc.: Adapted from Kantor, D. (2012) Reading the Room: Group Dynamics for Coaches and Leaders. Jossey-Bass;

Publisher's acknowledgements

142 Taylor & Francis: Genovese, M. A. (2015) The Future of Leadership: Leveraging influence in an age of hyper-change (Leadership: Research and Practice), Routledge.; 143–144 Renewal Associates Limited: Transforming David Kantor's Four Player model of Team Roles. https://www.renewalassociates.co.uk/2023/06/transforming-david-kantors-four-player-model-of-team-roles/; 145 Harvard Business Publishing: Katzenbach, J. R. and Smith, D.K. (2009) The Discipline of Teams, Harvard Business Review Classics.; 147 Henry Ford: Quotes by Henry Ford; 151 Penguin Random House: Sinek, S. (2009) Start with Why: How great leaders inspire everyone to take action, NY Portfolio.; 154 John Wiley & Sons, Inc: Adapted from Lencioni, P. (2002) The Five Dysfunctions of a Team: A leadership fable. John Wiley & Sons; 162–163 Robert Frost: Quotes by Robert Frost; 163 Stephen Covey: Quotes by Stephen Covey; 167 Penguin Random House: Adapted from Scharmer's model of the Four Fields appears in Isaacs W. (1999) Dialogue and the Art of Thinking Together. Bantam Doubleday Dell Publishing Group; 173 Taylor & Francis: David Bohm, On Dialogue, Taylor & Francis; 181 Nancy Rothbard: Quotes by Nancy Rothbard; 185 Alain de Botton: Quotes by Alain de Botton; 187 Springer Nature: Horst W. J. Rittel and Melvin M. Webber, Jun., 1973 Dilemmas in a General Theory of Planning, Springer.; 188 Keith Grint: Quotes by Keith Grint; 188 Harvard Business Publishing: Ronald Heifetz and Donald L. Laurie From the Magazine (December 2001) The Work of Leadership, Harvard Business Publishing; 190 Andy Cook: Quotes by Andy Cook; 194 Penguin Random House: Adapted from William Isaacs, Dialogue and the Art of Thinking Together, Journal of Organizational Change Management, Penguin Random House; 195 Eleanor Roosevelt: Quotes by Eleanor Roosevelt; 197 Palgrave Macmillan: Mike Clayton, The Influence Agenda: A Systematic Approach to Aligning Stakeholders for Driving Change: A Systematic Approach to Aligning Stakeholders in Times of Change, Palgrave Macmillan; 209 Pablo Picasso: Quotes by Pablo Picasso; 217 Peter Drucker: Quotes by Peter Drucker; 218 Mr Feelgood: Pete Samson MAY 20, 2022, Brompton

Bike CEO Shares His Vision For Cleaner, Happier Cities, Mr Feelgood; 219 Sift Limited: Sarah Rozenthuler 2016, Systemic dialogue: a gateway to purpose-led leadership, Sift Limited; 220 Southwest Airlines: Southwest Airlines: Our Purpose and Vision; 221 Steve Jurkovich: Quotes by Steve Jurkovich; 223 Chartered Management Institute: Ebert, C., Hurth, V. and Prabhu, P., (2018) The What, the Why and the How of Purpose: A guide for leaders, Chartered Management Institute and Blueprint for Better Business White Paper, https://www.managers.org.uk/~/media/Files/Reports/Guide-for-Leaders-White-Paper.pdf.; 223 Harvard Business Publishing: Polman, P. and Winston, A. (2021) Net Positive: How courageous companies thrive by giving more than they take, Harvard Business Review Press.; 225 Margaret Mead: Quotes by Margaret Mead; 229 Penguin Random House: Isaacs(1999), Dialogue: The Art of Thinking together, Doubleday; 233 David Thoreau: Quotes by David Thoreau; 234 Oliver Wendall Holmes: Quotes by Oliver Wendall Holmes; 240 Mahatma Gandhi: Quotes by Mahatma Gandhi; 241 The White House: President Barack Obama, Remarks by the President at Rally on Health Insurance Reform, THE WHITE HOUSE September 12, 2009.; 49 William B. Isaacs: Quotes by William B. Isaacs; 194 Taylor & Francis Group: Adapted from Bohm, D. (1996). On Dialogue, London: Routledge.; 194 Dialogue Associates: Adapted from Dialogue Associates; 106 Simon Horton: Quotes by Simon Horton; 109 Currency Doubleday: Isaacs, W. (1999) Dialogue and the Art of Thinking Together, Currency Doubleday.; 114 Hodder & Stoughton: Donald Walsch, N. (1997) Conversations with God, Book 1: An uncommon dialogue, Hodder and Stoughton.; 116 William Shakespeare: Shakespeare, W. (1596) The Merchant of Venice.; 121 Anonymous: Anonymous proverb; 132 Jeremy Clarkson: Quotes by Jeremy Clarkson; 8 University of Pittsburgh Press: Stafford, W. (2014), Sound of the Ax: Aphorisms and Poems, University of Pittsburgh Press.; 3 Harvard Business Publishing: Webber, A. (1993) What's So New About the New Economy?, Harvard Business Review, January–February.

What this book is about

As a leader, do you regret how you handled a difficult conversation? Perhaps you intended to speak your truth, only to find yourself losing your temper as the stakes went up. Maybe you caved in or avoided a tricky topic altogether, and a project fell apart as a result. In all such situations, people are often left feeling frustrated that they've let themselves down, damaged a relationship or not solved the problem they were facing.

If you've botched or bottled talking about a tough topic, you are far from alone. Research has shown that about 60 per cent of managers would like to increase their confidence to have a difficult conversation[3] and 70 per cent report avoidance.[4] Surely something as seemingly insignificant as a conversation cannot cause so much consternation or serious consequences, but the evidence tells us otherwise.

The good news is that there are things you can do to improve your ability to handle difficult conversations. Even when there are fierce oppositions, festering resentments and unresolved conflicts, change is possible. In my 20-plus years' work as a dialogue coach, I've seen that shifting from disabling patterns – talking tough, talking nice or not talking at all – to a real dialogue can occur rather quickly. It all pivots on cultivating a mindset and some simple conversational skills that many managers never learned in their family of origin or anywhere else.

First, consider some situations where what I call 'authentic dialogue' is needed and see if you can relate. Although some of the details may differ from your own, perhaps there are themes that seem familiar?

- Khaleb, a country director of a development bank, needs to implement an unpopular strategy which the board has signed off. It is now non-negotiable. Senior stakeholders are resisting collaborating with each other. Khaleb needs their insights to move forward but whenever he raises the topic, all stakeholders talk about are the risks of implementation, with rolled eyes and crossed arms.

- Lizzie has recently joined a senior management team. The team leader says he's not 'command-and-control' and yet calls all the shots. When he shouts out what he wants, often with a fist hitting the table, all the other execs fall in line. Decisions unravel as objections happen but only in the corridors, not in the meeting room. Lizzie wants to shift this pattern but is at a loss about how to intervene. She's afraid that the room will fall silent if she raises the issue of team dynamics.

- Lubna needs to have a performance appraisal but struggles to talk with her boss, who's often absent. When they eventually get round to having the conversation, Lubna says it took her three days to recover as her boss's tone of voice was so negative. She's worried about the impact the conversation will have on her performance rating and even her tenure.

- Charlie is so anxious about asking for a back payment for an overdue salary increase that it's keeping him awake at night. His energy is 'flat' and a colleague recently commented that Charlie came across as withdrawn. He knows he needs to find his voice but he's struggling to even get started with asking for what he's due.

These are all situations where discussing what really matters resolved the issues. While the stories in this book are taken from my experiences with clients, I have altered identifying features and, in some cases, created composites to protect confidentiality.

Sprinkled throughout the text are a few struggles of my own with difficult conversations and how I learned to resolve them through dialogue. I didn't want to write just from the outside, as a consultant or psychologist. When I'm faced with a tough conversation, not just showing up as a facilitator, my pulsing heart, clammy palms and dry mouth up the voltage. Finding a way to talk when my 'opponent' (or inner critic) is breathing down my neck has been a masterclass in communication over many years. This book, as much a product of personal reflection as it is rooted in experience and research, will equip you with tools for talking together, whether one-on-one, in teams or in larger groups. It covers face-to-face settings and online discussions.

Why you need to read this book

Many managers don't believe they have the tools to manage a difficult conversation well. This is often an accurate assessment as they have never been helped to develop the skills. These managers, who care enough to not want to make things worse, avoid tough talk. Other managers, who incorrectly self-assess, inflate their level of skill, plough straight in, often do it badly, and create the kind of mess that reinforces the perception among others that a difficult conversation is 'too tricky' or 'not worth it'.

A difficult conversation doesn't have to lead to avoidance or aggression. In exchange for your time (and money) spent reading this book, I want you to come away with three things:

1 **Confidence.** Over half of managers report that they'd value having the confidence to talk about tricky topics, such as discussing a pay packet or letting someone go.[5] With more than half of workers saying they deal with a difficult conversation at least once a month,[6] when you finally find a way to talk successfully, it's a real boost to your vitality and sense of self-worth.

2 **Competence.** A key reason managers give for avoiding talking about what matters most is lack of know-how. There are practical tools in every chapter that will help you master the essential things to do before and during a difficult conversation. You can take these transferrable skills with you into your next project, new role and even when you go home and talk with your partner or kids.

3 **Courage.** Many managers feel powerless and afraid when faced with a difficult interaction. Sticking your head above the parapet and saying what you really think *is* risky but so is staying silent and pushing issues elsewhere. Instead of running for the hills, quaking in your boots or going all out to 'win', this book will help you to cultivate an 'I've got what it takes' mindset.

Overall, this book will enable you, as a leader, to bring a better version of yourself to work. By developing your dialogic skills and deepening your authenticity, you'll release the potential that's locked up in a stuck situation through the power of talking and thinking together.

How this book works

'You're a magician!' a client said to me at the end of a two-day leadership retreat in the Middle East. There had been 'bombs going off' in the team and there was risk of people walking away from serious issues. During our time together, everyone stayed in the room and the conversation that was needed, happened. I'm not a magician but I do have a set of tried-and-tested tools to unlock difficult conversations.

Starting with Chapter 1, each chapter contains practical exercises for you to complete so that you develop a hands-on understanding of how to discuss what really matters (see pages ix–x for a list of the exercises). Each chapter ends with 'If you do only one thing now . . . ' to keep it simple. The exercises look both at holding effective one-on-one conversations and convening group dialogues, as the necessary skills are so similar for both. The skills required to navigate complex personal conversations will serve you well in leading group dialogues.

After this Introduction are ten chapters in three sections, as follows:

> **Part 1 The foundations.** This includes the theoretical foundations for the book and insights from psychological research and the leadership literature, out of which the four secrets in Part 2 arise. These four interventions are also based on my work with hundreds of leaders, managers and teams in organisations across the world. While the focus of this book is conversation in business, I refer on occasion to conversation in families and personal relationships. The principles of good dialogue are consistent across contexts, and leaders often need to deal with the wider issues that employees bring.
>
> **Part 2 The four secrets.** At the heart of this book are four interventions that make a tough conversation possible. One of the best-kept secrets of psychology is that minimal dialogue-centred interventions can be very powerful. They support you to find steady ground inside so you're ready to talk, build a bridge across a chasm when there's conflict, 'read the room' to transform a group of talented individuals into a top-performing team and 'hold space' so that the whole is more intelligent than the individuals present.
>
> **Part 3 Dialogic leadership in action.** This describes the core principles that leaders need to embody to co-create sustainable change. It shows how leaders can deliver purpose at three levels (the organisational, team and personal) through using the most accessible tool of all: conversation.

Here's a short overview of each chapter.

In Part 1, Chapter 1 outlines why authentic dialogue matters, when it's needed and how it differs from other forms of verbal exchange. Chapter 2 explores the obstacles to having a difficult conversation including lack of time and know-how. I cover several definitions of dialogue to arrive at 'authentic dialogue' as not just a verbal exchange but an open and honest conversation that creates positive change.

In Chapter 3, I introduce the notion of a 'container', a crucial element in creating the conditions for dialogue. This is a safe and energising space that enables people to open up and talk rather than retort. Paying attention to the more intangible aspects such as your tone of voice and the atmosphere in which talking takes place makes an impossible conversation possible. In Chapter 4, I share how understanding your 'reactive tendencies' reduces the risk of you derailing the conversation and enables you to respond more effectively to someone else's defensiveness.

In Part 2 The four secrets, are four interventions that disrupt stuck patterns of thoughts, feelings and behaviours to create a flow of positive energy that supports a generative conversation. I've called these 'secrets' as they are skills that are subtle, nuanced or underused. They might be approaches you never knew existed. Perhaps you already intuitively use them, and applying them more consciously will increase your confidence. These 'secrets' uncover the hidden creative potential in a situation, whether this is to create alignment, build trust or uncover new solutions.

Part 2 moves from handling your own inner dialogue (Chapter 5), to talking with one other person (Chapter 6), to team conversations (Chapter 7) and dialogue in a group of stakeholders such as a board (Chapter 8). Difficult conversations appear in all these different contexts and no other single book covers this spectrum.

The 'arc' begins with 'Find your ground', which involves doing some inner work – the precursor to all effective dialogue. This might be frustrating for high achievers who have a bias for leaping into action to solve a problem (and if that's you, you can always jump to the later chapters). However, as Bob Anderson (author, thought leader and Leadership Circle founder) says: *'Our bias is clear – there is no organizational transformation without a preceding transformation in the consciousness of the leadership.'*[7] Self-change is the prerequisite for external change, just as self-awareness sets the scene for awareness of what is transpiring in a group setting.

Without 'finding your ground', you risk repeating the same old stuck patterns of being compliant, defiant or avoidant.

Each chapter in Part 2 covers one secret:

1. Secret one: **Find your ground** – Cultivate a steady place inside by managing your inner dialogue, discerning what's true for you and staying present.
2. Secret two: **Build a bridge** – Generate trust by listening deeply, flexing your style, surfacing unmet needs and speaking authentically.
3. Secret three: **Read the room** – Notice what's going on as people communicate in teams or small groups and bring in the 'missing vitamins' to enrich the conversation.
4. Secret four: **Hold space** – Create an expansive emotional space where stakeholders honour their differences, navigate conflict, speak candidly and allow new possibilities to emerge.

The four secrets deal with increasing levels of complexity in interpersonal interactions. Each secret builds on the former, calls for a deeper skillset and requires a shift in focus. For this reason, the chapters are best read in sequence. You can, of course, jump around and dip into the chapter that's most relevant to you (conversation itself is far from linear, after all).

The four secrets invite you to develop both your self-awareness and systemic awareness. Both are needed. When you can listen to yourself and the whole room, when you can sense your own body and the collective energy field, you create a 'vessel' which can hold the heat of difference. It is this combination of inner and outer capacities that facilitates a discussion about what really matters. If this sounds daunting, know that everyone can do this, if they take the time to slow down and tune in, before and while they talk.

Part 3 widens the focus on authentic dialogue further with 'Dialogic leadership in action'. In Chapter 9, I recast the role of the leader for these disruptive times from manager or controller to convenor, catalyst, coach and co-visionary. A different kind of dialogue arises when a leader is willing to engage in a more participative, coherent, reflective and emergent way. I cover the four key principles of a dialogic process so that sustainable change becomes possible.

Finally, in Chapter 10, we arrive at 'Conversations about purpose'. Purpose is a conversation that, as the sub-title of this book says, 'really matters'. Research shows that while 85 per cent of executives and senior management experience living their purpose at work, only 15 per cent of frontline managers and staff do. This 'purpose hierarchy gap' points to massive untapped potential.[8] Without purpose, people lack direction. With purpose, people pull together to make a difference. Discussing purpose can, however, be tricky. Some people are cynical, others dismissive, and many leaders haven't got a clue about where to start. This chapter covers tools for talking about your raison d'être so that day-to-day work becomes energising.

What's new here?

I have written at length about dialogue in my two previous books; and I cover new ground here. In *How to Have Meaningful Conversations* (2012),[9] I focus less on workplace conversations and more on personal situations, such as speaking to an estranged family member, negotiating a change to a will, and bringing an unhappy, long-term relationship to an end. To increase wellbeing, deepen your confidence to talk was the key message.

Since then, good-news stories about conversation have become popular, perhaps in response to people's increased level of anxiety about starting a conversation with a stranger post-Covid-19. 'Jumbo supermarket opens new "slow lane" so lonely customers can stop for a chat' was the headline of a 2021 news story about a Dutch supermarket opening new 'chat checkouts' for people who had the time to talk.[10]

Conversation has become one of the most-read topics in the *Research Digest* of the British Psychological Society, which has run for over 20 years.[11] Their team of writers provide a summary of peer-reviewed studies, including a 2023 study that found having just one 'quality' conversation with a friend each day leads to people feeling happier and less stressed (where 'quality' means listening fully, demonstrating care and valuing others' opinions).[12]

In *Powered by Purpose* (2020), I explore how making dialogue authentic is essential for transforming daily work so that it becomes more meaningful.[13] In response to a growing body of evidence that challenges our collective notion that the purpose of life is to make ourselves as happy as possible, I outline how leaders can energise their people to do 'great work' (make a difference to people and the planet in a way that contributes to long-term wellbeing). Alongside authentic dialogue, I also write about three other capacities: cultivating leadership presence, engaging stakeholders and connecting on purpose.

While wellbeing and purpose are both important for having a 'good life', they are only two-thirds of the story. Recent psychological research has revealed another dimension to the good life, an aspect that is often overlooked. This additional territory refers to experiences that don't light us up or feel meaningful, but they deepen and broaden our lives by being novel, complex, unexpected and perspective changing.

'Psychological richness' is the term given to this third piece of the puzzle.[14] Valuable life experiences – such as having a difficult conversation – might not bring us great pleasure or even purpose, but they are enriching because they make us grow. This orientation – towards grappling with what's complex, uncertain, and perspective-changing and our becoming more mature – is the domain of this book.

In recent years, psychologists have focused more on 'what makes individuals and communities flourish rather than languish'.[15] Prior to this the profession was more focused on deficits and mental illness. In the words of Martin Seligman, who is often heralded as the founding father of this new movement, *'Positive psychology takes you through the countryside of pleasure and gratification, up into the high country of strength and virtue, and finally to the peaks of lasting fulfilment, meaning and purpose'*.[16] Mastering a difficult conversation takes you also into a rich and fertile valley.

Your descent might be scary but invigorating, nerve-wracking but nourishing, stretching but strengthening. Developing your capacity to lean into a difficult conversation is an empowering journey to take.

Notes

1. Gibran, K. (1923), *The Prophet*, Alfred A. Knopf, Inc.
2. Stafford, W. (2014), *Sound of the Ax: Aphorisms and Poems*, University of Pittsburgh Press.
3. https://www.managers.org.uk/knowledge-and-insights/news/top-10-difficult-conversations/.
4. Performance Coaching International (2008) found in a survey of 750 managers in public, private and voluntary sectors, that 70 per cent said that they were unable or unwilling to have the 'courageous conversation' needed to address poor performance in their staff.
5. https://www.managers.org.uk/knowledge-and-insights/news/top-10-difficult-conversations/.
6. https://www.managers.org.uk/knowledge-and-insights/news/top-10-difficult-conversations/.
7. Anderson, R. J. (2021). The Spirit of Leadership, https://leadershipcircle.com/wp-content/uploads/2021/07/Spirit-of-Leadership-Whitepaper-2021-07.pdf.
8. https://www.mckinsey.com/capabilities/people-and-organizational-performance/our-insights/help-your-employees-find-purpose-or-watch-them-leave.
9. Rozenthuler, S. (2012) *How to Have Meaningful Conversations*, Watkins.
10. https://www.dailystar.co.uk/news/world-news/jumbo-supermarket-opens-new-slow-25112892.

11. https://www.bps.org.uk/psychologist/20-years-british-psychological-societys-research-digest.
12. Hall, J. A., Holmstrom, A. J., Pennington, N., Perrault, E. K., & Totzkay, D. (2023) 'Quality conversation can increase daily well-being, *Communication Research*, *0*(0), https://doi.org/10.1177/00936502221139363.
13. Rozenthuler, S. (2020) *Powered by Purpose: Energise your people to do great work*, Pearson.
14. Oishi, S., & Westgate, E. C. (2021, August 12) A psychologically rich life: Beyond happiness and meaning, *Psychological Review*, Advance online publication, http://dx.doi.org/10.1037/rev0000317.
15. Boniwell, I. and Tunariu, A. (2019) *Positive Psychology: Theory, research and applications,* Second edition, Open University Press.
16. Seligman, M. E. P. (2002) Positive psychology, positive prevention, and positive therapy. In Snyder, C. R. & Lopez, S.J. (Eds.), *Handbook of Positive Psychology*. Oxford University Press.

part 1

The foundations

part 1

The foundations

chapter 1

Why dialogue matters

'In the new economy, conversations are the most important form of work.'

Alan Webber[1]

Real dialogue is a rare occurrence. Much more common in teams and organisations are ritualised or reactive interactions, which rarely reveal any new ideas. Authentic dialogue, where people speak candidly and listen effectively, reveals unanticipated possibilities. It is useful in some situations but not all. Dialogue can enable leaders to find a novel solution to a tough problem and empower a team to manage conflict. It is also invaluable for turning a difficult conversation into a creative exchange so that people can find a way through a stuck situation or complex challenge together.

Dialogue is a commonly used term – for example, an exchange at a UN summit or a meeting at Davos – but it's rarely a true dialogue. A real conversation builds a shared understanding and leaves people feeling more lucid than before they started talking. Much more frequent than dialogue are serial monologues or hostile debates, whether about artificial intelligence, global health crises (such as the recent Covid-19 pandemic), trans issues or immigration. Entrenched mindsets, rigid positions and trolling stifle even the possibility of talking together productively.

Take climate change. We are all familiar with the antagonism between sceptics and activists but the 'inner-circle' battles between 'feuding' climate activists who are 'tearing each other apart' are stopping sustainable solutions emerging at scale. Strong opinions, fixed positions, name-calling and a focus on 'winning' are preventing some of the best minds we have working together to tackle an existential threat that is facing us all. The way forward – not just with climate change but with all the critical, systemic issues we face – is not to stop the debate but to find ways of making the debate more productive.[2]

As is often pointed out, communication is a critical leadership skill. A recent book about former UK Prime Minister Boris Johnson revealed that one of his key shortcomings was his 'chronic inability to initiate difficult conversations'.[3] But it's not just politicians who need these skills. Leaders, managers and team members in organisations large and small, public and private all benefit from being able to communicate effectively in situations where people are toughing it out rather than talking.

A leader's lack of capacity for dialogue can derail a career; likewise, skill in this area is an underrated enabler of success. It is like a 'six-pointer' in football when there's a game between two teams with similar league positions. In a six-pointer, the result is particularly crucial, since the winning team denies three points to the close rival in addition to securing three points for itself. How you handle a difficult conversation is a corporate 'six-pointer'. Skill in dialogue – about important day-to-day topics as well as challenging issues – is a central factor that can make or break your career, team organisation or even government.

Leaders are waking up to the reality that the lack of skills to deal with difficult conversations bites into a business. Losing a senior executive (because they didn't get the feedback they needed to change their behaviour) or a valuable client (because you felt unable to share some bad news with them) is the costly consequence of not being able to talk when the pressure is on. A team beset with shouting matches, walls of silence, or people caving in to keep the peace pays a price. Performance and wellbeing both take a hit.

In this age of outrage, polarisation and 'post-truth', authentic dialogue is in short supply. Anger is on the rise at work, particularly in the UK. Data from Gallup in 2023 found that one in five UK professionals feel angry at work (19 per cent), a rise of 4 percentage points, when asked if they experienced the feeling 'a lot of the day yesterday'.[4] The global average is 19 per cent; the European average 14 per cent. It is not clear why anger levels are rising, perhaps even spiralling, but without finding healthy ways to vent, the anger won't go away.

Today's 'VUCA' world – volatile, uncertain, complex and ambiguous – is now the new normal in business and politics. Meeting the demands of our VUCA environments is raising the bar for day-to-day working, management and leadership, and new approaches are being developed to accommodate this.

Dealing with challenging conversations is now part of executive education programmes seeking to develop twenty-first century leaders. On the MBA programme at Stanford University's Graduate School of Business, students role-play scenarios such as how to lay someone off, decline unsolicited and unhelpful advice from a big investor, and respond to a noisy journalist.[5] Teaching dialogue skills to CEOs from across the globe at Saïd Business School, University of Oxford, has shown me first-hand the appetite senior leaders have to engage their stakeholders with a more human-centred approach to communication.

Command-and-control styles of leadership, which are more about making a monologue than having a dialogue, no longer work in many organisations. There is a growing antipathy towards heroic leaders and their ego needs. Those who are only out to build their own empires are finding it harder to garner support. We saw this in the 2020 collapse[6] of Sir Philip Green's Arcadia retail group, which included brands Topshop, Wallis and Burton, and the numerous staff complaints about Green's bad behaviour.[7]

Alongside this growing intolerance of 'I'm-the-boss' style of leadership is an increasing appetite for accessing collective intelligence to solve the multiple systemic problems our society faces. At the centre of better team working, collaboration and 'collective leadership' (a shift from fixed to dynamic hierarchies) is productive dialogue. In 'distributed' or 'shared' leadership, leaders invite their stakeholders to co-create a strategy, resolve an operational problem, or agree a future direction. Nestlé, for example, in their Beneath the Surface campaign have invited members of the public to join the conversation about their Environmental Social Governance dilemma: how to meet their target of 100 per cent palm oil from sustainable sources.[8]

Twenty-first century leaders must invest in the time needed to build a collaborative climate with their working partners. The failure rate of leaders implementing transformation programmes – whether a major change to a business model, customer experience or back office – has remained 'stubbornly high' despite advances in technology. Leaders who combine a rational with an emotional approach to making transformational changes (for example by collaborating on a compelling 'why', leaning into difficult emotions and creating safe spaces where people speak up) can increase their likelihood to success by two and a half times, from 28 per cent to 78 per cent.[9] This book builds on the lessons learned at the forefront of this new corporate environment, where both personal and corporate dialogue skills matter more than ever.

Why authenticity matters

Difficult conversations are all about truth-telling, interpersonal transparency and tolerance for difference. These attributes are also characteristic of authentic leaders. Authentic leadership is not a trait that some leaders have and other leaders don't. It is a way of leading that can be learned.[10],[11] Similarly, skills for authentic dialogue can be cultivated. While authentic leadership as a concept is still emerging, with many definitions that emphasise different attributes, there is clear evidence that authentic leaders are effective. Proven benefits of authentic leadership include increased wellbeing, more effective problem solving, better team working and enhanced employee engagement.[12]

Four themes converge at the foundation of authentic leadership and effective dialogue:[13]

1 **Self-awareness** – Having an accurate sense of your strengths and weaknesses, with a positive, confident view of yourself balanced with humility and self-regulation

2 **Interpersonal transparency** – Fostering trusting and collaborative relationships through disclosing agendas and matching behaviour with words and values

3 **Tolerance for uncertainty and difference** – Inviting diverse, even conflicting, perspectives, drawing on inputs from others and giving credit to others when due

4 **Strong ethical compass** – Behaving in principled ways, having a sense of right action, and demonstrating courage in the face of pressure to compromise integrity

Creating an environment where people feel safe to open up is within the reach of any leader who's willing to make themselves vulnerable by revealing more of who they are and letting go of the corporate mask. Without authenticity, a difficult conversation remains impossible.

What authentic dialogue is

Our ability to talk is often held out as a key characteristic of what makes us human. With the rise of chatbots this assumption is becoming questionable. Even a machine can learn to say, 'Happy to help!' and 'Is that OK for you?' without becoming cranky and reactive, like we humans.

In a fascinating account of her nine months spent being a stand-in for a property chatbot, Laura Preston described how, when the chatbot (called 'Brenda') tagged messages that she couldn't understand as 'HUMAN_FALLBACK', she stepped in to soften the exchange with a 'prospect'. [14] She, along with the other 60 operators, was paid to bring capacities that Brenda lacked: intuition, articulation and sensitivity to the more subtle aspects of communication so that prospects would remain convinced they were communicating with a human to maximise the likelihood of a booked viewing. It turns out that what makes us truly human is not so much our ability to talk but the more subtle aspects of communicating – to feel, listen, connect and understand one another – particularly when there's HUMAN_FALLBACK or tricky topics on the table.

I learned about the difference that dialogue makes in one of the most difficult situations life gives us: divorce. After seven years of marriage, we decided our lives were pulling in different directions and that a separation was the best way to draw a line under the marriage so that we could both move on. Having been brought up in a family where conflict was either swept under the carpet or, to my younger self, terrifying, the challenge of talking when emotions were running high and fears were rampant met me head on. Although guidance was in short supply, somehow my former husband and I were able to stay friends during this trickiest of times. Looking back with 15 years' hindsight, I now see that the reason we've remained friends to this day is because we were able to talk about what really mattered: the changing form of our relationship.

This experience taught me that a difficult conversation has the potential to be transformative. A challenging but open and honest conversation can actually bring us closer together rather than push us further apart.

Authentic dialogue goes against the grain of many corporate norms. A 'fix-it' mindset fires off advice more than asks questions. Politeness makes us stay on the surface rather than speak about the heart of the matter. Being oppositional means we show our 'edge' rather than our humility. Giving a quick response stops us slowing down to explore more deeply.

Offering someone our undivided attention is a rare gift, and yet is vital for dialogue. Being present, listening attentively, speaking candidly, respecting difference and suspending judgement are all hallmarks of authentic dialogue. It also helps when we bring in our curiosity more than our convictions. An open, unmade-up mind asks: What am I missing here? How does this other person's truth relate to the truth I am carrying? What's the bigger context that contains these different perspectives? There is a lightness to real dialogue, even if it feels clunky to start with, that revealing ourselves and seeing the larger picture brings. As Parker Palmer, an American author, educator and activist writes, *'the human soul does not want to be fixed, it wants simply to be seen and heard.'*[15]

Dialogue, particularly about difficult issues, is authentic when it is not about 'winning' but mutual discovery. The 'I'm-in-it-to-win-it' approach results in a combative exchange which leaves some people feeling they're the losers. Authentic dialogue is, by contrast, mutually beneficial, both in the moment and after the event. It leads to renewed relationships, resolved issues and clear decisions, not to mention flourishing teams and brilliant boards.

Our desire to express ourselves is the essence of being human. While many of us shy away from, or even loathe, having a conversation that could be self-revealing, deep inside we have a yearning to be known and heard respectfully. This impulse to evince ourselves, when fused with tools for talking openly, overcomes the sense of being ill equipped, whether to discuss a promotion, inappropriate behaviour or poor performance. Authentic dialogue lifts us out of a difficult situation and helps us to find our unique place in the scheme of things. It is, as George Sanfacon writes, *'a conversation in which the human spirit is evoked and present'*.[16]

From monologue to dialogue

Dialogue differs from other verbal interactions. Understanding this helps to cut through dysfunctional team and group dynamics, which are particularly problematic in today's highly interconnected world. The problems facing leaders are too complex for any one person to solve. Challenges such as developing a sustainable business strategy, cleaning up a supply chain and recruiting the best talent in a global marketplace are not limited to the borders of a single country or the boundary of an organisational department. Cutting a swath through these issues requires a multitude of stakeholders thinking and talking together in unprecedented ways.

Keith Grint and Clare Holt, researchers at Warwick Business School, define contemporary leadership as '*The art of engaging a community in facing up to complex collective problems*'. They note the growing antipathy towards heroic leaders and the increasing interest in collective or distributed leadership and working in partnership.

Despite this new approach to leadership having the potential to be the 'universal future', Grint and Holt also underline the current reality. Partnerships are often paralysed into inaction. Many organisations still operate on the basis of traditional hierarchies, and the widespread application of 'command-and-control' decision style, while perhaps unpopular, seldom gets replaced with any clear collective decision-making mechanism.[17]

The optimum leadership style is circumstantial. For example, an effective leader with a young team may well lead them better with some 'command-and-control'. More experienced and flexible people can be left to self-organise. I've coached some high-performing leadership teams where the team leader (who said to me, 'We're not going on a journey from good to great, but from great to exceptional') found out that letting his team members self-organise their work 'streams' was vastly more effective.

The real skill, then, is having the right leadership style for the people concerned given the situation faced. This is known as 'Situational Leadership'. That said, authentic dialogue comes into its own in a team which needs to pivot away from a 'command-and-control' way of working towards a flatter hierarchy with collective decision-making. Many leaders I've worked with – not just in business but in NGOs, government departments, schools and not-for-profits – have shared how tough it is to move their people towards a collaborative way of working. Their comments have included, 'They're so used to command-and-control, it's better-the-devil-you-know', 'My team feel out of their depth being asked rather than being told what to do', and 'Some of my direct reports say "You're the boss and that's your role."'

While I agree that collective leadership is a difficult 'nut to crack', I've also seen enough evidence as a leadership consultant to know that this form of engagement is definitely possible. When a whole team is fully involved in an authentic dialogue about thorny issues, drawing on leadership qualities sourced as a group rather than as individuals, outcomes that stick are created.[18]

Powerful leaders understand that each person has a piece of the puzzle, and that it's in the mix of diverse perspectives that innovative thinking emerges. They know how to restore a sense of unity by bringing people together. They can transform stagnant energy into a greater vitality. They are able to turn fragmented thinking into a coherent way forward.

In short, these leaders have the ability to access the collective wisdom of the people around them to create new possibilities, whether this is a shared purpose, new strategy or a ten-year vision. The only way to do this is to have a dialogue.

As I observed in my previous book, *Powered by Purpose*, dialogue differs from other forms of verbal interaction. The conversation continuum in Figure 1.1 is one way to understand this difference.

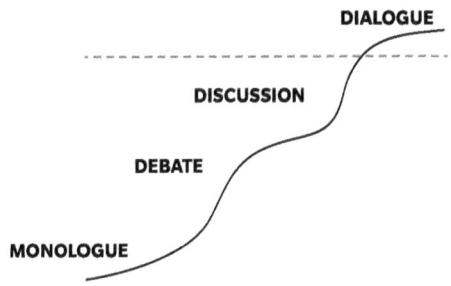

Figure 1.1 The conversation continuum

The continuum moves from the simplest form of verbal interaction (monologue) to the most skilled (dialogue). None of them are 'bad' and each has their place. As we move up the continuum, an expanded skillset is needed. The continuum is cumulative and the gradient gets steeper to represent the more complex the skillset that dialogue demands. The four interaction patterns are:

- **Monologue.** One person speaks and the other/s listen. This can be an effective way to communicate when a leader needs to transmit a message to a large audience. In a team meeting, however, if a monologue goes on too long, others switch off.
- **Debate.** An exchange where one person asserts their opinion and another person challenges it with a counterargument. While this can be high-energy, it can become fractious, and 'winning' or 'beating down' your opponent becomes primary.
- **Discussion.** A conversation which emphasises individual points of view. People try to convince one another of their position and often become identified with their perspective, albeit unconsciously. People tend to talk past one another rather than with one another. The word *discussion* shares the same root as *percussion* and *concussion* and means to 'shake apart' or 'break down'. While it can be useful for coming to a decision about a clear-cut issue or when limited time is available, a discussion often goes awry when there are difficult topics or complex issues. People are often left feeling *shaken*, mentally, emotionally and socially, and without a satisfactory way forward.[19]
- **Dialogue.** A meaningful conversation where people talk and think together. Coming from the Greek, *dia*, meaning 'through' and *legein* meaning 'to speak', *dialogue* is, in essence, finding a way through by speaking. Other interpretations of dialogue's roots emphasise that dialogue is about the 'flow of meaning': *logos* is 'word' or 'meaning'. Dialogue is meaning moving through yourself or a group. It energises and changes people, through building a shared understanding rather than agreement. It is less helpful (or necessary) when problems are routine or well understood. Dialogue is invaluable for addressing complex or controversial

issues where there are multiple points of view without any obvious solution. By becoming aware of the source of thinking behind the words, including your own, new possibilities for co-ordinated action surface. Dialogue does, however, take time and needs a 'container' or supportive holding environment in which people can find their voice, listen to one another and deepen their understanding about what it means to create together.

There is a line across the continuum to represent that there's a threshold to cross to be in dialogue. Most teams know how to have a monologue, debate and discussion but struggle to have a dialogue. As it has been said, 'Two monologues do not make a dialogue.'

Dialogue differs from other verbal interactions. As David Bohm writes, '*In a dialogue . . . nobody is trying to win . . . There is a different sort of spirit to it. In a dialogue, there is no attempt to gain points, or to make your particular view prevail.*'[20]

There are three qualities that differentiate dialogue from discussion, debate or serial monologues. You can use these 'signs' to 'read the room' (more on this in Chapter 7) and inform yourself whether you're really having a creative exchange. A dialogue is:

- **Reflective.** The conversation is slower and includes the bigger picture. People aren't lost in the weeds. They're looking 'up and out' at the larger context and starting to see how fragmented points of view hang together. This happens when people pay attention to the invisible, becoming aware of how their internal thoughts and feelings impact others and the world around them.

- **Generative.** A dialogue leaves you feeling more lucid. It is not always comfortable or 'nice' but it feels 'true'. As people become more 'present', new thinking replaces habitual reactions and dug-out positions. Insights arise that one individual could not have arrived at by thinking alone. As people sense into what the potential is in a situation, and build alignment around it, there is a coherence to the ideas and actions they generate.

- **Dynamic.** Dialogue has a sense of 'flow'. A shared understanding emerges out of individuals sharing their perspectives. Instead of being on autopilot and operating from memory and well-worn thought patterns, people tune into what's actually here *now* and what might be possible in the future. There's a rich 'field' of energy exchange in the room and even a sense of fellowship. As people expand their bandwidth of what they can accept and seek, new creative action becomes possible.

Dialogue is an art and a skill that can be learned. What's more, conversational skills are not only for senior executives leading corporate teams but for all managers and leaders, whether in business, politics or the not-for-profit-sector. The challenges are too big, the times are too urgent, and the human capacity locked away inside us waiting to be used is too great for us to continue falling into the trap of thinking or working alone. Expanding our capacity to engage in dialogue is beneficial for us all.

To reflect further, see Exercise 1 – Conversation continuum.

Exercise 1
Conversation continuum

Think about a team or group you are part of (or lead). Look back at the conversation continuum and reflect on these questions:

1 Where's the centre of gravity in your team? Are you mostly in serial monologues, debate, discussion or dialogue?
2 What would it take to nudge it towards dialogue (when dialogue is needed)?
3 What could *you* do to make the conversations you have more reflective, generative and dynamic?

For example, you might set aside some time for a free-flowing conversation without an agenda. You might encourage people to bring a question to the meeting to set a tone of curiosity. You could share a context (or ask someone else to) and then ask others to share what stood out for them.

Building a culture of dialogue

There has been much discussion over the past decade about creating a culture of coaching in organisations. This is closely related to building a culture of dialogue. A simple definition of corporate culture is 'the way things get done around here'.[21] Key features of a corporate coaching culture are to create an environment where each person is able to maximise their potential, where the default style of leadership and employee engagement is coaching, and where people are supported and challenged to increase their self-awareness and autonomy in order to achieve workplace goals.[22]

Inspired by this articulation, I define a culture of dialogue as being a place where creative conversations rather than reactive interactions happen. Rather than people reacting with well-worn behaviours and rigid positions, they feel safe to speak up and raise issues. Teams discuss what really matters. Leaders 'hold space' for building a shared understanding. They role model attentive listening, authentic speaking, respecting differences and suspending assumptions in order to find common ground.

The workplace, and the world, is hungry for this shift. The runaway success of the podcast *The Rest is Politics*, which regularly tops the charts in the UK, reflects the appetite people have for discussing what matters in a world of online echo chambers, constant distractions and culture wars. Hosts Rory Stewart and Alastair Campbell launched the podcast in February 2022, and their in-person events consistently sell out in record time.

When Campbell and Stewart reflect on their unexpected success, chief among the reasons they give is their ground rule to 'disagree agreeably'. This creates an energising and engaging atmosphere. Their dialogue, which stretches across the traditional political divide with Stewart inhabiting the 'right' and Campbell the 'left', is rich with insight. So much communication in the public space (and organisations) is stilted, stale and scripted. As Stewart and Campbell say, a "dialogue of the deaf" is pervasive.[23] It is impossible to make change happen when people stick to a script of talking points and take fixed positions.

What are we left with?

Our inability to talk about what really matters cuts across families, organisations and even nations. One of the striking paradoxes of family and organisational life is how groups of people can spend so much time together without ever really talking and getting to know one another. It's a set-up for silence, silos, power struggles, turf wars or worse, an empty life.

The rise of social media has made us poorer at having difficult conversations rather than increasing the richness of them. While online platform X, formerly known as Twitter, was heralded as being the world's town square, by Twitter's founders and Elon Musk, this has proven to be wrong. *'Twitter makes it easy to discuss hard topics poorly'*, Klein writes in *The Great Delusion Behind Twitter*.[24] With only 140 characters to express yourself, bite-size bluntness crowds out nuanced thinking. The quote tweet function promotes mockery rather than conversation. The drive to get more 'likes' drives polarisation. Negativity and character assassinations capture our attention rather than deepen it. Impulsive reactivity replaces sober consideration. Klein concludes, *'Civilization does not depend on a place to gather. It depends on what happens when people gather.'*

If we fail to overcome the many reasons we can't talk together about our difficulties, we risk ending up like the society in the sci-fi story 'The Machine Stops'. Written by E. M. Forster in 1909, in this story humans live in isolation below ground and rely on a giant machine to provide all their needs, physical and spiritual. In a chillingly prescient story, people communicate via a form of instant messaging and video conferencing, where nuances of expression are blurred. The subtle essence of communication has been lost, *'just as the imponderable bloom of the grape was ignored by the manufacturers of artificial fruit'*[25] that the underground residents consume. At the end of the story, the machine collapses and brings down humanity with it, but not before the realisation that our connection to the natural world and to one another is what truly matters.

'When systems collapse, what are we left with?' asks Otto Scharmer (American academic and co-founder of the Presencing Institute).[26] Scharmer rightly points out that what we are left with is each other, our relationships and how we relate to Mother Nature. I am convinced that at the root of us being able to draw on all these precious resources is a single, critical capacity: our willingness and ability to turn a difficult conversation into an authentic dialogue.

Summary

1 Dialogue is an over-used and often misunderstood term. Not every verbal interaction is a dialogue.

2 Dialogue happens when people talk and think together. Dialogue creates a shared understanding by a flow of meaning moving through people, whether this is in a one-on-one setting or a larger group.

3 Dialogue requires authenticity. It is more reflective, generative and dynamic than the typical conversation that happens in an organisation.

4 A difficult conversation requires dialogue. With dialogue, new ideas and unanticipated possibilities emerge.

5 Shifting a conversation from serial monologues, oppositional debate or febrile discussion to authentic dialogue calls for an expanded skillset.

6 Authentic dialogue is a way of leading that is fit for the current turbulent times. It provides an opportunity for more collaboration and co-creation than a 'command-and-control' approach.

7 Personal and corporate dialogue skills matter more than ever if we are to solve the complex, systemic problems our society faces.

> **If you do only one thing now . . .** Authentic dialogue is your aim. This means making your conversation a co-creation. Pay attention to two areas. If you tend to over-talk, pull back. Focus on the other people, listen to them, then summarise what you've heard others say before giving your own opinion. Practise this: 'It seems like you're saying . . . ' If you see someone else being too dominant, encourage others present to contribute by saying 'I wonder what others are thinking? Let's bring them in.'

Notes

1 Webber, A. (1993) *Harvard Business Review*, January–February, https://hbr.org/1993/01/whats-so-new-about-the-new-economy#:~:text=conversations%20are%20the%20most%20important%20form%20of%20work.

2 https://www.theguardian.com/books/2023/jul/10/the-big-idea-why-climate-tribalism-only-helps-the-deniers.

3 Seldon, A. and Newell, R. (2023) *Johnson at 10*, Atlantic.

4 GALLUP, State of the Global Workplace 2023 Report, THE VOICE OF THE WORLD'S EMPLOYEES.

5 Schumpeter Column (2023) 'Managing expectations', *The Economist*, April 8th.

6 https://www.ft.com/content/cd2e9b8a-c9b6-4a2f-8810-cb749ea37421.

7 https://www.ft.com/content/374a08ac-7d61-11e9-81d2-f785092ab560.

8 https://www.nestle.com/beneath-the-surface.

9 EY and Saïd Business School (2022) *The Future of Transformation is Human*, https://assets.ey.com/content/dam/ey-sites/ey-com/en_gl/noindex/ey-the-future-of-transformation-is-human-report.pdf.

10 Beddoes-Jones, F. & Swailes, S. (2015) 'Authentic Leadership: Development of a new three pillar model', *Strategic HR Review*, Vol. 14 (3), pp. 94–99.

11 Fusco, T., Palmer, S. and O'Riordan, S. (2016) 'Assessing the effectiveness of authentic leadership group coaching, *International Coaching Psychology Review*.

12 Beddoes-Jones, F. (2022) *Authentic Leadership: The courage to lead*, British Psychological Society webinar, January 28th.

13 Luthans, F., & Avolio, B.J. (2003) Authentic leadership development, In K. S. Cameron, J. E. Dutton, & R. E. Quinn (Eds.), *Positive Organizational Scholarship* (pp. 241–258), San Francisco, CA: Berrett-Kochler.

14 https://www.nplusonemag.com/issue-44/essays/human_fallback/.

15 Palmer, P. (1998) *The Courage to Teach*, John Wiley & Sons.

16 Sanfancon, G. (2015) *The Council of Equals: A guide and handbook for shared governance*, Charing Cross Press.

17 Grint, K. and Holt, C. (2012) *Scientific and Medical Network Review* (Winter 2012), p. 21.

18 Rozenthuler S. (2013) 'Collective leadership: From silos to shared intelligence', *Network Review* no.111, pp. 8–9, Scientific and Medical Network.

19 SanFacon, G. (2015). *The Council of Equals: A guide and handbook for shared governance*, Charing Cross Press.

20 Bohm, D. (1996). *On Dialogue*, London: Routledge.

21 Deal, T. E. and Kennedy, A. A. (1983) Culture: A new look through old lenses, *The Journal of Applied Behavioural Science*, 19(4), pp. 498–505.

22 Passmore, J. and Crabble, K. (2020) Developing a coaching culture in your organisation. In Passmore, J. (Ed), *The Coaches' Handbook: The complete practitioner guide for professional coaches*, Routledge.

23 *The Rest is Politics* podcast, 16 November 2022.
24 EZRA KLEIN, The Great Delusion Behind Twitter Dec. 11, 2022.
25 Forster E. M. (1909) 'The Machine Stops', *The Oxford and Cambridge Review*.
26 Otto Scharmer, Sep 7, 2022, Protect the Flame Circles of Radical Presence in Times of Collapse Otto Scharmer.

chapter 2

What stops us from talking

'What do we live for, if not to make life less difficult for each other?'

George Eliot

It's not uncommon for talented leaders and managers to avoid or botch difficult conversations and then to regret the missed opportunity. After all, most managers receive no training in how to talk and, more importantly, listen. Conversation is a crucial activity in any team or organisation. By talking and thinking together, people stop being stuck and instead solve problems, whether for their team, organisation or wider society. If you're a leader who struggles to have conversations that matter, it helps to understand what stops you from talking about the tough stuff and then work to overcome that block. There are six main obstacles to be aware of and some accompanying small 'wins' that will enable you to start expanding your skills in authentic dialogue.

> Here's an email that landed in my inbox. It is typical of the requests that I receive:
>
> *'Sarah*
>
> *I hope that this finds you safe and well. I wondered if you can help me?*
>
> *I understand you're an occupational psychologist. Google tells me that "Occupational psychologists" (often called industrial-organisational psychologists) study humans in work-related settings. They examine the ways people behave as individuals and in group settings, and then they use their findings to solve problems for companies.*
>
> *Your website offers this and I think you might be able to look over my shoulder. I am anticipating the risk that I might have problems with my team in the future, or even now. Perhaps my challenge is that I do not know what my problems are in this area? I am trying to understand and anticipate the likely negatives before they blindside me.*
>
> *The next couple of years are going to be difficult commercially and I need to know my team will not "fall over". How*

> they communicate with each other will be crucial – and this is exacerbated by us all being remote workers. If my Senior Management Team (SMT) is beset with tensions and personality clashes, cracks will emerge under pressure.
>
> I understand that better dialogue will help us to reduce stress points but there are multiple challenges. One team member throws hand grenades when they don't get their own way. Some are inscrutable and I never truly know what they're thinking. Others have a strong need for validation, which distorts their approach. Others listen but don't actually hear what others are saying, so they fail to understand the consequences of their actions beyond the next (obvious) milestone.
>
> I want to understand better each of their bandwidth and how I can support them to thrive in their role. Developing the capacity to have difficult conversations has a central role in this. I want to ensure that they/we remain a cohesive team in the future without avoiding the tricky topics or have them blow up in our faces.
>
> Please excuse the layman's brief but your help in navigating this would be appreciated. I wanted to start the conversation so that I can understand your thoughts on this matter. When could we have a chat?
>
> Regards,
> Amal'

It might have been a layman's brief but Amal's note nails why his team needs to talk. He's aware of the costs of not being able to have a difficult conversation and of the benefits of being able to talk. He's also willing to face the current reality without flinching. There's no rushing to fix his team and find a solution that would end up missing the mark.

Amal isn't alone in his struggle and we'll return to Amal's story later. I observe many leaders and managers in organisations of all different sizes and across all sectors facing communication challenges. Here are some of the comments I've heard over the years:

> **'We can talk but we can't dialogue.'**
> **'We tend to talk *about* each other rather than *to* each other.'**
> **'All we do is talk!'**

Just because people are talking doesn't mean that they're communicating. As the old saying goes, 'Two monologues do not make a dialogue.' In two decades of team coaching, not a session goes by without someone concluding that 'it's all about communication, really.'

Given that many managers know that better communication is the difference that makes the difference, why are difficult conversations such a pervasive issue? At this point you might like to complete Exercise 2 to reflect on what a difficult conversation means to you.

Exercise 2
What is a difficult conversation?

1. What would you identify as a 'difficult conversation'? (e.g. saying no to a request, dealing with a grievance, handling a sensitive personal issue)
2. When you think about having a difficult conversation, what happens in your body? (e.g. heart races, palms become sweaty, stomach goes in knots)
3. How do people behave during a difficult conversation, including yourself? (e.g. go silent, start shouting, burst into tears, have a sulk)
4. What are the risks if it doesn't go well? (e.g. situation deteriorates, team member leaves)
5. What are the benefits if it does go well? (e.g. sleep better at night, improved performance)

Here are six obstacles I've seen among the leaders I've worked with. Understanding what gets in the way of having a difficult conversation throws light on finding a way to talk. I give some 'small wins' below and there are many more in the rest of the book.

Obstacle 1: 'I don't have time'

'People are stacked' a CEO said to me recently. Her team was trapped in firefighting. They dealt with the urgent-but-not-important and struggled to find time for the important-but-not-urgent. Many conversations that would add value fall into the latter category including: articulating a compelling purpose for an organisation, identifying performance metrics for a team or improving relationships with critical stakeholders such as non-executive directors.

One of the ironies of not making time for a difficult conversation is that it perpetuates the vicious cycle of not having time to talk. We can see this clearly in the case of dealing with underperformance. The Future Foundation, commissioned by global consultancy SHL, surveyed 700 executives across seven countries including the US, UK and India to look at 'The hidden cost of poor people management'. They found that managers in the US spend an average of 34 days per year dealing with poor performance. This figure rises to 41 days per year in larger organisations (where the turnover is above $8.5 m).[1]

That's a staggering amount of time wasted. Imagine you got back seven or eight weeks of your time each year. What would you be able to do with this freed-up time and energy? Would you finally get round to writing that strategy paper, go on an extended leadership retreat or spend time with your team in an agenda-free space?

It might be counterintuitive but leaning into a difficult conversation returns time to you. Check out Figure 2.1, which Dr Claus Springborg and I developed in our work together:

Time spent on having dialogue	Time spent due to lack of dialogue
Building rapport	Managing resistance
Designing session	Navigating conflict
Establishing great outcomes	Dealing with misunderstandings
Preparing materials	Wasted work
	Dealing with frustration
	Business stalling
	Managing disaffected stakeholders

Figure 2.1 Time spent on having dialogue vs. Time spent due to lack of dialogue

The time spent on having dialogue (in column 1) is significantly less than the time wasted due to lack of dialogue. The costs of not talking are harder to see but more costly in the long run. To create some momentum, see Exercise 3 – Find time to talk.

Exercise 3
Find time to talk

If you're struggling to find time to talk, ask yourself these questions to mobilise your energy:

1 What is it that I really want to change?
2 What can I contribute to this situation regardless of how I feel about it?
3 What's getting in the way of me finding time to talk?
4 What blocks are others creating?
5 How could I overcome these obstacles?

Reflect on your answers. Identify one thing you can take away from your responses and put into action.

Obstacle 2: 'There are some people you can't have a dialogue with'

A Learning & Development Director of a large retail organisation, with stores spread across the UK, recently said to me that they could trace all the leadership issues in their organisation back to a single source: the reluctance or inability to have difficult conversations.

At the heart of this is a common perception among some managers that there's a 'difficult person' on the team who makes dialogue impossible. Perhaps someone immediately springs to mind? Maybe there's someone in your team who's the naysayer, grumpy person or troublemaker? It could be your boss who repeatedly turns up late, a colleague who has a habit of making inappropriate remarks or a supplier who blocks conversations.

Left unaddressed, there are several dangers. Meetings are run with the sole intention of not upsetting that person. Team members become frustrated with the lack of progress. The atmosphere turns toxic as people gossip rather than discuss what really matters. There is a principle in psychology which states, 'What you focus on, expands.' If we backbite, others bitch. If we complain, others gripe. If we go grumpy, cold shoulders set in.

Instead of focusing on the 'difficult person', place your attention on what's happening inside you. While it's true that some people are disrespectful, volatile or undermining, you can't do anything to change them; all you can do is to 'keep your own side of the street clean.' For support with this, see Exercise 4 – Dealing with a difficult person.

Exercise 4
Dealing with a difficult person

Bring to mind someone you find tricky to deal with (Person 'X').

1. Notice the story you hold about X. This internal commentary, left unexamined, operates on autopilot. Bring it into the light ➤

of awareness by asking yourself: Who am I taking X to be? For example:

- A troublemaker – 'They block what I want because they're obstructive and want their own way.'
- A competitor – 'They feel threatened by my work, so they undermine me in public.'
- A know-it-all – 'They think their opinion is superior and have to have the last word.'
- A judge – 'They always focus on what's wrong because they want to keep me in my corner.'

2. Now switch your focus. If you stay stuck in your 'story' about X, it will be hard (if not impossible) to have a productive conversation. Remind yourself that you can never fully know what that person is thinking or going through. Consider the possibility that they're doing the best they can, no matter how they're coming across. Identify something you don't know about them – the knowing of which could change your attitude (maybe their partner just left them, they got passed over for a promotion or they hate the way their job has changed). Notice the impact that this expanded focus has on you.

3. Challenge yourself to see X as a person beyond their personality or behaviour. Cultivate 'unconditional positive regard'[2] (the great psychologist Carl Rogers coined this term in his human-centred approach). This means accepting and supporting someone, regardless of whether they deserve it or not. Think of a question to ask X that you wouldn't typically cover, coming from this place, for example:

- What's your main challenge right now?
- What resources would help you to manage this?
- What can I do to support you?

When your tone changes, it can be contagious. If you show respect to the other person, they are more likely to be more respectful to you. By changing your 'story' about X, you're more likely to have a more meaningful conversation.

Dialogue turns 'difficult people' into valuable assets. I've coached many teams where there's been a so-called 'bad apple' upsetting the applecart. When team members have the tools to give each other feedback (in a short, structured, safe one-on-one setting), it lifts and shifts the whole team dynamic. After I'd led an IT team through a 'feedback carousel process' (where they each paired with every other person), one 'difficult' person reflected:

> **'It's easy to ignore another person's comments about you but when I hear the same thing seven times over, I have to pay attention.'**

As a result of making it safe to share feedback, collaboration among team members significantly improved. It's possible to draw the brilliance out of bolshy people by having a real and respectful conversation.

Obstacle 3: 'Nothing will change anyway'

Resistance to having difficult conversations is rife. Objections include: 'Won't it just turn into a "talking shop" where nothing really changes' 'Might talking open a can of worms and make matters worse?' 'Dialogue is "all-talk-and-no-action" and what we need is action.'

Without dialogue, however, nothing really changes. Just because dialogue is difficult, it doesn't mean we have to fight shy of talking together. As David Bohm, the quantum physicist who developed some powerful insights about human interaction, observed in his influential paper, 'Dialogue – A Proposal' (co-authored with Peter Garrett and Donald Factor in 1991):

> **'In our modern culture men and women are able to interact with one another in many ways: they can sing, dance and play together with little difficulty but their ability to talk together about subjects that matter deeply to them seems invariably to lead to dispute, division and often to violence. In our view this condition points to a deep and pervasive defect in the process of human thought.'[3]**

With the global challenges we face – social inequality, climate change, global poverty, mass migration and world hunger – it is a critical moment for individuals, teams and organisations to talk and think well together. In 2022, Collin's Dictionary identified as their Word of the Year: permacrisis. This is a prolonged period of volatility and uncertainty, especially when it's the result of a series of disastrous events. For moving forward in this environment, better dialogue will be crucial.

To overcome resistance to dialogue, leaders need to attend to not only the tangibles but the intangibles too. To borrow an analogy from David Bohm, when we plant an acorn and it grows into an oak tree, we typically think of the seed as the source of the tree. It is, however, more accurate to see the total environment as giving rise to the tree – the moisture in the air, the nutrients in the soil and the energy from the sun. The seed is the *aperture* through which the tree unfolds.

In a similar way, dialogue is the portal through which new thinking and fresh innovations are released. For a conversation to become this opening, it helps to be aware of how we talk (which could be compared to the seed), and the setting in which the conversation takes place (the room, atmosphere and mood). Personal inputs – our tone of voice, presence and receptivity – also significantly shape a conversation.

Realising that even a single conversation could open or shut the door on a whole new future helps leaders to become more conscious of the impact of what happens when they do talk and when they don't.

Obstacle 4: 'It's just too tricky'

Lack of know-how is a big block to having a difficult conversation. As Sir Ian Blatchford, chief executive of the Science Museum Group, observes:

> 'Boards are vital to our lives, but they can drive every chief executive absolutely round the bend . . . It's the one thing about being a boss that no one ever trains you for . . . The moment you become chief executive, people

will cease to tell you the truth and that is the greatest risk . . . Dissenting voices need to be heard.' (*Financial Times*, 27 November 2022)[4]

Research carried out by workplace resource company Bravely has found that 70 per cent of managers avoid having difficult conversations.[5] Managers were either unwilling or unable to have more tense conversations due to a lack of trust or fear of reprisal, particularly when confrontation is required. Unresolved crucial conversations lead to poor decision-making, a cynical atmosphere that rots communication, and people competing rather than collaborating.

This pattern of not-talking is compounded by senior leaders who avoid or mess up difficult conversations. One of the truths of being a leader is that you're always a role model, whether you like it or not. What you do – throw a tantrum, swear at people, thump your fists – you give others permission to do. What you fail to do – say it as it is, share information, name an issue – you give others permission not to do.

The reluctance to talk seems to make sense. Learning how to navigate 'boardroom psychology' is one of the trickier aspects of a leader's role. But think about this: If you're 'on withhold' and not speaking out, how can you expect the people you lead to find their voice? If you interrupt people and don't let them finish their sentences, no wonder others don't listen and 're-load'. If you take up most of the airtime in the meeting room, what space is there for others to share their ideas?

One leader I worked with who wanted to do better identified that he wanted to improve listening in his team so he decided to deepen his own listening first. Many leaders are practised in demonstrating the behaviours that indicate they are listening – not interrupting, eye contact, nodding – but, in reality, are still only waiting to deliver their next point. They are not really hearing, engaging with and building on the contributions of others.

In our coaching conversations, we identified small changes that would strengthen listening.

Instead of jumping in with his own opinion, this leader challenged himself to replace his next assertion with a question. This can be as simple as saying 'What makes you say that?', 'Tell me more. I'm curious about the bit when you said . . . '.

When someone gives an opposing view, the temptation is to jump right in. But when, in a high-energy moment, we choose to be responsive rather than reactive it keeps the conversation on track rather than derailing it. Healthy self-regulation changes a conversation for the better.

In another team I worked with, the Finance Director had a lightbulb moment.

'If managers paid more attention to the tangible costs of meetings, there would be more impetus to make them more productive' he said.

Doing a quick sum on a pad of paper in the meeting room, he worked out the rough cost of a meeting by estimating the cost per hour of each person's time (there are online tools to help you with this if your mental arithmetic needs a helping hand).

'For a two-hour meeting of eight directors who earn £100k each, at an hourly rate of £50, the cost of the meeting is nearly £1000 before you've added any other costs like travel, venue and refreshments.'

It was a sobering pattern to see. Businesses lose money when meetings are unproductive. There's the 'opportunity cost' because these directors could be doing value-adding work. There are also invisible costs associated with not reaching a decision, the inability to discuss complex change to resolution or the lack of understanding about perceptions of inequality.

While it can be tricky to measure the impact of having a difficult conversation, progress is happening. Dik Veenman, founder of The Right Conversation, has shown that a 15 per cent increase in conversational effectiveness translates into a 17 per cent improvement in the bottom line.[6] Having used their tool, the Team Dialogue Indicator, with teams that I've coached I've seen first-hand the value of a team being able to talk about how they 'talk'. Going 'meta' enables a team to identify unproductive conversational habits (such as being distracted) and to pinpoint drivers for better dialogue (e.g. asking more questions).

Obstacle 5: 'I'd rather not have *that* conversation'

Tackling poor performance is one of the most common conversations that managers dread. As organisational psychologist and Stanford Professor Robert Sutton once told the *New York Times*: 'If the performance review (as usually done) was a drug, it wouldn't be approved by the Federal Food and Drug Administration because it's so ineffective and has such vile side effects.' Reflecting on this much-quoted perspective, Sutton writes that it's not a case of getting rid of all annual performance evaluations but asking, 'what would happen if we didn't do them?'[7]

The inevitable impacts of not tackling poor performance include unresolved issues, customer complaints, duplication of work, time wasted correcting mistakes and frustration among team members who have to fill in the gap others leave behind. Moreover, lack of respect for senior leaders who don't tackle underperformance is insidious.

A study commissioned by CPP Inc, publishers of the Myers-Briggs Assessment and the Thomas-Kilmann Conflict Mode Instrument, found that US employees spent 2.8 hours per week dealing with difficult situations, equating to approximately $359 billion in paid hours in 2008.[8] A 2016 study of over 1000 employees by VitalSmarts concluded that each conversation failure costs an organisation $7500 and more than seven working days in lost time and resources.[9]

Companies are increasingly recognising that in our digitalised, disruptive and fast-moving world, established ways of giving feedback – particularly the once-yearly, form-filling 'download' – are no longer fit-for-purpose. Hybrid working brings further challenges, as Amal highlighted, with team members in different geographies, time zones and offices.

Making the feedback process more conversational, frequent and informal is on trend. Gap encourages feedback to be delivered monthly, rather than annually, and to give it outside of the office environment in order to develop deeper relationships.[10] Culture Amp have developed an employee performance review tool to make the feedback process more engaging and remove any stigma behind it.[11]

Netflix asks managers and employees to have conversations about performance as an organic part of their work and to undergo a 360-degree performance review where they're able to provide feedback to anyone else based on their rationale that people can handle 'anything' as long as they're told the truth.[12] Others have questioned 'radical candour' such as Miranda Green at the FT who points out that this latest version of 'tough love' could, at times, become emotionally exhausting, leaving us too depleted to do our day-to-day work.[13]

Managers providing feedback with more frequency and skill than in the typical annual review structure is a real step forward. I have seen the careers of senior leaders derail and the businesses of founders fail in large part either because they didn't receive the feedback they needed or because, when they did, they dismissed it. It's true that a feedback conversation costs time and energy but not as much as poor performance does.

Obstacle 6: 'Better not rock the boat'

Fear of conflict keeps many people stuck in jobs they don't enjoy or doing projects that feel meaningless. This particularly applies to people wanting to give upward feedback to a leader or engage in constructive conflict in a meeting with more senior leaders.

Avoiding conflict also undermines team performance. As Patrick Lencioni, best-selling author of the book *The Five Dysfunctions of a Team*, observes this is often a result of lack of trust in a team. He writes:

> **'Trust is critical because without it teams are unlikely to engage in unfiltered, passionate debate about key issues. This creates two problems. First, stifling conflict actually increases the likelihood of destructive, back-channel sniping. Second, it leads to sub-optimal decision-making because the team is not benefiting from the true ideas and perspectives of its members.'**[14]

Even the word 'conflict' has many running for the hills. When someone opposes our point of view, we go tense and contract. "I'll go along to get along" we say to ourselves, "best not rock the boat". We do what others want to keep the peace. But constantly acquiescing to the wishes of others will never provide the kind of relationships that will really satisfy.

Others, when they encounter opposition, 'discharge' and dump their anger onto other people. They become 'street fighters' rather than sparring partners and repel others with their aggression.

Another response to conflict is stony silence. As soon as a conversation starts to get uncomfortable, people stop talking. A tense atmosphere fills the room and pushes out the possibility of talking to resolve a disagreement.

We'll explore these three reactive responses in Chapter 4. Understanding that there are three different needs that people seek to meet – for approval, control or protection – helps you to stay in the game. A difficult conversation doesn't have to turn into a full-blown conflict. Differences don't have to create divisions.

Many managers and leaders fail to understand the risks associated with not being able to handle conflict. A robust dialogue is often cut off at the pass for fear of relationship damage, being rejected or losing our position of power. When team members start to see that the risks of stifling conflict are often greater than the risks of leaning in, a difficult conversation becomes possible. Without leaders developing this capacity, an organisation will never build an inclusive culture where people can self-express fully and so feel valued and respected.

Taking stock

Given that senior leaders can spend up to 80 per cent of their time talking, dealing with these obstacles even to a small degree can have a huge impact. Take the opportunity to pause and reflect by completing Exercise 5 – Taking stock of obstacles.

Exercise 5
Taking stock of obstacles

----

1. Identify a difficult conversation at work that you're facing. Go for the one where you feel most stuck. It might be:

   a) Asking for something that you really want such as a pay rise or perk

   b) Telling your boss that you're going to leave

   c) Speaking 'truth to power' to reveal a blind spot or new opportunity

   d) Giving someone challenging feedback

   e) Delivering bad news about a team's performance to senior leaders

   f) Telling a supplier that you're ending their contract

   g) Letting someone know they haven't got the job/promotion/assignment

   h) Articulating the purpose of a team or organisation beyond making money.

2. Review the six obstacles above and identify the one/s that most apply to you. What clues have you gleaned already about how to move forward? What do you already know how to do that could help you to overcome this block? Bring your 'unconscious competence'[15] (skills or strategies that have become 'second nature' and can be performed easily) to mind.

3. Ask yourself: What would it take for me to have this conversation? For example, 'I would have to say what I really think' or 'I'd have to really pick my moment' or 'I'd need to be prepared to walk away from the situation once I'd said my piece'.

4. What else might support you to overcome the obstacle/s you identified? For example, spending time preparing what I need to say, going off-site to talk.

5 Reflect on what you want to move towards not just move away from. For example, you might want to hand in your notice and set up your own business so that you have more autonomy. Maybe you want a pay rise so that you feel more secure. Perhaps you want to make someone redundant as they're consistently underperforming and you want to be fair to the other team members who are performing. If you dig a little deeper, you'll often discover that underneath the surface of a difficult conversation, there's a longing for a deeper desire. Seeing this helps you to lean in and talk rather than stay stuck and dissatisfied.

The pervasive problems that beset our ability to talk with one another aren't surprising. Eighty per cent of managers are 'accidental' managers, according to the Chartered Management Institute, who coined the term. They lack the necessary skills because they've never had the opportunity to learn them, having risen up the 'managerial escalator' without formal training, including in difficult conversations. No wonder national productivity in the UK is lagging.[16]

There is growing recognition of the gap this leaves behind. Deloitte and PwC are giving extra coaching to their youngest UK staff after noticing recruits whose education was disrupted by lockdowns have weaker teamwork and communication skills than previous cohorts.[17] Organisations are increasingly valuing essential human skills, whether it's public speaking, conflict resolution or non-verbal communication such as eye contact.

With conversation, the intangible becomes tangible. An FT article (23 May 2023) shared that ETF (exchange-traded fund) investors are increasingly paying attention to companies with a strong corporate culture where 'our people are our best asset' is not just rhetoric but real. *'The strongest share price signals were derived from harder-to-measure metrics such as employees' perceptions of autonomy, fairness, trust, alignment of interests and psychological safety. More easily measured metrics such as job titles and benefits provide weaker performance signals.*' Corporate scandals, such as the VW emissions cheating, destroy value whereas satisfied and motivated employees create value.[18]

Psychologists have pointed to the power of the subtle for decades. 'Unconditional positive regard' being critical for positive human interactions, as Carl Rogers proposed, is one example. Now managers and leaders are experiencing for themselves the difference that these more invisible dimensions to our interactions bring.

Getting to authentic dialogue

To create change through conversation, we must move beyond seeing 'talk' as merely an exchange of words. Definitions of dialogue point to several important dimensions of a difficult conversation to which we need to pay attention. Bill Isaacs, author of the seminal text *Dialogue and the Art of Thinking Together*, offers the following definition:

> **'Dialogue is a conversation in which people think together in relationship . . . The art of thinking together.'[19]**

Notice the emphasis on relationship. We need an atmosphere between us that can hold the charge of differences of opinion and the heat of strong emotions.

David Bohm, in his book *On Dialogue*, states:

> **'Dialogue kindles a new mode of paying attention – to the assumptions taken for granted, the polarisation of opinions, the rules for acceptable and unacceptable conversation and the methods for managing differences.'[20]**

Here is the need to pay attention to *how* we're talking and thinking. Our heads are full of assumptions that we take for granted; we don't even notice that they're there until we 'bump into' someone else's thinking. When we bring our underlying assumptions into a conversation, it deepens our thinking.

Theodore Zeldin, philosopher and author, emphasises the emergent quality of talking:

> **'Conversation is a meeting of minds with different memories and habits. When minds meet, they don't just exchange facts: they transform them, reshape them, draw different implications from them, engage in new trains of thought. Conversation doesn't just reshuffle the cards: it creates new cards.'**[21]

True dialogue is generative. It has a dynamism and freshness to it that many meetings lack.

Finally, Paulo Freire, the Brazilian educator and philosopher, writes about dialogue being a more human way of interacting. He writes:

> **'Dialogue cannot exist without humility.'**[22]

When we put being right ahead of being in relationship, talking goes tense. When we set out not knowing, ask questions instead of giving answers, and bring open hearts and minds, we build connection and have a real conversation.

Drawing on all the definitions covered so far, here's how I define 'authentic dialogue', which is what every difficult conversation calls for. Authentic dialogue is:

> **'A conversation that generates positive change by people listening and thinking together.'**

The positive change could be a new insight, novel solution or strengthened relationship. Great outcomes occur only when a conversation goes beyond being an exchange of words, a shouting match or a bear pit where people tear chunks out of each other.

An authentic dialogue is a conversation that involves one or more of these components:

- Grappling with real issues. People not only talk together but think together to arrive at a way forward that everyone has brought into.
- Dealing with troublesome emotions. People share how they feel, listen to what's true for others and find ways to contain the 'charge' of difference.
- Creating something new. Out of a shared understanding, fresh insights emerge which one person thinking alone couldn't have come up with.

Talking together is action. It carries power. It affects material reality. The rest of this book explores how.

From falling over to flourishing

The fundamental purpose of an organisation is for a group of individuals to create something together that they are unable to produce by working in isolation or in parallel. In this sense, the collective really is more powerful than the individual. And without dialogue to facilitate this, a team risks 'falling over', as Amal put it in his note to me. Work is duplicated, mistakes fall through the cracks and conflicts fester.

After I completed a two-day dialogue skill-building programme for Amal and his team, we had a catch-up a few weeks later. Amal thanked me for the session and said, 'People really need to do this sort of thing more often. It's a waste to let a team breakdown when positive experiences like the time spent with you can so readily motivate and strengthen a group.'

Amal also shared that he'd just received a promotion. He was soon to lead a much larger team, which also had a pattern of hybrid working.

'My decision that I needed to create a more cohesive team arrived in the nick of time', he reflected.

'I trust that the skills you've learned will stand both you and your existing team in good stead', I replied.

'One hundred per cent', said Amal. 'I've learned that people will 'open up' and flourish if put in a safe space with a nourishing and interesting facilitator.'

Or leader, I thought.

When I gathered feedback from the rest of the SMT about the session, people spoke about receiving new insights into their daily management role and making changes in their behaviour to improve their professional and home life. Other comments included:

> **'Effective leadership is all about teamwork. Teaching the team how to talk and how to listen has been invaluable. There was a sub-plot too which was the bonding experience.'**

> **'We developed communications skills using techniques and practices you probably never even knew existed.'**

> **'I'm now more aware of my behaviours during meetings and how these can make me a better leader.'**

> **'It was great to share this experience as it brought everyone closer together.'**

Their observations were a great reminder of the benefits of dialogue. Individuals feel a sense of belonging, teams are more cohesive, and organisations deliver quality goods and services. All this flows from people overcoming the blocks to talking and experiencing a real sense that 'we're in this together.'

Summary

1 There are many obstacles to having a difficult conversation including lack of time and know-how. Many managers avoid having a difficult conversation because they believe it's too tricky or that it's too difficult dealing with a certain person.

2 Without tried-and-tested strategies to overcome these blocks, stuckness sets in and problems remain unresolved. They may even escalate.

3 In an age of increasing polarisation and 'permacrisis', skilful dialogue is needed more than ever.

4 'Authentic dialogue' is not just a verbal exchange. It creates positive change by people talking, thinking and acting together.

5 A difficult conversation saves valuable time. Robust conversations will, in the long run, save far more time than they take.

6 Dialogue can turn 'difficult people' into valuable assets. To draw out a person's potential, bring 'unconditional positive regard' to the conversation.

7 Dialogue increases wellbeing and productivity. It creates positive change in individuals, teams and organisations.

> **If you do only one thing now . . .** When you're avoiding or messing up a difficult conversation, identify what's getting in the way. Take your time to reflect calmly. At the root of the issue, there's likely to be some fear (of rejection, loss of control or damaging a relationship). Name your fear without trying to change it. See if it loosens its grip.

Notes

1 Karsh, L. (2004) The Hidden Costs of Poor People Management. *Inc.* https://www.inc.com/articles/2004/12/karsh.html.

2 Rogers, C. (1957) 'The necessary and sufficient conditions of therapeutic personality change', *Journal of Counseling Psychology*, 21, pp. 95–103.

3 Bohm D., Factor, D. and Garrett, P. (1991) Dialogue – A proposal, https://aofpd.org/library/public-resources/dialogue-a-proposal/.

4   Anjli Raval, Science Museum's Ian Blatchford: 'If the arts world is not careful, it will be eaten alive by its own piety, Financial Times, 27 November 2022.
5   https://learn.workbravely.com/hubfs/Understanding-the-Conversation-Gap.pdf.
6   https://www.therightconversation.co.uk/downloads/team-dialogue-indicator-case-study.
7   Bob Sutton, Nov 24, 2013. If Performance Evaluations Were a Drug, They Would Not Receive F.D.A. Approval," But They Aren't Always Bad.
8   CPP Global Human Capital Report (2008) *Workplace conflict and how businesses can harness it to survive*, https://www.themyersbriggs.com/-/media/f39a8b7fb4fe4daface552d9f485c825.ashx.
9   https://www.vitalsmarts.fr/wp-content/uploads/2020/12/Costly-Conversations-Ebook.pdf.
10 https://www.fastcompany.com/3051779/3-ways-companies-are-changing-the-dreaded-performance-review.
11 https://www.cultureamp.com.
12 https://hbr.org/2014/01/how-netflix-reinvented-hr.
13 https://www.ft.com/content/d2a3e4d5-f9e2-426c-9c20-d5cd149137ec.
14 Lencioni, P. (2002) *The Five Dysfunctions of a Team: A leadership fable*, John Wiley & Sons.
15 De Phillips, F.A., Berliner, & W. M., Cribbin, J. J. (1960) 'Meaning of learning and knowledge', *Management of Training Programs*. Homewood, IL: Richard D. Irwin.
16 https://www.ft.com/content/4cd32315-a3e4-4768-9f31-fa3e7466f728.
17 https://www.ft.com/content/a8b20502-8238-4655-ba82-30d6243332d9.
18 Chris Flood, Corporate culture ETFs aim to gain from happier employees, The Financial Times Limited, MAY 5 2023.

19 Isaacs, W. (1999) *Dialogue and the Art of Thinking Together*, Currency Doubleday.
20 Bohm, D. (1996) *On Dialogue*, Routledge.
21 Zeldin, T. (1988) *Conversation*, Harvill.
22 Freire, P. (2005) *Pedagogy of the Oppressed*, Continuum.

chapter 3

What every conversation needs

> 'All great failures in life stem from failures in conversation.'
>
> Bill Isaacs

The quality of the atmosphere in a room can make or break a difficult conversation and is an essential component of authentic dialogue. Creating a 'holding environment' for authentic dialogue enables people to feel safe and talk rather than get defensive and shut down. Leaders need to pay attention not just to the content of their conversation but to subtle aspects such as the 'field' in which the talking takes place. We'll explore what a 'container' is, why it matters and how you can build a container in practical ways.

> 'Bombs have been going off', my co-facilitator told me. 'There have been shouting matches and now it's getting personal. There's a real undercurrent of people not feeling seen or heard. Time to fasten our seatbelts.'
>
> When I walked into the meeting room on the first day, the atmosphere felt chilly even though it was a sunny 22 degrees Celsius outside. My palms felt clammy. I reminded myself how meeting in groups, even mid-size such as the 15 team members we had, stimulates anxiety in individuals. Fears of attack, of being lost in a crowd or of rejection are rife.
>
> By the second day of our leadership retreat, the ice had started to thaw. We'd spent a couple of hours naming the difficult conversations that the team needed to have (using the Critical conversations grid, which I'll cover in Chapter 9) when suddenly we ended up diving into one of them.
>
> The CEO spoke about an unexpected call he'd received on the golf course from the bank's main client. A transaction involving $93m dollars had failed.
>
> 'My own father wouldn't speak to me like that.'
>
> His voice was getting louder, his speech faster and his face more flushed.
>
> 'I cannot believe that we still don't have systems in place to deal with a future incident.'

> As he paused to draw breath, the youngest and most junior member of the team turned to him and said in a much lower voice,
> 'M_____, you're starting to intimidate us.'
> A hush swept across the whole room.
> He looked the CEO right in the eye and said firmly but kindly:
> 'I hear what you're saying but the way you're saying it makes it difficult to hear.'
> I waited with bated breath for what would happen next. Would the CEO attack, go silent or pooh-pooh the observation? The rest of the meeting would pivot on this moment.

Many of the more difficult conversations explored in this book, such as asking for a pay rise, giving someone challenging feedback or delivering bad news to a stakeholder, are delicate and complex. There's a real risk that the essence of what needs to be said remains unspoken or that when it is shared, people get triggered and the conversation derails.

While there are never any guarantees about how a conversation will progress, attending to the conditions in which the talking takes place maximises the likelihood of success. The quality of the 'holding environment' directly impacts the quality of the conversation. Just as a seedling doesn't grow unless the soil, moisture and sunlight support it, so human interaction depends on the quality of the surroundings.

Leaders often overlook the importance of the environment. With their drive to meet objectives, make assertions and push through an agenda, they often fail to notice the subtle change in tone when a conversation goes tense or they're at a loss regarding what to do about it. We'll address this gap by unpacking the most neglected dimension of authentic dialogue: the setting in which it takes place.

There is a dearth of spaces for rich conversations in our families, organisations and society. People feel more frustrated than lucid once they've tried to talk. According to Rishi Sunak, at the heart of the government's Covid response in 2020, there was no real forum for debate where people could speak freely, ask questions and offer a dissenting opinion. Discussion was stifled, trade-offs weren't aired, and options weren't fully explored. When asked how he would have handled the pandemic differently, Sunak's response was, *'I would just have had a more grown-up conversation with the country.'*[1]

In the BBC Radio 4 series *A Long History of Argument*, Rory Stewart, host and former Member of Parliament (MP), reflects on how the ability to govern well is directly related to the ability to argue well. Polarised positions, populism and post-truth politics all hamper politicians' ability to talk together, which is having severe consequences for our democracy. The rise of social media platforms such as X (formerly known as Twitter) since 2014 has exacerbated the lack of productive dialogue in politics as algorithms promote divisive content rather than 'reward' communicating meaningfully about what really matters.

Stewart points out that the rules of engagement in the Houses of Parliament, such as no one being allowed to call another MP a 'liar', were created so that the members could debate effectively in the chamber. However, rather than MPs debating face-to-face in parliament, Stewart observes:

'Nowadays it feels much more like people are performing, not for the people in the chamber with them but to be overheard in a clip on television or on Twitter. When that happens, you're no longer really engaging as a human being, you're no longer really trying to persuade someone or being persuaded in turn.'[2]

Sound bites have replaced substance. Tweets have taken precedence over in-person conversation. Conflict online has stymied face-to-face communication, all because of a lack of know-how about how to create an environment that sustains a difficult conversation. As Andrew Marr has observed:

> 'Social media, far from providing a digital version of the town square, is driving us away from a common conversation... [we have been] ... giggling too much about the latest scandal to think about the most important things – too distracted to have essential, calmer conversations.'[3]

This pattern of getting distracted, poor debate and bad decision-making is pervasive in our government, organisations and teams. Our 'trigger culture' extends way beyond X, previously known as Twitter. As Nina Power has said, we're unlikely to get far if we resort to fighting instead of talking.[4]

But it doesn't have to be this way. While I agree that productive dialogue, particularly in the public square, is a difficult 'nut to crack', I've also seen enough evidence as a dialogue coach to know that a different form of engagement is not only worth pursuing, but decidedly possible.

What every difficult conversation needs

In dialogue work, the word that's used to capture the notion of the space that 'holds' a conversation is a *container*. It is, in many ways, not a great word as it can conjure up images of metal boxes in shipping or plastic boxes to store food, neither of which are helpful associations. Yet the word, originally used in a therapeutic context to describe a relationship in which a client feels accepted no matter what they share, has stuck. Bill Isaacs summarises its importance as follows:

> 'As the container is, so goes the conversation.'

Having worked with Bill and his team at Dialogos, I appreciate that without a strong container, authentic dialogue doesn't happen.

Without a supportive 'holding environment', our verbal interaction will disappoint rather than inspire. This applies to all difficult conversations, whether in one-to-one, team or multi-stakeholder settings.

I'll more fully define a container in a moment, but first I want to share a personal experience that underlined how critical a strong container is. And you might like to pause and reflect on where in your life and leadership you've seen the difference that a 'container' has made to a difficult conversation (see Exercise 6 – Create a container).

Exercise 6
Create a container

Think about conversations you've had whether at work, home or in your wider life. Go for conversations that you can replay in your mind as easily as possible.

1. Recall a conversation that energised you and engaged the other person (or persons).
    - Identify the tangible factors that contributed to you talking together effectively. This includes the physical space you were in (e.g. you had the meeting offsite rather than in the office and this reduced the amount of distraction; or the room had lots of natural light, which created a great ambiance; or you were online and everyone turned up and engaged).
    - Identify the *intangible* factors that had an impact. This includes the human dynamics at play (e.g. there was roughly equal airtime between participants that led to a trusting atmosphere; or someone took the risk to share something meaningful about themselves and this set an authentic tone for others).
2. Recall a difficult conversation you had that left you feeling dissatisfied, regretful or drained.
    - Identify the tangible factors that got in the way of you talking together effectively (e.g. you were online and the other person

had their camera switched off so it was difficult to understand what was really happening or there wasn't enough time for a free-flowing discussion).
- Identify the *intangible* factors that contributed to the conversation going off course (e.g. one or two people dominated the airwaves; there was a tense atmosphere and many people stayed silent; or two of the team members had fallen out and no one was willing to say anything about the 'elephant in the room').

Reflect on your answers to the questions. What can you learn from your experience about creating a 'container'? How could you apply this learning in the future?

Why a container is critical for dialogue

I can remember the first time I felt the atmosphere in a room shift. I was at school in a music room which wasn't our regular classroom. We were with our teacher, but the unfamiliarity of the space had my seven-year-old being on high alert. For some unknown reason, our teacher had had to step away and unusually we were teacherless for a few minutes.

The noise level quickly got louder as kids started talking over one another. There was a sense of excitement and nervousness as a couple of kids tried to make their voices heard over the din of drums playing, recorders piping and cymbals clashing. The fragile melody that had begun to emerge when the teacher had been in the room was lost to a noise fest. The cacophony subsided as soon as the teacher walked back in but our tune didn't return. With the teacher's exit, we'd lost our container and our capacity to make music together.

It was my first experience of how the output produced reflects the conditions in which it's created. No container, no music. No container, no conversation. No container, no coherence.

What is a container?

If you've walked into a room and felt the atmosphere was so thick that you could cut it with a knife, you already have a feel for the energy 'field' of a container. Maybe you've been lucky enough to walk into a room and feel love, energy and excitement? Your 'felt-sense' picks up on the presence of a container.

When I reflect on my work as a dialogue coach, it's all about creating the conditions for a meaningful dialogue to ignite. If you've ever talked to a teenager in a car and discovered how the eye gaze isn't so intense and the sense of motion keeps the talk moving (not to mention the lack of an easy exit), you already know how conducive a 'container' is.

Our thoughts and words have a presence; they're like currents moving through the air, capable of drawing others to us or driving them away. A container feels expansive and spacious when there's trust in the room. When the atmosphere tenses up and people withdraw, it's much harder to talk.

We create change in our lives, teams and organisations through the creation of a 'container'. Coming from the Latin, *'con-tenere'*, the root of the word means 'to hold with or within'. Developmental psychologists have found that a 'containing relationship' between an infant and caregiver is key to the growth of a healthy self, as it manages the infant's anxiety, settles their frustration and frees their capacity for curiosity and exploration. A 'container' is also critical for the healthy growth of groups and teams through a coaching process.[5]

Bill Isaacs describes a container in the following way:

'A field of shared meaning and intense personal and emotional energy, in which [participants] can safely generate insightful conversations that are powerful enough to spark change, while remaining within the bounds of mutual respect. These are the kinds of conversations that bring unrealized potential into being.'[6]

Creating and maintaining a container is an act of leadership. When I've led dialogue programmes, whether for CEOs, bishops and cathedral deans or for groups of psychologists, it has struck me that there's always at least one participant who says, 'I've never thought about creating a container for a conversation.'

Containers are vital for dialogue for three key reasons:

- Firstly, they 'hold' difficult feelings. Being in a group, particularly a larger group of 15 or more, routinely frustrates our needs for recognition, intimacy and even our sense of identity. A container handles this pressure so that people can express how they're feeling through dialogue rather than anxiety and frustration becoming destructive and derailing the dialogue.

- Secondly, with a container, it's possible for the warmth of human connection to emerge. Longitudinal research has shown that having a 'warm surround' of healthy relationships is key to our wellbeing. A vital tool for creating this is conversation. Connections with other people predict how long you stay healthy, how long your brain will stay sharp and makes you less likely to get coronary heart disease (see box below for more information).

The value of a 'warm surround'

Way ahead of the curve of the current positive psychology movement, the Harvard Study of Adult Development (HSAD), which began in 1938, is the longest scientific study of happiness ever conducted. The study began with 268 undergraduate students at Harvard College, whose lives have been tracked for over 75 years. In addition, 456 14-year-old boys from some of the most disadvantaged neighbourhoods in Boston, Massachusetts were included in the study. All had interviews and medical tests on joining the study as well as regular brain scans, blood tests and further interviews throughout their lives.

Eight decades later, HSAD has expanded to include three generations and more than 1300 offspring of the original participants. Whereas the initial study looked only at white men, more than half of participants are now women. Various books have documented the findings of the study with its insights on what makes a happy, meaningful and successful life; findings that have been corroborated by other research with more diverse groups.[7]

In his 2012 book *Triumphs of Experience*, George E. Vaillant shares the factors that are both irrelevant and relevant for living a contented and long life.[8] Having been involved in the study for 45 years, Vaillant found that a clear pattern of results emerged. Variables reflecting social class (e.g. the level to which their mother or father was educated) had no bearing on success later in life. Neither did variables that reflected constitutional factors, such as having a strongly masculine physique. The variables that reflected the quality of the men's relational lives, however, were very strong predictors. This led Vaillant to conclude that the real 'antecedent of flourishing' was the capacity for positive, close and loving relationships.

The value of 'warm relationships' also shows up in the incomes earned by the men. The 58 men who scored most highly for warm relationships earned an average maximum income of $243,000 per year whereas the 31 men who scored the lowest earned an average maximum income of $102,000 per year. By contrast, there was no significant difference between the maximum earned incomes of the men when divided by IQ.

What differentiated the most successful from the least successful men wasn't so much the presence of one relationship, such as a lifelong marriage. Flourishing later in life was associated with a man's capacity to value others, whether his partner, parents, siblings, children, colleagues or friends. Creating a loving surround, whether within your family or at work, is what matters.

Robert Waldinger, another researcher involved in the study and professor of psychiatry at Harvard Medical school, also

> highlights how having warm connections with other people predicts how long you stay healthy. 'Warm' is a relationship that feels engaged, nourishing and supportive, whether this is emotionally, financially or practically; rather than draining, acrimonious or exploitative. In his book, *The Good Life*, co-authored with Marc Schulz, 'social fitness' is the term they use to describe how we can improve our lives through strengthening our social connections, just as we can improve our physical fitness through taking action.[9] Our wellbeing and happiness aren't static or determined solely by our genes or disposition. We can, as Waldinger says, 'move the needle'. Conversation is a key tool for developing life-enriching, as well as career enhancing, warm connections.

- Finally, a coherent 'energy field' generates alignment. Psychologists Losada and Heaphy have demonstrated that the quality of atmosphere is a key difference between high- and low-performing teams.[10] Low-performing teams get stuck in negativity, which creates restricted emotional spaces that close possibilities for action. Top teams operate in an expansive emotional space that opens the way to newness: people speak their truth even when it's uncomfortable, or a team finally agrees a way forward for an issue that's been undiscussable.

> Continuing on from the music room experience, the next time that the notion of a container appeared in my awareness was during an informal conversation on a dialogue training programme. The programme took place in the town hall of Chipping Campden in the Cotswolds. There were latticed windows which looked out onto honey-coloured stone houses with narrow pavements and hanging baskets.

With 25 chairs in a circle, a large bunch of flowers on a side table displaying a range of books, it felt like a perfect setting for dialogue. I could smell the freshness of the freesias and the warm orange carpet made me think of sitting around a campfire. It had of course been intentionally chosen by our trainer, Peter Garrett. Peter was at that time working with Bill Isaacs at Dialogos, a niche consultancy based in Boston, USA, and he had excellent radar for creating an environment that supported generative dialogue.

One evening over dinner, Peter and I were chatting about how I might take what I'd been learning about dialogue into the Cabinet Office, where I was working as a psychologist. I felt alive with the possibility of no longer 'chasing the expert' by bringing in external consultants to solve the complex recruitment problems we were facing. Over 15,000 graduates had applied for the 400 places on the 'Civil Service Selection Board' (CSSB), and the number of applicants for this graduate Fast Stream selection process were expected to rise year on year (it now stands at more than 30,000 for around 800 places). The chief psychologist and I had been tasked with redesigning the whole selection process, including reducing the two-and-a-half-day assessment centre down to a single day.

With a dialogic approach, I was starting to see how we could harvest the collective intelligence of the civil servants involved in the project to come up with our own solutions. These were likely to be a better cultural fit than any expert solution delivered from the outside. More crucially, the tranche of retired senior civil servants who were assessors at CSSB (and heavily invested in keeping the process as it had been for decades) were more likely to accept design ideas that they'd had a part in generating.

My conversation with Peter suddenly took an unexpected turn.

'Now tell me about doing street shows', Peter said.

I'd spoken earlier in the circle about my four years living on the road in Spain, earning my keep as a street circus performer. It had been an unexpected chapter that followed my graduation from the University of Nottingham's psychology department. Instead of taking a graduate job or starting a PhD, the spirit of adventure had turned into a plan to teach English for a year, which had morphed into becoming a fire juggler.

The long hot Spanish evenings, the smell of paella cooking mingled with diesel from the trucks and the intoxicating scent of fiery torches tossed high into the air stays with me still. We'd been discussing insights from the emerging science of complex adaptive systems. I'd shared how, during my time as a traveller, I'd come to appreciate how life lived 'at the edge of chaos' is truly enlivening, just as complexity science was discovering. I hadn't imagined that we'd return to the topic of busking over the candlelit dinner with some local musicians softly playing flutes in the background.

I sat up a little straighter, excited by Peter's inquiry. There was also some shakiness inside. I'd been back from Spain for two years and was still transitioning into mainstream work and society. The years on the road might have sounded romantic but they'd been more a masterclass in resilience, as had my return to the UK.

It had taken me a year to find a job having sent off dozens of applications and CVs. I'd eventually landed a position at the Department of Work and Pensions in Sheffield where I worked with the HR team on the more technical aspects of selection systems and then transferred to the Cabinet Office on secondment. I was painfully aware that regarding career progression, I was way behind the other psychologists I'd graduated with. They had done the sensible thing and taken up jobs at consultancies or posts in academia rather than driven off into the sunshine in an old camper van as I had done.

▶

'You must have learnt how to build containers quickly', Peter said.

I'd never thought about my time as a busker in that way and yet Peter's observation rang true. Street circus is a raw art. If you don't capture people's attention, they walk away. If you're not entertaining, your crowd quickly disperses. If you don't connect with your volunteer, you'll be heckled. If you try to pass the hat too soon, people will hurry away.

I described to Peter how the turning point in my busking career had been meeting an American magician, *El Mago*, as I had come to call him. He had travelled for 20 years all over the world with his street show and was a veteran performer. I'd spotted him in the central plaza in Pamplona during the San Fermin fiesta, where the bulls run through the streets along with locals dressed in white waving red flags to tease and taunt *los toros*.

I watched as El Mago picked his pitch, put down his bag, put on his top hat and blew up a balloon. As he twisted it into an elephant, the three kids who'd stopped by to watch laughed and clapped. Their applause drew in a few more kids and out came another balloon which turned into a giraffe. Mums and dads, aunts and uncles, grannies and granddads came to see what the fun was all about. Soon the crowd was several rows deep with people straining to see what was happening. There were more tricks, gasps and chuckles as more and more people joined the throng. El Mago got people to stand back to create a bigger space for him to perform, which, in turn, attracted a larger crowd. In less than five minutes, he'd turned a public square into a pop-up theatre. The gathered crowd were enthralled.

I wasn't a magician but I was a keen student. I gradually applied the art of 'doing a show' to my juggling skills over a summer season. Instead of 'doing time' (as buskers call it) juggling at the side of the street, I learned how to pull, build and entertain a crowd and then pass the hat (before they walked away). By carefully choosing a volunteer and raising a round of applause for them as they stepped into the 'ring', I doubled my winnings overnight.

For my finale I rolled out a mat, asked the volunteer to lie down and juggled knives over the top of him, from his toes to the tip of his head. In dozens of shows, there was only one volunteer who, on seeing the knives flash in the dark, got up and walked away. It wasn't me that kept the other volunteers in place, it was the strength of the holding environment.

The space created was the intangible X-factor that held a street show together. The micro-economics of busking were starker. 'Doing time' I'd get 1000 pesetas in the hat for each hour I juggled (and what hard work that was). Doing shows of 15 minutes would land me 5000 pesetas in the hat. On a good night, with the right pitch, I could do four or five shows in two hours and take home 25,000 pesetas. Showtime!

I saw jugglers who tossed seven balls in the air, clowns who rode unicycles as tall as a lamppost and acrobats who climbed on top of each other's shoulders but no matter how brilliant their technical skills were, if they didn't know how to create and hold space, their street show never took off. Similarly, if a leader or manager doesn't learn and use the skills of container building, a difficult conversation will never have a successful outcome.

How to build a container

There is an art and science to container building that many leaders have never learned, the learning of which can change everything. We arrive on this earth through the container of a womb. The natural world abounds with containers. A river needs its banks otherwise it's a marsh. A seedling grows in a pot or a greenhouse, protected from vicissitudes of the wider environment. Every significant creative endeavour also starts life in a holding environment, whether it's a novel, poem, song, strategy or passionately declared purpose. With a container in place, what's been impossible to talk about becomes possible.

A container has both physical and non-physical dimensions. On a more tangible level, the container is the room we're in, but also the lighting, sound and air quality. If there's natural light, it helps to bring a sense of spaciousness. A quiet room, away from the banter of an open-plan office, enables people to think together as they talk together. An open window letting in fresh air stops the conversation from going stale. The cost of an offsite venue yields a return as it reduces the distractions of the business-as-usual environment.

As a leader or convener of a dialogue, it pays to think through how you'll set up the room. Make a conscious choice about how chairs are laid out – a circle of chairs creates a sense of intimacy that rows of chairs will never replicate. A conversation that takes place in a room with no table to hide behind can reach places that a boardroom discussion typically cannot.

A container also has more intangible dimensions. We hear so much these days about how important it is to have psychological or emotional safety in the room and rightly so. But safety alone doesn't cut it. A difficult conversation needs an atmosphere of possibility, not just protection. Dialogue calls for energy as well as for engagement. Talking and thinking together needs not just our heads but our hearts and our guts too. The street show experience taught me that while safety is fundamental, on its own, it's not enough.

I'll say more about creating a container for dialogue in teams in Chapter 7 (Read the room) and in multi-stakeholder groups in Chapter 8 (Hold space). In the next chapter, I unpack container building in two more fundamental ways: for yourself and for talking with another one-to-one.

Returning to the 'hot' moment of the story with which I started this chapter, all eyes were on the CEO as he took his time to respond. He looked down and then around the circle at his team. I had the sense that a moment before he'd been out on the golf course re-living the phone call but that now he was back in the room, being fully present.

'I'm sorry', he said. *'I can understand why that way I was talking wasn't helping.'*

This simple, humble and authentic acknowledgement was the turning point of the meeting.

The atmosphere, which my co-facilitator and I had carefully built with the group, had been strong enough to hold the discomfort of someone 'speaking truth to power'. We'd started both days with a 'check-in' to bring all the voices into the room and encourage equal airtime. We'd set some clear ground rules to establish safety and placed the phones of team members in a 'nursery' in the next room to minimise distractions and encourage people to be present (See Chapter 8, Hold space, for more information on these tools).

With our 'container' in place, the team was then able to talk about what really mattered to them. Our dialogue named the issues that would help catapult the bank in the right direction. The team had talked about how fast they could fix what was broken – together. They'd also agreed to hold another leadership retreat in six months' time; a sure sign that the team had started to form.

'Transformation in action', my co-facilitator said when we talked on the plane going home. Some words of Ursula K. Le Guin (American author) came to mind:

> *'Words'*, she wrote in her moving piece on the magic of real human conversation, *'transform both speaker and hearer; they feed energy back and forth and amplify it. They feed understanding or emotion back and forth and amplify it.'*[11]

When there's a 'container' to hold our words and emotions, our dialogue comes from – and goes to – a very different place. Reactivity reduces and creativity infuses and enhances our conversation. We stop feeling anxious and frustrated and look for solutions that work for everyone, releasing untapped potential.

Summary

---

1 A 'container' is a safe and energising space that enables people to open up and talk rather than get defensive and shut down. When a container is missing, a difficult conversation becomes even more tricky or impossible.

2 Leaders need to pay attention not only to the content of their conversation, but to the more intangible aspects such as the atmosphere that the talking takes place in. Many managers and leaders ignore or overlook the more subtle dimensions of a conversation even though they significantly shape the quality of the talking.

3 With a positive atmosphere, where there's safety, energy and possibility, talking together, even about the tough stuff, becomes possible. An 'expansive emotional space', which is a key characteristic of high-performing teams, opens up possibilities for action.

4 A 'container' has physical and non-physical dimensions. Physical elements include the room you're in, the quality of the lighting and sound and the room set-up. Non-physical dimensions include the tone, atmosphere and degree of positivity. Both matter.

> **If you do only one thing now...** It is vital your conversation takes place within a supportive container. How you yourself speak has a crucial role in generating this. Pay attention to your tone of voice. Cultivate an attitude of respect, openness and honesty. Don't be domineering or a pushover. Come from a place of curiosity in what you say and how you say it. Try 'tell me more about...'

Notes

1. Nelson, F. (2022) Lockdown: the inside story, *The Spectator*, 27 August.
2. Cunliffe, R. (2022) Encounter with Rory Stewart, *The New Statesman*, 22–28 July.
3. Marr, A. (2022) Politics column, *The New Statesman*, 22–28 July.
4. Power. N. (2023) in an interview with McRedmond, F., *Prospect*, April.
5. Thornton, C. (2016) *Group and Team Coaching: The secret life of groups*, Routledge.
6. Isaacs, W. (8 February 2017) Conversations that Change the World, *Strategy+Business*.
7. Flood, A. (2023) How to be happy, *New Scientist*, 14 January 2023.
8. Vaillant, G. E. (2012) *Triumphs of Experience*, Belknap Press of Harvard University Press.
9. Waldinger, R. and Schulz, M. (2023) *The Good Life: Lessons from the world's longest study on happiness*, Rider.
10. Losada, M. and Heaphy, E. (2004) The role of positivity and connectivity in the performance of business teams: A nonlinear dynamics model, *American Behavioural Scientist*, Vol. 47, 6, pp. 740–765.
11. Le Guin, U. (2004) *The Wave in the Mind: Talks and essays on the writer, the reader, and the imagination*, Shambhala Publications Inc.

chapter 4

Turn down the heat

'Whatever is triggering you, is on you.'
Richie Norton

When we are 'triggered' by the behaviour of someone, instead of a kneejerk reaction, a more effective response is possible. Knowing your triggers enables you to create a pause so that your 'reactive self' no longer sabotages your conversation. There are three reactive patterns (to attack, withdraw or acquiesce) and we ignore them at our peril. By seeing your reactivity more clearly, you can take a step back and tap into your 'creative self'. As your inner state changes, it becomes easier to talk when there's tough stuff on the table.

> She was called Bridget, and before we had exchanged a word beyond 'hello', I could feel her sadness on the screen. It was like listening to someone who hadn't spoken in depth for years. Bridget was searching for words in an unfamiliar situation – with someone she hardly knew. As the words suddenly came tumbling out, she began ending the pretence that everything was OK. Another shuddering sigh and silence. Very gently I said,
> 'Take your time. Tell me as much as you want.'
> 'I feel like. . . I feel like. . . My whole life is passing me by. *It's going. . . I'm going. . . . Nowhere.*'
> Bridget paused, and her slowly spoken words made the silence stretch out between us.
> 'I feel so . . . stuck. Personally, professionally and spiritually – *stuck*. I'm frustrated with myself and scared to take the next step.'
> 'What do you want?'
> 'I want to be able to move forwards – in my life, in my work and in my relationship.'
> 'How will you know you have done that?'
> 'I'll feel lighter and freer in myself.'
> 'So what gets in the way?'
> 'I make excuses for myself. I have got IBS, I'm dyslexic, I. . . '
> 'And what would taking the next step give you?'
> 'A greater sense of connection – with my work, with my creativity, but most of all, with my partner. It feels magical when it does happen. I'd like to expand that.'

'So how may I be able to help?'

'I really struggle having conversations... My partner and I find it hard to communicate. It's difficult for me to find the words... Having better conversations, and a better relationship, feels like the next frontier.'

Bridget described how she'd recently left London to live in Ipswich and set up her own business. To subsidise her fledgling start-up, she had taken a part-time job locally. It was hard going and taking its toll.

'I'm the bread winner', Bridget said. 'My partner, Liam, is a musician who doesn't earn very much. I get really frustrated about how little money we have. I have nowhere to dump my stuff, so when we argue I accuse him of holding me back.'

Bridget started to cry quietly. I could see the tears falling in her lap.

'I have been a such a witch!' Bridget said, plunging straight in. 'I have so many fears about money. I feel resentful that Liam has less work and earns so little. We argue and I explode. My parting shot is "I'm leaving!" and yet I stay... It's a vicious cycle we've played out time and time again.'

I waited for Bridget to continue on her roll.

'I'm not achieving what I really want to achieve. I don't send the emails I need to send, I don't pick up the phone to create new contacts and I don't grow my business in the way I know I could.'

'What gets in the way?'

'I make excuses for myself: "I'm a disorganised dyslexic!" Or I tell myself that I can't work when my home is in a mess so I tidy up instead of work. And when I have finished tidying up, I tell myself that I'm too tired to do any real work. I lose momentum.'

I was impressed with Bridget's self-honesty.

'I'm stuck in a cycle of self-sabotage. I ignore my own needs, because I *do* need to work in an ordered environment, but

> I also need to earn my living. When I don't get down to working, it triggers all my fears that I'll end up broke, alone and in a homeless shelter.'
>
> Bridget took a long breath.
>
> 'Liam and I both work at home in a small house. We have separate rooms but I find it really frustrating when Liam comes in and interrupts me – even if he is offering me a cup of tea!'
>
> 'How do you respond?'
>
> 'I say something like, "Don't talk to me right now!", "Go away!" or "Leave me alone!" We've had problems in the past when I have cut him off completely and he's like a child that picks, picks, picks at me. I detach further and then our relationship gets in a real mess. I want to change that pattern, but I don't know how. Do you?'
>
> I had an idea, but it probably wasn't what Bridget was expecting. Turning down the heat – whether in a business setting or an intimate relationship – involves directing our attention on the place where we have most leverage: ourselves. As Ryan Roslansky, CEO, LinkedIn, observed, *'It's probably not on my LinkedIn profile, but I think the most important skill I had to pick up early on was learning how to manage my psychology.'*[1]

Know your triggers

You know that your buttons are being pushed when your inner state doesn't serve you or the situation. You move from a healthy emotion to an unhealthy version. Fear paralyses you instead of creating alertness. Anger becomes rage rather than a way of setting boundaries. Sadness turns into chronic depression. If you express these high-octane emotions, you're at risk of 'acting out' and hurting someone else. If you suppress these emotions, you risk hurting yourself, for example by creating an illness.

Recent research from neuroscience shows how specific threats in a social situation affect our ability to talk together. Financial uncertainty or speaking to someone more senior stimulates brain networks similar to threats to our primary survival needs (such as for food and water). Once our limbic system (which houses our emotional reactions) is activated, it seeks to minimise the threat by avoiding a situation. All this happens unconsciously, automatically and very quickly – in less than 1/5th of a second!

Our over-vigilant amygdala (in our limbic system) is easily triggered as it is more tuned to threats than rewards. Once our reactivity kicks in, our cognitive performance decreases as we have fewer resources available – less oxygen and less glucose – in our prefrontal cortex (our thinking brain). We overthink the situation without any new insights.

There are five key social threats that act as potential stressors, which David Rock has summarised with the acronym SCARF.[2] These impact your ability to have a difficult conversation. Without raising your awareness of them, you're more likely to stay stuck in a habitual reaction rather than break through to a creative response. The threats are to your:

- **Status.** For example, speaking to your boss, receiving a performance review or being left out of a meeting
- **Certainty.** For example, concerns about money, someone acting incongruously, not knowing others' expectations or sensing someone is not telling you the truth
- **Autonomy.** For example, feeling micro-managed, unilateral decision-making or being told what to do
- **Relatedness.** For example, feeling isolated doing a project, information being withheld or someone acting in an untrustworthy way
- **Fairness.** For example, different sets of rules for different people, moving the goalposts or a gap between what's said and what's done.

Once you raise your awareness of these triggers, you shift from being 'had by' to 'having' your inner experience. This subtle but powerful internal change enables you to find some steadiness inside. When you know your triggers, you are better able to:

- **Bring objectivity.** You see the situation in the here-and-now. You acknowledge your sense, for example, of being micro-managed or believing a situation to be unfair. This gets you out of denial or getting caught up with pointless finger-pointing
- **Take stock.** Recognising these trigger points for what they are – threats to your social standing – helps you manage how you deal with your 'fight', 'flight' or 'freeze' reaction kicking in. You remind yourself that there is no overt threat to your wellbeing or safety, despite the adrenalin coursing through your veins
- **Create a pause.** Re-engaging your 'thinking brain' when it has been hijacked by your 'emotional brain' takes time but even a brief pause helps. Taking a couple of deep breaths, counting to ten or getting a glass of water generates a 'moment of choice'. You can then choose what to do or say next.

To explore what rattles your cage, see Exercise 7 – Notice your triggers.

Exercise 7
Notice your triggers

1. Recall or anticipate a difficult conversation. Reflect on what you experience as a threat. The SCARF list of possible activators isn't exhaustive. Use it to spark your own thinking. Are you experiencing the conversation as a threat to your Status, Certainty, Autonomy, Relatedness, Fairness (or a combination)?

2. Now observe your reaction. Notice what's going on inside you in four ways:
   - **Physical.** These are the sensations in your body. For example, pounding heart, faster breathing, tightness in chest, or rolling your eyes.

- **Emotional.** This is your energy in motion (your 'e-motion.') For example, anxiety, anger, fear, hurt.
- **Cognitive.** These are your thoughts. For example, disbelief ('How dare they...'), dismay ('I'll never be able to say what I really think'), dread ('I'm going to embarrass myself').
- **Narrative.** The story you're telling yourself about yourself or the other person (for example, 'I'm terrible at this sort of thing' or 'They never listen'). Ask yourself: Who am I taking myself to be? Who am I taking this other person to be? Are you, for example, casting one of you into the role of victim or villain?

3 Once you sense your reaction, write it down. This will help you 'own' it. When it's laid out on a page, what do you notice? What difference does it make to name the stressor? For example, you might realise that a threat to your autonomy is understandable and so you relax a little. If you 'see' your projection of 'villain' onto the other person, does this leave you feeling more lucid?

4 Now reflect on the exercise. See if there's more understanding and compassion (for yourself) once you see what is stressing you. How might you experience the subtle shift from you being 'had by' your inner experience to you 'having' it? How can you use this awareness to create a 'moment of choice' for yourself?

When Bridget and I explored her triggers, she zoomed in on the 'C' in the SCARF model.

'Speaking with Liam feels difficult', Bridget said. 'But the driving force is my lack of certainty about our financial situation.'

I left a pause to let that insight sink in.

'It's so easy for me to distract myself by focusing all my anxieties on him', Bridget continued. 'I'm starting to see that I could be a lot more focused. I'm not very disciplined. It's my own lack of focus that's really annoying me. I don't want to drift any more!'

When the temperature goes up

Knowing what triggers you paves the way to examining your reactions more closely. When talking about the tough stuff, there are many obstacles that can get in the way. Someone might walk out of the room, raise their voice or thump the table in frustration. The reaction happens in an instant, but its impact can last a lot longer. If it was you who threw your toys out of the pram, you might know that awful feeling of 'I'm never coming back from this'.

Or you might have a strong reaction inside. You cave in and don't say what you really want to say. Rather than having the real conversation, you give in to keep the peace. Then regret gnaws away at you, impacting your very being. Resentment festers and issues remain unresolved.

Or maybe you know a manager (or maybe you are that manager) who avoids having a difficult conversation altogether? Operating in splendid isolation might bring short-term relief – not having to deal with the mess of hurt feelings – but in the longer term performance drops, mistakes happen, and relationships fall apart.

If you can see yourself in any of the above three scenarios, you're not alone. A 2015 study of global leaders found that 70–80 per cent of leaders operate in a 'reactive' mode where the focus is on 'quick wins' rather than long-term success.[3] Add in demanding clients, a stroppy CEO or an aggressive competitor, little wonder that many leaders are consumed by firefighting, problem solving and thinking quickly. When it then comes to talking together, latent emotional reactions can scupper a necessary but difficult conversation. Whether tempers flare, walls of silence go up or defensiveness cuts in, the situation derails.

Raising your awareness about your reactive tendencies makes it possible to shift these patterns. Instead of speaking over others, you speak up for others. Rather than prioritising others' needs, you sensitively make a case for your own. Instead of withdrawing, you bring the wisdom of detachment when you talk.

Knowing your 'reactive tendency' is key to moving past a specific limitation and leveraging your strength instead. It also enables you to create a container for yourself: a place of internal steadiness. The less reactive you are, the more creative your conversation will be.

The two selves

Look at the two words below. They describe the two mindsets that can be brought to a conversation:

REACTIVE
CREATIVE

Notice how the 'C' is in a different place. As Neale Donald Walsch, says, *'When we C things correctly, life becomes Creative instead of reaCtive.'*

To handle a difficult conversation successfully, it helps to 'C' how you can move from being in a reactive place to a creative place. You then play to win rather than play not to lose.

The key to real winning takes place inside us not outside us. The development of inner skills unlocks our energy, as Timothy Gallwey wrote in his best-selling book, *The Inner Game of Tennis*.[4] Published in 1975, Gallwey's book has been credited with launching the whole coaching movement. His observation that tennis players who cultivated inner skills, such as relaxed concentration, accomplished more than players who focused only on technical skills, such as hitting a hard backhand, applies not just to tennis but to dialogue too.

The essence of the *Inner Game* is a model of two inner selves that we each have. Our reactive self (Self 1) includes our judging mind, inner critic and 'efforting'. On the tennis court (and in the meeting room), it leads to lapses of concentration, nervousness, self-doubt and self-condemnation. Self 1 can 'shoot both ways' with its stinging criticism that can attack inwardly ('I'm such a loser') or others ('they're a real idiot'). When we go tense, overthink or overly control a situation (such as barking at our partner for bringing us a cup of tea), Self 1 has the upper hand. In a tennis game, it interferes with how we play, making our backhand too rigid or our serve too stiff. In the boardroom, Self 1 shoots others down, meddles with an agenda, and tries to force the action.

Our creative self (Self 2) is both spontaneous and calm. Free of judgement, it has a natural focus which is effortless and relaxed. Self 2 allows the game to happen rather than trying to make it happen. Our attention is in the here-and-now with effortless concentration. We direct our thinking rather than stewing or ranting. In a conversation, when we speak from Self 2, we say what we need to say clearly but kindly, honestly and sensitively. We allow a meeting to unfold, trusting that what needs to be said is spoken.

The figure below (Figure 4.1) gives the key features of Self 1 and Self 2.

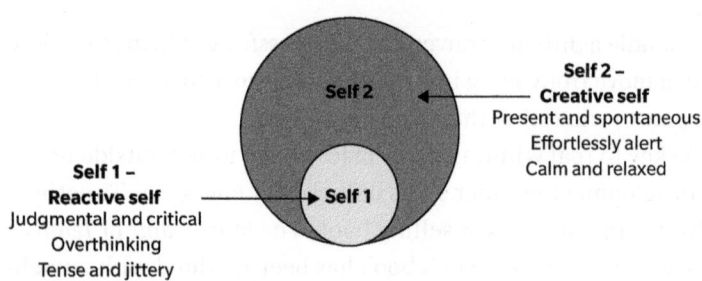

Figure 4.1 Self 1 and Self 2

The key to better tennis – and better conversations – is improving the relationship between the reactive self and the creative self. It is not about trying to get rid of your Self 1. There are good reasons we have a reactive self (we'll come back to this in the next chapter when we take a look at the 'superego'). The work to do is understanding your reactive patterns and then staying in awareness of them. This quietens your Self 1, allows your Self 2 to emerge, and enables you to handle defensiveness in others.

The three reactive tendencies

We have already talked of reactive tendencies. There are three key ones which get in the way of us being able to handle a difficult conversation successfully. You could see these as three different versions of Self 1. The German psychoanalyst Karen Horney first articulated this framework in 1945.[5] She observed that children develop three defensive reactions in response to the threatening world of adults. They can move towards people, away from people or against people. Bob Anderson and colleagues at The Leadership Circle have adapted this framework for leaders. I unpack it below to explore how you can better see your own emotional reactions.

A reactive tendency is a survival strategy probably developed in childhood to cope with stress and anxiety. What was functional then is often dysfunctional now, particularly if left unconscious. The three reactive tendencies are:

- **'Moving towards'.** This tendency is strongly driven by the need to be liked, loved and safe. Individuals with this tendency put the needs of others ahead of their own needs in their search for approval. In a conversation, they're less likely to raise contentious issues or speak out.

- **'Moving against'.** This tendency is fuelled by the need to maintain control of oneself and others. What matters is winning, sometimes at all costs. Individuals with this tendency can be critical and perfectionistic when they talk to others. They might fail to acknowledge their own part in a difficult situation.

- **'Moving away'.** This tendency values independence and self-sufficiency. Individuals with this way of operating prefer to deal with the rational rather than risk high-stakes conversations where people can get irrational. They resist talking about feelings and feel uncomfortable when others emote.

Bridget was more of a 'move against' type with her angry attitude towards her partner. Her inability to manage this volatile emotion was scuppering her conversations and her relationship. Whatever shape our reactivity takes, the first step is always the same: to see and name it clearly so that it doesn't keep on rupturing a connection with another person.

Quietening Self 1

By making your reactive self more conscious, you create the possibility of transformation. Each reactive tendency has a core belief and set of needs (see Figure 4.2 for more information). In the context of difficult conversations, I call these three modes 'Appeaser' (moving towards), 'Confronter' (moving against) and 'Avoider' (moving away).

	'Appeaser'	'Confronter'	'Avoider'
Mode/ tendency	Complying: Moving towards	Controlling: Moving against	Protecting: Moving away
Core belief	'I'm OK if you like/love/accept/ approve of me'	'I'm OK if I'm in charge, get results and win'	'I'm OK if I'm smart, self-sufficient and keep my distance'
Needs	Love, affection, harmony, approval, relationship	Personal achievement, task accomplishment, admiration	Independence, rational perspective, detachment
Limitation	• Fears rejection • Gives up too much power • Keeps peace at any cost • Escalates issues inappropriately • Shows up cautiously • Doesn't speak out	• Fears failure • Takes up too much power • Perfection orientation • Shuts others down • Stops listening • Wins at cost of others • Criticises without seeing own part	• Fears vulnerability • Ignores power dynamics • Know-it-all • Likes to be right • Picks holes in others' arguments • Comes across as cold and distant • Hard to reach and get to know

Strength	• Loyal • Empathic • Senses others' needs	• Energy and drive • Speaks up • Makes things happen	• Remains calm • Sees the big picture • Brings detached clarity

Figure 4.2 Three reactive modes in difficult conversations
(Based on the work of Karen Horney and Bob Anderson)

To work out your tendency/tendencies, complete the free self-assessment that the Leadership Circle offers (https://leadership-circle.com/free-self-assessment/). You'll receive a 'graph' which will show the strength of how you see your tendencies across the three areas (as well as your self-evaluations across 18 creative competencies). These will have a direct impact on your approach to dialogue.

Whether you have your graph or not, think about your reactive patterns when a conversation starts to get difficult. When the pressure is on, what happens next? Explore Figure 4.2 and the core beliefs, needs, limitations and strengths that most closely reflect you.

Trusting Self 2

Seeing your tendencies more clearly creates the possibility of leveraging them for positive change. When you know what your reactive tendency is (or your combination of tendencies), you can use this awareness to strengthen your ability to have a difficult conversation. As Marcus Aurelius, the Stoic philosopher and Roman emperor, observed: *'The impediment to action advances action. What stands in the way becomes the way.'*[6]

Each of the reactive tendencies also carries a hidden gift:[7]

- 'Appeasers' who 'move towards' (or comply) also bring the gifts of their heart: loyalty, sensitivity to others and emotional intelligence.

- 'Confronters' who 'move against' (or control) bring the gifts of will, such as energy and drive, making change happen and the desire for outstanding results.
- 'Avoiders' who 'move away' (or protect) bring the gifts of their intellect including detached clarity, perspective, and the ability to step back and see the big picture.

Instead of storming out, going silent or giving in, you can find a more creative response. See Figure 4.3 on Creative responses for some ideas.

Mode/ tendency	'Appeaser' Complying: Moving towards	'Confronter' Controlling: Moving against	'Avoider' Protecting: Moving away
Try this instead	• Set a boundary and keep to it, e.g. 'I only have an hour for this conversation so let's start to wrap it up' • Make a clear request, e.g. 'What I'd really like is . . . ' • State your opinion, e.g. 'What's not working so well is . . . '	• Listen and summarise before jumping in, e.g. 'To recap, what I think you're saying is . . . ' • Check your understanding, e.g. 'It seems like you're saying . . . ' • Let the other person finish their sentence before diving in	• Find a way to say what's going on for you without feeling too exposed, e.g. 'The impact on me has been . . . ' • Observe what's happening and share what you see, e.g. 'I'm noticing that . . . ' • Name a dilemma when you see one, e.g. 'There are two options and I wonder which is the less painful'

Figure 4.3 Creative responses

For example, if you know that you tend to appease and 'move towards', you take the compassion that you feel for another and direct it towards yourself. Before having a difficult conversation, you ask yourself, what are my needs? If I didn't need their approval, what would I ask for? This self-inquiry reduces the risk that you'll be compliant when you talk.

One coaching client I worked with wanted to work a three-day week to support a healthier lifestyle. Whenever she thought about discussing this with her boss, she became anxious. When she recognised her tendency to back down at the first hint of rejection, she wrote down all the positive reasons she wanted to change her working pattern to strengthen her resolve. Using her natural gift of inclination to think about the other person, she identified several ways to offer support to her boss during a handover. When the conversation came, knowing how to handle her reactivity kept her steady. Her boss agreed to the three-day week.

If, on the other hand, you tend to avoid and 'move away', you could challenge yourself to jot down what the risks and benefits are of talking and of staying silent. Many coaching clients have discovered that the risks of staying silent turn out to be greater than the risks of talking, even if there's some discomfort.

The key shift that takes you from being reactive to being creative is in how you see yourself. You 'unhook' yourself from your emotional needs for approval, control or distance. You no longer define yourself in relation to what others think about you. Your self-worth bubbles up from within. This shift in outlook creates a steady place where you can respond rather than react, and this transforms your ability to have a difficult conversation. To explore more, complete Exercise 8 – Shift from reactivity to creativity.

Exercise 8
Shift from reactivity to creativity

Identify a conversation when you were triggered into a reactive mindset (whether move towards, move against, move away or a combination).

Complete the following sentences:

1 What got in the way of me dealing effectively with this conversation was . . .

2 What was *right* about me behaving in that way was . . .

3 One strength I can draw on to behave differently in a similar situation is . . .
4 I can leverage this by . . . .

Seeing another's reactivity

When you've settled your Self 1 and started to trust your Self 2, you experience your mind as quiet and clear. Your body has less noticeable tension. You sense what 'right action' is. Your energy field has a coherence that invites others to feel more centred.

I'll say more in the next chapter about what else you can do to 'find your ground' (such as find your opening line). Below I cover how you can draw on the Reactive/Creative framework to prepare for a difficult conversation by asking yourself which of the three reactive tendencies the other person is most likely to demonstrate. If they get triggered, are they more of an 'Appeaser', 'Confronter' or 'Avoider'? By tuning into their profile, you can identify strategies to use, particularly if the conversation starts to get tense (see Figure 4.4 Addressing reactive tendencies in another). The strategies and sentence suggestions are intended to create a space that is safe and energising enough to keep the conversation going.

The coaching client I mentioned earlier, who wanted to work a three-day week, pinpointed that her boss was more of an 'Avoider'. She anticipated the reluctance to share their concerns about her proposal, which could stall the decision for her to work part-time. If it was necessary to keep the momentum going towards the end of the conversation, she planned to say something like:

'Take your time to reflect and let's talk again when you're ready.'

She followed this up with an email. Thanking her boss for the conversation, she wrote that she'd catch up in a week's time. Accepting

	'Appeaser' **Complying:** **Moving towards**	**'Confronter'** **Controlling:** **Moving against**	**'Avoider'** **Protecting:** **Moving away**
Try this	• Provide reassurance and support • Make it safe for them to challenge • Encourage them to give an alternative view	• Say when they need to back off • Say how they can help • Intervene if they start to monopolise the conversation	• Share how much you value their perspective • Prod them to speak up • Make time for them so that they make time for you
What you might say	• 'I appreciate that you . . .' • 'What do you need?' • 'How can I help you?'	• 'Here's how you can help . . .' • 'I'd now like to say how it is for me' • 'What result could we create together?'	• 'I'd value your observations' • 'What information can we use here?' • 'Take your time to reflect and let's talk again when you're ready'

Figure 4.4 Addressing reactive tendencies in another

her boss's tendency to be distant meant that she could adjust her own communication to keep things moving forward.

From charged to centred

My coaching conversations with Bridget continued over several months. During that time, there were significant changes in her relationship with Liam. The two of them came to see me for a session on how to improve their dialogue skills. They made a clear joint decision to start trying for a baby and to put money aside regularly towards a deposit for a house.

'My communication with Liam has really changed', Bridget reflected on our last call. 'In the past, we'd often end up in an argument. These days, we can actually stay in the room together and talk.'

'How has your communication changed?'

'I'm more supportive. Not so judging. We recognise how our differences can make us stronger. Liam's a deep thinker; I'm a quick thinker. Put us together, and we can be a great combination.'

'What's been the turning point?'

'Seeing and then taking responsibility for my shortcomings. Once I'd seen my patterns, I slowly found the courage to admit them. I started to see how I'd become trapped in a cycle of needing to be right. I realised that wasn't healthy for me or our relationship.'

I could sense Bridget's sense of relief radiating out from her. I felt warmed by the glow.

'I walked down the street today with a smile on my face', Bridget said. 'It's been amazing to realise that it wasn't Liam that I had to change. It was me. I feel at peace.'

'Well done', I said. 'What rich learning.'

'Business is getting better too', Bridget shared. 'I've updated my website, got some new clients and have lots of bookings for the next few weeks.'

Bridget had done her work. She'd learned to disengage from her reactivity, allowing her to step into her creativity. It was terrific to see this transformation.

Summary

1 Pinpoint what pushes your buttons. Use the SCARF framework to identify threats to your Status, Certainty, Autonomy, Relatedness and Fairness. This awareness enables you to see what the driving force is that's making a conversation appear so difficult.

2 When you get triggered, understand your 'reactive tendency'. There are three key tendencies: appeasing (moving towards), confronting (moving against) and avoiding (moving away).

3 Raising your awareness about your own pattern reduces the risk of an emotional outburst derailing the conversation and makes other behaviours possible.

4 Appeasing (moving towards) is driven by the need for approval, safety and support. If this is your pattern, challenge yourself to raise an issue or speak out during a difficult conversation.

5 Confronting (moving against) is fuelled by the need to be in control, win and get results. Individuals with this tendency benefit from softening their approach and acknowledging their own part in a difficult situation.

6 Avoiding (moving away) is a reactive tendency that seeks independence. If you identify with this pattern, stay in the conversation and allow others to talk about their feelings even if this feels uncomfortable.

7 Understanding the other person's reactive tendencies helps you to keep a dialogue going. Think ahead about what you'll do and say if they get triggered so as to increase your confidence and ability to respond more creatively.

> **If you do only one thing now** . . . When you notice yourself overreacting, take a pause. Scan your body to find where you have a strong sensation (knot in stomach, racing heart, shortness of breath). Focus your attention there. Take a deeper breath before you speak to make what you say less of a retort and more of a balanced response. As you do this more and more often, notice the gain in being calmer, more present and more relaxed.

Notes

1 Andrew Edgecliffe-Johnson JULY 16 2023, LinkedIn's Ryan Roslansky: 'You can only learn how to be a CEO by being a CEO, The Financial Times Limited.

2   Rock, D. (2009) Managing with the brain in mind, *Strategy+Business*, Issue 56.

3   Anderson, R. J., Adams, W. A., & Adams, B. (2015) *Mastering leadership: An integrated framework for breakthrough performance and extraordinary business results*, Wiley.

4   Gallwey T. (2014) *The Inner Game of Tennis*, Pan Books.

5   Horney, K. (1945) *Our Inner Conflicts: A constructive theory of neurosis*, New York: WW Norton & Company Inc.

6   Marcus Aurelius, *Meditations*, Book 5.20.

7   Anderson, R. J. and Adams, W. A. (2016) *Mastering Leadership: An integrated framework for breakthrough performance and extraordinary business results*, Wiley.

part 2

The four secrets

chapter 5

Find your ground

'I am always in conversation, and sometimes other people are involved.'

Mark Twain

To build your confidence for conducting dialogue, 'finding your ground' is essential. So often we are not fully present due to the chatter in our heads about what's happening and easily lose our footing. By increasing your awareness of your own dialogue, you can deal with your inner critic, enabling you to have a better conversation with someone else. Doing some prep before you talk enables you to find your opening and then talk about what matters.

> Looking back (it's over 20 years ago now), it wasn't a good moment. I'd caught my boss in a corridor just after she'd climbed three flights of stairs, having been at a monthly departmental meeting of psychologists. I'd forgotten about that meeting (they were above my pay grade) and the stressful dynamics she said that they often involved.
>
> Before she'd reached her office door, I launched in without pausing for breath myself. Did she know that the civil service had set up a new secondment scheme if someone proactively found a 'host' department? If I can get the chief psychologist at the Cabinet Office to agree to me moving to London from Sheffield, would she back me?
>
> Nicole, my boss, was no longer breathless when she replied 'no' but I could hear the tightness in her voice. She replied that there were too many projects in our department and too little psychologist resource for me to leave the team even for three months. With that she turned and shut the door, not just to her office but to my next chapter.

Unsteady ground

Speaking to your boss can feel threatening given their senior status (remember the 'S' in the SCARF model? See Chapter 4). Many managers deal poorly with people wanting to move on or resign. As the departing person, it's tempting to either walk away or to let rip with your parting shot. As Dylan Thomas wrote, *'When one burns one's bridges, what a very nice fire it makes.'*

Both the walk-away and the no-holds-barred approach are ineffective. You might, in the future, be denied a reference or miss out on turning your former employer into a client. There can be a tricky balance to strike between being clear about your reasons for leaving and yet not too candid, particularly if you're feeling sore, angry or hurt.

When you hit a block, it helps to tune into what your inner dialogue is telling you. Becoming aware of your inner chatter is a 'high leverage' tool. If you don't have this awareness, there's the risk that the conversation you're having with someone else is drowned out by the conversation you start having with yourself.

'Finding your ground' is essential for a difficult conversation. You 'have' your 'ground' when you:

- **Harness your inner dialogue.** Our incessant mental chatter shapes our conversation in unseen ways. Seeing your inner dialogue creates the possibility of changing it.

- **Suspend self-defeating thoughts.** Left unaddressed, the default setting of our inner dialogue is overly critical. When the tone of it changes, so do outward possibilities.

- **Find your opening.** The hardest part of a dialogue is often the start. Knowing what you'll say to begin helps you cross the threshold and into discussing what matters.

We'll take each of these in turn.

Harness your inner chatter

Many conversations are difficult because we think that they will derail. Our expectations shape what happens in a conversation, just as they do in other areas of life. If you enter a conversation expecting it to be a nightmare, it usually is. If you lean into a conversation feeling calm, you're much more likely to get a great outcome.

Learning to manage your inner dialogue is crucial to making a success of a difficult conversation. An inner voice is perfectly normal. It is, as neuroscientist and experimental psychologist Ethan Kross says in *Chatter: The Voice in Our Head and How to Harness It*, 'a basic feature of the mind'.[1] Many of us have it and it doesn't make us mad or bad.

Your inner dialogue is both a liability and an asset. Your awareness of your inner chatter tips the balance. The incessant stream of words inside your mind can be your worst critic and best coach, your most helpful superpower and destructive kryptonite (this was the alien mineral in *Superman* that has the property of depriving Superman of his powers).

There are specific things people say or do which improve their inner conversations and their conversations with another person. This includes having a rant (to yourself), noticing bodily sensations and using your awareness to redirect your focus (more on this later).

You might take a pause right now to listen to what your inner voice is saying. Imagine placing a microphone inside your head: what would it pick up? It could be 'I haven't really got time for reading this book. How self-indulgent of me.' Or, 'I wish she'd hurry up and get on with some more tools and strategies.' Or, 'I meant to call home and I've wound up reading this book instead. Just like me to forget.'

You might notice that this inner commentary tends to have a more negative than positive tone. This isn't surprising given that this 'structure' of your psyche, which psychologists call your superego (or inner critic) has its roots way back in your childhood when you absorbed, by osmosis, the energy of your parents or main caregivers, teachers and other authority figures (see box on Understanding your superego). In the previous chapter, I covered a model of Self 1 (the 'reactive self') and Self 2 (the 'creative self'). Our 'superego' inhabits Self 1. When we have some distance from our superego, we move into our Self 2.

Understanding your superego

When you go tense and become overly critical (whether of yourself or another), this 'egoic activity' makes dialogue difficult. To address this, you need to deal with what psychologists call your 'superego'. Otherwise known as your

> inner critic, this 'structure' is pervasive in your psyche – so much so, that you might not even recognise it's there.
>
> The superego often speaks to you in terms of should and shouldn't, and ought and oughtn't. Tonally, it sounds like an internalised parent or authority figure with its harsh admonitions and even 'attacks'. Meetings are full of superego activity when people pull rank, talk down or big themselves up.
>
> Seeing your superego reduces the risk of 'toxic leakage'. Your body transmits contempt with a raised eyebrow, anger with a red face, withdrawal with crossed arms, even without you saying anything. Others pick up on your body language more than you realise.
>
> Leaders who want to have better conversations need to become aware of this punitive inner judge. In *Soul without Shame*, Byron Brown describes how the superego operates like a 'warped lens' that distorts reality. When our superego is running us, we distrust our intuitive contact with life. We resist movement towards growth and development as the superego wants to maintain the status quo. It keeps us away from what it considers to be dangerous, such as having an honest conversation and saying what we really think.
>
> Brown urges us to 'disrobe' what he calls 'The Judge'. Bringing the usually hidden, unspoken voice of judgement, harsh criticism or condemnation into your awareness helps you to step away from these superego 'introjects'.[2]
>
> Awareness of your inner critic creates space inside you for something new: more objectivity, understanding, discernment, hope and possibility. This movement internally makes it easier for you to talk with someone about what really matters.

An unharnessed inner voice is troublesome when you need to talk about a tough situation, particularly if it spirals into unrelenting, punitive thoughts. If the voice inside becomes a frenzy of negativity, whether it's directed at you or the other person, it drowns out the voice of the person you're talking with. Cyclical negative thoughts and emotions turn our capacity for introspection into a curse rather than a blessing.

Where you place your attention is crucial. It's not about trying to get rid of your chatter, which is mission impossible. It's about developing an easier relationship with your inner voice so that your superego doesn't hog all your neural capacity. If you've ever struggled to think straight after a heated argument, you'll have a sense of how the 'executive functioning' of your mind – thinking, planning, strategising – is a limited capacity resource.

Keeping the 'executive functioning' of your mind online enables you to stay in the game. It will help you to prepare for a difficult conversation and stay grounded during the interaction. You're able to respond creatively rather than comply, shout or stonewall (remember those three reactive tendencies?). As Kross observes, a pained, negative inner voice 'divides and blurs' your attention. A harnessed inner voice gives you your ground.

'Suspend' your inner dialogue

We have seen how the quality of the conversation you have with yourself directly affects the quality of the conversation you have with another. Attending to this inner dialogue goes against the grain of the conventional corporate world. Many managers mistakenly associate self-reflection with vanity or self-absorption and stay stuck as a result.

In his book *On Dialogue*, David Bohm uses the metaphor of a polluted river to underline the importance of attending to how we're thinking not just to what we're saying. If you focus on cleaning the water, you'll find that the river quickly gets contaminated again. Better to 'go upstream' and remove the toxins at source. To stop subverting a conversation, clear up your inner dialogue, rather than focusing only on how you talk.[3]

A key capacity to cultivate is what David Bohm calls 'suspending'. This involves laying out your thinking in front of you so you can examine it. Just as a chandelier is 'suspended' from the ceiling so that you can walk around it, see it and examine it, when you 'suspend' your chatter, you can see whether it undermines or strengthens a conversation. Suspending is the middle ground between repressing and acting out. It is a subtle skill and yet one of the most powerful to develop to make a difficult conversation go well.

There's a great tool that helps you to 'suspend' and attend to your inner dialogue. It involves looking backwards to go forward with a greater sense of ground. Chris Argyris (a professor at Yale School of Management and Harvard Business School) originally developed the Left-Hand Column (LHC) exercise, which Peter Senge and colleagues have popularised.[4] In the LHC you write out the unexpressed thoughts and feelings you had during a difficult conversation. In the right-hand column, you write out the words that were spoken as best you remember them.

If you'd like to harvest the learning from a difficult conversation, see Exercise 9 – Left-hand column case to complete one for yourself.

Exercise 9
Left-hand column case

1 Identify a challenging conversation that you've had. This could have been with a colleague, client or in any other setting. It may have been face-to-face, on video conference or on the telephone, with one other person or several others. It might have involved dealing with criticism, conflict among team members or another situation involving difficult emotions.

2 Take a sheet of paper and create a table with two columns. Fill in the two columns as follows. The case does not need to be long and may even be a few sentences:

- **In the right-hand column**, write out the conversation as best as you remember it. Try to make it as accurate as you can but don't worry if you can't remember all the details. Focus on the essence of the exchange.

- **In the left-hand column**, write out what you were thinking and feeling *but not saying*. It's important to include any feelings, particularly difficult feelings, that you were experiencing such as frustration, anger, disappointment, sadness or embarrassment, fear or withdrawal (remember those three reactive tendencies from Chapter 2?). Be as authentic as you can.

3 Take a pause and come back to your 'case' when you're feeling fresh. Now ask yourself, if I faced a similar situation again, what would I say or do differently? Other reflections that could be helpful include:

- To what extent did I voice my LHC? What stopped me?
- On reflection, what would have been helpful to voice from my LHC?
- What would have been better to 'bracket' (keep in the LHC)?

To help one client, Vivien, to prepare for her conversation with her boss (William), I suggested that she complete an LHC exercise. By being in touch with her inner dialogue, I trusted that the bigger picture could come into view.

Vivien decided to focus on a conversation where it had become apparent that she and William had different understandings of what a new CRM (Customer Relationship Management) exercise would involve. There were also budgetary limitations which affected the scope of what could be done. Figure 5.1 gives the first few lines of Vivien's LHC.

Having written her LHC, Vivien reflected:

'I always let William have his way. It's not just me he sees as a slacker, it's everyone. That's why he called us all back into the office after Covid. He doesn't trust us to work at home and he doesn't trust my professional judgement either.'

Vivien sat back in her chair and looked out of the window. We were sitting in the lounge of a hotel overlooking a quiet street where people were walking by in the morning sunshine.

What I was thinking and feeling but not saying	What was said
I need to raise this issue, otherwise I will feel even more resentful that my time is being wasted while William gets his act together.	Vivien: As we know, this project has taken a while to get off the ground and we've had several conversations to help clarify the approach to the CRM exercise within the budgetary parameters. As a result, the scope has changed. I need to include some extra resource for bringing in an external consultant. How might we acknowledge this in the budget?
That's not how I see it! I feel really affronted. He makes me feel so stupid. I just want to do a great re-brand that will be really impactful.	William: Well, it's a bit late in the day to be bringing this up. Greedy consultants want to get all the work they can and I don't want us to be milked by them. We should be doing the work ourselves.
I need to make my case now.	Vivien: That's not quite how I see it. Putting in extra consultant resource up front is key to doing good work. With the changing brief, it has only become clear now that we need this.

Figure 5.1 Left-hand column case example

'What can you learn from this interaction?' I asked.

'When I cave in, it costs me.'

I could hear the ring of truth in Vivien's words. As a 'move towards' type myself (remember the reactive tendencies in Chapter 3?), I could relate to her 'setting' of appeasing.

'How can you take that insight into your next conversation with William?' I asked.

'I need to find ways to stop being a "good girl"', Vivien said. Her voice sounded calm and warm. Her tone had strength. 'If only I knew how.'

Next steps are easier to see once you're grounded inside. By seeing your inner dialogue, you can see what's 'true'. This data helps you to discern your 'move' in a clear-sighted way.

Deal with self-defeating thoughts

If you're tense, you cannot have an expansive conversation. If you find a way to feel rooted in yourself, even if just a little, talking with someone about the tough stuff becomes easier.

In their book *Life Coaching: A Cognitive-Behavioural Approach*, Michael Neenan and Windy Dryden observe how much of our inner dialogue is made up of ANTs: Automatic Negative Thoughts. These are incessant, invisible and unnoticed. They are, however, very powerful. ANTs shape our interactions with others without us realising.

In Vivien's case, her ANTs, such as 'He makes me feel so stupid', were stopping her from speaking out about her need for more consultant resource.

'What would you rather have in your Left-Hand Column?' I asked.

Vivien took the piece of paper and looked again at what she'd written.

'Take your time', I said. 'Do whatever it takes to get centred and feel calm inside.'

This is not about trying to 'trick' your psyche into believing something it knows isn't true. It is, however, about shaking yourself out of your mental well-worn grooves. I wanted Vivien to feel 'all of a piece', to quote Yeats. When our body relaxes, so does our psyche. The somatic route into authentic dialogue is often overlooked.

Vivien sat back in her chair. She paused and then wrote out these new replacing thoughts:

- I have a request and I want to share it.
- There's no need for me to justify myself. Speaking my truth is valuable in itself.
- I'm not comfortable with how this meeting is going but I'll see it through.

'One way to improve your conversations is to turn your ANTs into PETs', I said.

'PETs?'

'Your Automatic Negative Thoughts become Performance Enhancing Thoughts', I said, inspired by the cognitive-behavioural approach.

Vivien looked thoughtful. I wondered if that sounded a bit heady so I decided to try again.

'Your inner critic becomes your creative ally.'

A smile spread across Vivien's face.

'I'll probably have another conversation with William next week', she said. 'It feels scary but what else can I do if I want to progress the project?'

For more examples of negative self-talk and positive self-talk, check out Figure 5.2. See what resonates for you as a way of surfacing your own inner chatter.

Find your opening

Once you have resolved to have a difficult conversation, some prep is essential. The challenge is that conversation is an 'improvisational art' that cannot be scripted in advance. It unfolds moment by moment. As I said in *How to Have Meaningful Conversations*, 'True dialogue is, in its best moments, techniqueless.'

Negative self-talk (ANTs: Automatic Negative Thoughts)	Positive self-talk (PETs: Performance Enhancing Thoughts)
• You always make these mistakes • Never let your guard down • You knew that! • It's all your fault • You haven't got any skills to offer • Things never go to plan • Ugh not again • I have a lot more work to do on myself • How the **** am I supposed to do this? • Everyone is judging you • You're simply not good enough!	• You'll be able to find a way through • This is not that important • You'll get it next time • You've got this • Get on with it • It's OK. Try again. Keep going • I knew that would work • Things work out in the end or it's not the end • Just do your best • Well done for saying that • It's just someone's opinion, not fact • Everyone's different

Figure 5.2 Negative and positive self-talk

That said, doing some preparation helps. Unclear messages, an absence of evidence and lack of preparation all cause a conversation to derail. You might for example:

- **Gather facts and information.** For example, if you want to ask for a pay rise, find out what other organisations are paying people who do similar work to you.
- **Check policies.** For example, if you want to resign, check what your notice period is and how the HR process works.
- **Schedule a meeting.** For example, if you want to give someone some challenging feedback, choose an office where you can shut the door.
- **Pick your moment.** For example, if you want to turn down a request for annual leave, you might decide that the start or end of the day or shift is best.

There's a balance to strike between preparation and improvisation. Do enough prep to feel grounded without being thrown if your talk goes down a different track. Do whatever it takes to be 'present' so that you respond in the moment to whatever arises. Don't, however, rely too much on your ability to think on your feet if this means doing no prep whatsoever.

Simple techniques such as taking a deeper breath, counting slowly to three, or pausing before you speak all help you to stay present. Physical actions such as sitting up a little straighter in your chair, uncrossing your arms and legs, and placing your feet flat on the floor are all ways to stay grounded. In *Powered by Purpose* I included a whole chapter on 'cultivating leadership presence'.[5]

An essential piece of prep is to think carefully about what you want to say. You might even write down an outline. At the very least, work out your opening line. Take your time to do this. You might even find it energising. Possible opening lines include:

- Thank you for agreeing to meet today, there is something I want to discuss with you . . .
- There's something I'd like to talk about with you that I think will help us work together more effectively.

- I appreciate your willingness to talk about _____ I think we see things differently and I'd like to understand more your point of view.
- I'd like to explore if we might reach a better understanding about _____. I really want to hear your point of view and share my perspective as well.
- It seems that there's a pattern (conflict, disagreement, problem) that's emerged. I'd like to talk about what's led to it happening.

Go for an opening that has curiosity, respect and authenticity. Before you try to stand in another person's shoes, make sure you're standing in your own. To explore further, complete Exercise 10 – Beginning a difficult conversation.

Exercise 10
Beginning a difficult conversation

'The hardest part is getting started' applies to a difficult conversation as well as many of life's other challenges. The upside is that when you've found your opening, you're over the biggest hurdle. To identify your first words, there are three steps.

1 First, think through the situation. As you mull over the conversation, see what words come to you. Put your mind into 'soft focus' so that you're receptive without trying too hard.

2 Secondly, write down your words (see above for some inspiration). As you do this, check your own motivation. You are not there to punish the other person or just to get things off your chest. The conversation should be mutually beneficial. Check your words reflect how you really want to show up.

3 Finally, practise saying out loud your opening line so that you no longer need any notes. You might even record your voice and listen back to what you've said. See if you can transmit a genuine desire to connect and move things forward.

Having a difficult conversation is a journey to authority; the kind of authority that arises inside when you know who you are and what you want. This ballast makes a difficult conversation possible.

The release

Returning to the failed conversation I'd had with my boss about going on secondment, I felt crushed but determined to learn my lesson. I decided to let the matter lie until there was a better time and place to talk (remember the importance of a container as we saw in Chapter 3? I wasn't onto that back then).

A few months later, I decided to brace myself for the conversation again. I made sure we had an allocated, uninterrupted time for our one-to-one in her office. Putting aside my inner critic ('How can you even think of bringing this up again, you idiot!'), I said out loud my well-rehearsed opening line. By the end of our 20-minute chat, Nicole said she could see how keen I was to go and readily agreed to my offer to do a full handover and regular keep-in-touch calls. Success! This time, I'd found my ground.

'To fail to prepare is to prepare to fail' applies as much to a difficult conversation as any risky endeavour, if not more so. Being off-centre can be costly when you talk. You might regret what you say, damage a relationship or limit your options if you botch it. Had I not found my calm place inside and redone the conversation with my boss, I'd never have made the move to London and become a dialogue consultant and you wouldn't be reading this book.

Summary

1 You 'find your ground' by seeing your incessant mental chatter, addressing self-defeating thoughts and doing some prep before a difficult conversation.

2 To harness your inner voice, write a 'left-hand column' case. See your superego at work. If you are riddled with negativity, your conversation will unravel. Make your inner chatter more conscious to create more choice about how you show up.

3 Set the direction of your inner dialogue by 'suspending' it in front of you. Challenge yourself to transform your automatic negative thoughts (ANTs) into performance enhancing thoughts (PETs). Turn your inner critic into a creative ally.

4 Do your prep before having a difficult conversation. Work out your opening line. Choose your words carefully without doing too much 'easing in'. Write down your first words and practise saying them out loud to see if they ring true for you.

5 Remember that when you change what you say to yourself, you change what you say to another. A difficult conversation becomes possible when you find your ground.

> **If you do only one thing now** . . . You need to ensure you are grounded before you open that all-important conversation. Do some preparation before you talk, so you feel steadier at the start of a difficult conversation. Work out your opening line and practise saying it out loud. If it doesn't ring true, change it until it does. Plan it without overly scripting it.

Notes

1 Kross, E. (2021) *Chatter: The voice in our head and how to harness it*, Vermilion.
2 Brown, B. (1998) *Soul without Shame: A guide to liberating yourself from the judge within*, Shambhala Publications Inc.
3 Bohm, D. (1996) *On Dialogue*, Routledge.

4 Kleiner, A., Smith B., Roberts C., Senge, P. and Ross, R. (2011) *The Fifth Discipline Fieldbook: Strategies for building a learning organisation*, Nicholas Brealey Publishing.
5 Rozenthuler, S. (2020) *Powered by Purpose: Energise your people to do great work*, Pearson.

chapter 6

Build a bridge

'I believe we can change the world if we start listening to one another again.'

Margaret Wheatley

When the stakes are high, it can be challenging to stay in connection with the other person, and with yourself. Foundational to bridge-building in a conversation are attentive listening and authentic speaking. Bringing these skills to bear turns a heated argument into a shared understanding. We will explore three allies of deep listening: mirroring, validating and empathising. We will also examine two allies of voicing: using collaborative language and finding your flow so that you say what you really want to say.

> Jegan and Mea met on the dance floor of a weekly jive class. Jegan, who'd been brought up in London, had lived in Manchester for several years whereas Mea, who was Italian, had recently moved there. They were both in their mid-thirties and interested in business, the arts, sustainability and personal development.
> There was an immediate sense of connection. Jegan had been looking for a 'spiritual partner' to enrich his life in ways that a regular practice of meditation couldn't reach. Within the first few days of their meeting, Mea had had a powerful dream about Jegan.
> 'It was my soul who noticed him, not my mind', she told me.
> Three months after they met, they moved in together. Within a year, they were married. Shortly after their wedding, Jegan and Mea went into business together. They took on the publication of an established 'green living' online magazine. Jegan, who'd been a chartered accountant for several years, left his job to run the business full-time. Mea, who'd trained as a massage therapist, moved happily into her new line of work, excited by the opportunities it brought. Keen to double their circulation, they started to host events in their local community including workshops on permaculture, healthy eating and holistic lifestyles.
> At the time I met Jegan and Mea they'd been married for seven years. When they came to my dialogue workshop, they

shared with the other participants that, during the last year, their struggles had been so challenging they'd contemplated divorce and yet their love was so strong they'd also considered starting a family. The warmth of the early years of their relationship had been replaced by a cooler climate, which they were at a loss to change.

We stayed in touch after the workshop as Jegan and Mea were keen to learn more about how they could make their relationship less stressful and more satisfying. They decided that some coaching for them as a couple and as business partners might help.

'We're arguing a lot', said Jegan. 'I'm also really worried about the business. We're losing money, and that often fuels the arguments. We seem to be failing on all fronts.'

'There's a stuckness in our relationship', said Mea. 'We repeat the same old boring patterns and we don't know how to break out of them.'

As I listened to them, I found myself wondering about the impact that their relationship had on the rest of the team. The dynamics of an intimate relationship 'bleed' into a business. As founder Estée Lauder said, 'There are two things that can destroy a family business. The family or the business.'

The upside is that if you upgrade your dialogue skills, it benefits your personal relationship and your business too. We'll return to the story of Mea and Jegan a bit later in the chapter. But first, some context about the skills that build a bridge when spiralling conflict occurs.

One of the most powerful 'bridges' you can build in a difficult conversation is to deepen your listening. Even more than skilful speaking, helping the other person to feel heard and understood puts out fires. It calms the atmosphere and restores a relationship, which in turn breathes new life into a business.

When I heard Simon Horton, who teaches hostage negotiators, share his insights about how to navigate entrenched conflicts I had a powerful reminder about the difference that listening makes. We were both giving talks at an event hosted by our publisher, Pearson. Simon is author of *Change Their Mind* and a Visiting Lecturer at Imperial College, London. His five-word summary of his tried-and-tested approach was:

'I listened them into it.'

The much more common phrase 'I *talked* them into it' shows our cultural bias. We give so much more attention to producing speech than receiving it. 'He needs a good talking to', 'She's a good talker', 'Can we talk?' are all phrases with which we're familiar. Rarely do we hear comments such as 'He needs a good listening to', 'She's a good listener', 'Can we listen to one another?' They can even sound a little odd.

All good dialogue begins with good listening. We don't have to agree with someone to understand them. Even when there's a difference of opinion, building a common understanding is possible. We'll come to the skills of authentic speaking also but first I cover how to connect with the other person when you're at risk of a disconnect through the power of listening.

Why listening builds bridges

Heated arguments, bickering and even edgy banter all risk fracturing relationships. While conflict is a natural and unavoidable part of our lives, it can be destructive. Left to fester, conflict can ruin a relationship whether in a business, community or family. Learning how to reach across a chasm when differences divide can be the biggest stretch – and the biggest gain – ever.

Foundational to this bridge-building is listening and really hearing what the other person says. I experienced the difference that deep listening makes when I desperately needed it in my own relationship. My partner (at that time) and I were struggling to deal with some issues and incompatibilities for which there were no easy answers. My pain felt raw, as did his. My anger flared into rage, as did his. My defences got triggered, as did his. We ended up in a mess. 'Hurt people hurt people', he said to me after yet another argument.

Being in a volatile relationship was a new experience for me. I felt out of my depth at handling the red-hot emotions that moved through me and the spiky space between us. I'd been brought up in a family where anger was rarely expressed. In this relationship, I didn't have the knowledge or tools to handle my own anger and was at a complete loss at how to deal with the full blast of his.

Given our inability to overcome the conflict, we went to see a therapist who introduced us to 'Imago dialogue', the creation of the American psychotherapist Harville Hendrix. The 'marriage whisperer', as Oprah Winfrey calls him, has helped thousands of couples to develop a 'passionate friendship' when communication has broken down. This carefully structured dialogue process, with its three active listening skills, has proven to be transformative in situations where people press each other's buttons.

Although my relationship with this partner didn't work out in the long term, what I learned about listening lies at the heart of the work I do, whether with senior leadership teams or coaching individuals in conflict. Feeling heard and understood was the only thing that enabled us to break out of the vicious cycle of daily arguing and the cold shoulder. By slowing down and learning to listen, we were able to have a meaningful conversation. Our hard-won communication clarified my decision to leave the relationship, confident that no stone had been left unturned.

By finding a way to air and share frustrations, I have seen that it is also possible to save a business and a relationship. Issues that we might let roll off the table with other people, for example, disagreements about money, can become major stressors in a business partnership that is also an intimate relationship. Problems at work often have problems at home at their core. And problems at home can often create problems at work. Either way, the tools needed to transform a relationship through deeper conversation are the same. For a whistle-stop tour of Harville Hendrix's theory, see the box on Why conflict occurs.

Why conflict occurs in intimate relationships

In *Getting the Love You Want* Hendrix describes how we choose our partner from a 'cast of thousands' because of an unconscious drive to find our *Imago*. Coming from the Latin for *image*, this is a fusion of the key characteristics of our primary caretakers, which could be our parent, grandparent, sibling or someone else who was close in infancy.[1]

Our unconscious creates a single image of the person we'd love to love, in a similar way to how the psyche merges one person into another in a dream. When we fall in love, it's because that person 'fits' the template of our Imago. They might have the same ability to work hard like our mum, the kindness of our dad and the fun loving nature of our sister.

The rub is that our partner embodies the *negative* as well as the positive traits of our caretakers. They might also have Mum's stinginess, Dad's stubbornness and our sister's impatience. Once the honeymoon period is over, we might find ourselves feeling anxious or uncomfortable around our partner in ways we could not have imagined when we were swooning. As they fail to meet our needs, our response is typically to 'cry or criticise', like a young child. The grim determination of a power struggle sets in.

Many intimate relationships wind up in a place where frustration and scratchiness dominate the atmosphere. Our partner activates the lack of gratification that we inevitably experienced with our mother (or main caregiver) in our infancy. As adults, we become engaged in fights, arguments and negative conflicts with our partner, which are difficult to exit unless we do our 'work.'

The dynamics in our intimate relationship often have a strange sense of the familiar. Because our partner resembles our primary caretakers, they have the potential to re-injure us

> in the same way in which we were hurt as a child. It's this double whammy of wounding that makes problems in our work and personal relationships so painful.
>
> The purpose of our relationship, according to Imago theory, is to heal these unresolved issues. We recreate, without realising, the environment of our childhood to complete our unfinished business. When we see that our partner is not to blame for our (archaic) distress but is picking at wounds that we brought into the relationship, this understanding changes our perspective. We become aware that we're being given another chance to deal with what we were unable to cope with as a child. This orientation helps us to find our way out of the power struggle and into a healthier relationship rooted in the present.
>
> Although Hendrix's focus is on intimate relationships, his theory applies to the wider context of business. If you've ever had a boss who resembled your father or a colleague who had a similar feel to your sister, this will make sense. In building a bridge to another person, we need to relate to them not as who we take them to be but as who they really are. To make this shift, deep listening has an essential part to play.

How deeper listening works

At our first coaching session, I asked Jegan and Mea to each bring an issue they'd like to discuss. I explained that we'd use the three active listening skills of Imago dialogue that they'd learned at the workshop. They decided that Jegan would bring his topic first. I reminded them that it helps to have two distinct roles: the 'Speaker' and the 'Listener', which they would both take turns to occupy. Separating out the role of the speaker and the listener is key for deeper listening to take place. As Bill Isaacs, my former colleague, often said, *'Most people don't listen, they reload.'*

Having a separate speaker and listener, at least to begin with, allows people to speak without fear of interruption and to listen without the pressure to respond. It helps to build 'calm and connect' neurobiological states, which have been shown to be a prerequisite for accessing our creativity, kindness and compassion.[2]

As the speaker, the focus is on voicing your own feelings, thoughts and concerns, not to blame, shame or criticise the other. The listener's task is to receive what the speaker has to say without interrupting or correcting. They are to be as receptive and non-reactive as possible. Once the speaker has finished sharing their thoughts, the listener reflects back what's been said so that the speaker feels heard.

Instead of setting up our next point we, as the listener, focus on what the other person is saying. When we're 'required' to play back what we've heard, this cuts across our tendency to tune out what the other person has said and instead be thinking about what we want to say next.

There are three active listening skills that enrich the quality of a conversation. Here's an overview:

- **Mirror.** We repeat back to the other person the key things that they've said. We put aside our own stuff to concentrate on what the other person is saying. This attentive listening helps people to become more aware of how they are thinking.

- **Validate.** We affirm that what the other person has said makes sense, even if we don't agree with it. We seek to understand their viewpoint and acknowledge it as legitimate. By seeing the other as an equal, we come to understand their own 'model' of the world.

- **Empathise.** We share how we imagine the other person is feeling or has felt. Here, for the first time, we add something of our own perspective to the conversation. We take a guess about how the other person has been impacted emotionally and voice it, tentatively.

Figure 6.1 on Active Listening gives some words you might use to demonstrate them.

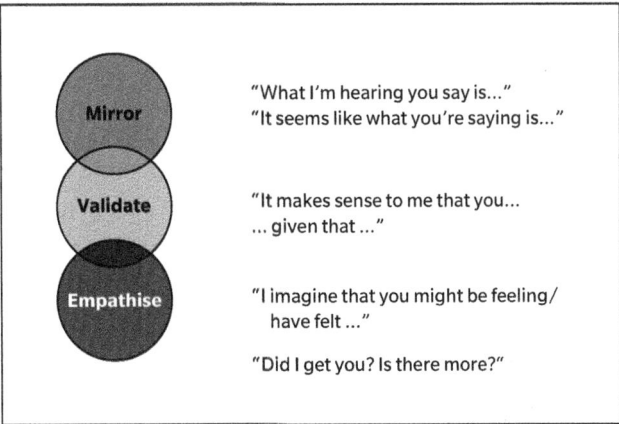

Figure 6.1 Active listening

How mirroring creates a shared understanding

Mirroring is important for several reasons, not least because it slows down the interaction. When people hear their own words played back, it clarifies their thinking. The speaker has the rare opportunity to explore what's often remained invisible to them. Difficulties in communication often stem from assumptions, and making these explicit unravels the knots.

There are benefits too for the listener. Instead of giving a knee-jerk reaction when it comes to our turn, we can offer a more considered response. To mirror well, the listener needs to listen carefully, check their understanding and reflect back what they heard without inserting any of their own 'stuff'. By doing this, the listener learns how to manage their reactivity. Their toys stay in the pram.

While mirroring may sound simple, it is often not easy to do. It requires the listener to put to one side their own thoughts and feelings and instead to concentrate on what the other person is saying.

When the listener is able to step into the other person's shoes and see the relationship through their eyes, a real conversation becomes possible.

'If it gets too much to hold', I said to Mea, 'you can send a signal to Jegan to stop speaking. Perhaps you could raise your hand.'

'I'd rather touch his knee', Mea said, with a sparkle in her eye.

After taking a moment to gather his thoughts (and maybe muster some courage), Jegan began. He sat facing Mea and spoke directly to her.

'Work is constantly on my mind. We really need to get the business going and sort out the finances. And you're sleeping a lot. You don't seem to be that interested in making money. It's worrying me a great deal. I feel I have to push you all the time. You seem very reluctant to be involved anymore.'

Tension filled the air. I found myself reflecting on the 'C' in the SCARF model (see Chapter 4). When our financial certainty is threatened, it can really raise the stakes.

'I'm seeing how little money we have, how much is going out and how much we're struggling to make ends meet. I really had to drag you to do the article for the magazine. It feels like I'm constantly having to get you to do things for the business.'

Mea's hand touched Jegan's knee.

'Remember', I said, 'don't "insert" you. Only focus on what Jegan's saying. Your turn will come.'

There was a thoughtful pause.

'What I'm hearing you say is that you're very worried about the business. You constantly have to drag me to do things. You think that I don't want to be involved anymore. You're seeing a financial collapse and it's really concerning you.'

I suggested to Mea that she checked whether Jegan agreed that what she'd said was an accurate reflection of what he'd said. Creating a shared understanding takes time but it's where the bridge-building starts.

'Did I get you?'

'Yes', Jegan said. 'You got me.'

I suggested Mea ask Jegan what else was on his mind. As therapists are fond of saying, the 'presenting issue' is often not the real issue at all. There can be many layers to uncover.

'Is there more?'

Jegan looked thoughtful.

'I feel you always get angry with me whenever I mention the business and criticise me for doing too much. It makes me feel rejected because I'm working hard to improve our financial situation and you don't seem to appreciate that. I feel lost and powerless about what to do next and it's getting worse and worse.'

Given the opportunity to talk without being interrupted, Jegan shared more about how he was really feeling.

'I have this sense that it's all on my shoulders. I'm carrying all the responsibility, all the stress, all the worry and that you don't care.'

Mea listened, without flinching. She mirrored what she'd heard and asked again if there was more.

'I find it hard to relax. You tell me to relax all the time but I'm carrying all the weight. You tell me to have more fun but you're not taking any responsibility!'

With a fluency that took me by surprise, Jegan continued.

'I know I've been working too much. I've been putting too many hours into the business. We haven't been spending enough time together. There hasn't been the energy for us.'

I noticed no one jumped in to fill the empty space.

'I've been trying to fit you into a way of working and then I'm angry with you because you're not up at 9 o'clock like me. I'm trying to fit you into a box of a working pattern that works for me but isn't your natural working pattern.'

I saw an appreciative look in Mea's eyes as Jegan focused his attention on his own shortcomings rather than pointing the finger at her.

With several more rounds where Mea reflected back, checked her understanding and asked if there was more, Jegan dug deeper and deeper into the issue.

'I can go on and on but that's probably enough', he eventually said.

How validating and empathising work

I sensed Jegan had said all he needed to say for the time being so I suggested that we move to the next part of the dialogue, known as 'validation'. This is where the listener affirms that what the speaker has shared made sense. Validation is not about agreeing (or disagreeing) with the other person; it is about confirming that their way of seeing the world is coherent, even if, especially if, it is different from yours. As Neale Donald Walsch says, *'Nobody does anything wrong given their model of the world.'*[3] What helps, then, is to come to a better understanding of their 'model of their world', in other words, their thoughts, feelings and needs.

'It makes sense to me that you feel unappreciated because you feel you're contributing so much and you feel that you have to keep driving me.' Mea said.

'I can understand that you feel angry', she continued, 'because you see me not doing what you'd like me to do, and you feel that you don't have me alongside you. Did I get you?'

Jegan nodded.

The three of us sat in silence, realising the truth of Jegan's feelings.

With hardly a prompt from me, Mea had moved seamlessly into the third part of the dialogue by showing some empathy. This is also a critical part of the process as difficult emotions are at the heart of a difficult conversation. If we exclude them, they hang around in the air like 'free radicals' and refuse to go away (drawing on the metaphor that Douglas Stone and his co-authors from the Harvard Negotiation Project use in their book, *Difficult Conversations*).[4]

'I imagine you might also be feeling burdened, given how much you're having to carry', she said gently.

'Yes', said Jegan. 'It's inside me all the time but I don't express it and it makes me frustrated. It's good to express the frustrations and for you to acknowledge them. I feel enabled to speak in a way that you're able to really hear.'

I watched as they held each other's gaze for a long time. Jegan had unfolded his arms and leaned forwards in his chair. Mea's shoulders had dropped and her hands rested gently on her lap. The silent conversation of their bodies said that their bridge-building was underway.

To explore how you could use the three skills of listening, see Exercise 11 – Deepening your listening.

Exercise 11
Deepening your listening

This exercise is best done with someone else with whom you have a contentious issue to discuss. Make sure you both have enough time and feel emotionally available to talk.

There will be two distinct roles, which you'll both take turns to occupy. For the first 'round', decide who will be the Listener and who will be the Speaker. In the second round, swap roles.

You might choose to set a timer (e.g. for 20 minutes) so that your two 'rounds' are of the same length.

As the **Speaker**:

1 Set some context but make it succinct.
2 Keep the focus on yourself. You could start your sentences with:
   - *I'm feeling . . .*
   - *My part in this has been . . .*
   - *The story I tell myself is . . .*
   - *What I'd like is . . .*
3 Keep what you say short. Don't blame, shame or criticise.
4 Modify the Listener's understanding if needs be.
5 Be receptive to their validation, empathy and perspective. Thank them for listening to you.

As the **Listener:**

1. **Mirror.** Reflect back what you've heard, particularly any feelings. Don't 'insert' you.
2. Check your understanding: *'Did I get you?'*
3. Continue to mirror until the Speaker says yes.
4. Ask, *'Is there more?'*
5. Summarise *'Let me see if I've got all that ... Did I?'*
6. **Validate.** *'It makes sense to me that ... given that ... '*
7. **Empathise.** *'I imagine you might have felt/be feeling ... '* (insert a real feeling such as angry, sad, fearful)
8. Check again *'Did I get you?'*
9. If time, provide an alternative perspective, tentatively. *'It may also be possible that ... '*

If you have time, spend a few more minutes reflecting together on how you're now feeling and what you learned from your speaking and listening.

Voicing

Alongside active listening, authentic speaking is essential for a difficult conversation to be a success. The speaking of truth, while uncomfortable, is rarely damaging to a relationship in the long run. The withholding of truth, however, often turns out to be damaging – and pointless. As Shakespeare said, *'the truth will out'*.[5]

Sharing what you see from your unique vantage point is known as the practice of 'voicing'. Speaking authentically sounds simple but isn't easy. Some of us stay silent and fear putting our heads above the parapet. Others are vocal but aloof and arrogant. Other people talk too much, sucking all the oxygen out of the room.

Speaking openly and respectfully is a huge achievement, when we are able to do so.

Bill Isaacs observes how voicing *'sets off new order of things, opens new possibilities'*.[6] I would add that it also restores relationships that have gone awry. Having coached many different teams, the turning point in their conversations happens when someone 'names an elephant' and dares to say what others know but don't want to say.

While the benefits of voicing are huge, so are the potential blockers. Organisations give mixed messages, wanting people to be empowered but shooting down voices that show too much dissent. Our self-images get in the way as inner voices hold sway ('Who do you think you are?'). Bosses 'shift the burden' saying that 'My door is always open' and make it the responsibility of others to speak out when the barriers to doing so appear insurmountable.

Remembering that your unique voice has magic in it helps. Isaacs traces the 'spell' *abracadabra* back to its Aramaic root, an ancient Middle Eastern language that was spoken from around the seventh century B.C. to the seventh century A.D. The phrase comes from the Kabbalistic tradition, a form of Jewish mysticism, to remind people of the power of their speech. *Abra* means to create, *ca* means 'as' and *dabra* comes from the verb 'to speak'. The essence of *abracadabra* is 'I create as I speak'. Sharing words is an act of creation.

Voicing calls for courage, determination and humility. As Jim Collins identified in *From Good to Great*, leaders who take people with them on the journey of transformation embody the qualities of fierce resolve and grounded humility.[7] Cultivating this combination of qualities is what a difficult conversation calls for; the question is, how?

There are two allies that support voicing. The first is to use collaborative language and the second is to structure what you say so that you cover all the ground you need to. We'll take each of these in turn.

Using collaborative language

In a heated exchange, it's very tempting to point the finger and make it all about the other person. More challenging and much more effective is to turn the focus on yourself. It's like taking a selfie on your phone. You hit the button that swivels the lens to focus on you not what you're looking at. It makes your message clearer. It reduces the risk of the other person getting defensive. You feel stronger and more 'planted' in yourself.

When you're not speaking from your authentic self, there is a risk that you come across as judging or even 'attacking' the other person. An 'attack' might be a blurt, rant or careless comment rather than an all-out verbal assault, but it causes damage nonetheless. It can stop a dialogue dead in its tracks. This is because you aren't really voicing at all; you are 'projecting' onto the other person your judgements, opinions and condemnations.

The real 'flashpoint' is when we come across as making moralistic judgements about the other person. In his best-selling book *Nonviolent Communication*, Marshall B. Rosenberg underlines the importance of using language that is as free of judgement and superiority as possible.[8] Language that insinuates that the other person is wrong, defective or bad injures others and ourselves. It ruptures a relationship rather than repairs it.

A simple way to use collaborative language is to replace 'You' statements with 'I' statements. For example, saying 'You weren't listening to me, were you?' is likely to get someone's back up. If they react negatively and then you do the same, you end up in the same hole you were trying to exit.

Meet the moment instead with 'I' statement. Saying 'I'm feeling impatient because I'd like to feel more connected with you and the way we're interacting isn't creating the kind of connection I want' is much more likely to keep the dialogue going.

Returning to Mea and Jegan, here are some statements Mea could have made when it was her turn to talk (see Figure 6.2 on Judging and Voicing). The more Mea could be in 'voicing' and less in 'judging', the more successful her conversation with Jegan was likely to be.

Judging: Attacking or condemning the other person by coming across as superior	Voicing: Sharing what you see from your unique vantage point
You've got lost in working long hours	I miss you being involved in the more practical side of things
You need to man up	I feel your absence. I'd like a strong male presence in the business and our home
What an attitude! Where's your compassion?	I want you to show more care about our relationship
You're not being very understanding	I want to feel more 'me'. I have a fear that if I do that now, I'll overpower you
You used to be much more attentive	I've not been asking for help
Are you crazy? That's a stupid idea	Now you've got me thinking.

Figure 6.2 Judging and Voicing

There are several other ways to make your language considered and compassionate. Making this shift means that your conversation stays focused on what matters rather than derailing into a 'car crash' of reactivity. These other ways are to:

- **Replace statements that contain 'Should' or 'Shouldn't'.** Assertions such as 'You should have told me...' or 'You shouldn't have lost your temper' carry a punitive tone, which makes the other person more likely to be defensive. Saying 'I would have preferred to know sooner' or 'There's been some real fallout from you getting angry' helps to keep the door to dialogue open.

- **Eliminate 'Always' and 'Never'.** 'Blanket' statements such as 'You never listen to other people's point of view' are likely to trigger the other person because they are rarely true. Better to be specific about the time and context in which the behaviour you want to address arose. For example, 'When you interrupted the

customer several times at last week's meeting, I felt concerned about the impact you were having.'
- **Avoid inflammatory words or phrases.** Phrases such as 'You've clearly lost the plot', 'Only an idiot would...' or 'Duh! Hello!' might help you let off steam but this is at the expense of the other person. Being on the receiving end of these phrases will make some people blow, others recoil and others cave in. If you notice you're getting agitated or they're becoming defensive, better to stop, breathe and ask for a short timeout. Give the other person time to cool down, if they need it.

Finding your flow

Having a structure to what you want to say will help you to keep your focus when you talk, but it's important to keep a balance. You want to be prepared without being too controlling. It's helpful to find some words as long as you don't slip into ruminating. You want to be focused without becoming rigid. The conversation needs to flow.

Difficult conversations rarely go as planned. If, for example, the other person appears not to be picking up on what you're saying, ask them to share their understanding of what you've said before you carry on. If you need to 'decode' what the other person is saying, ask questions, paraphrase and summarise to check your understanding. A constructive conversation has an affirming, back-and-forth quality for which you can't fully prepare.

Working out a general outline is supportive. Having a beginning, middle and end gives a difficult conversation some shape and will help to hold you steady. In the previous chapter, I covered how to find your opening to a difficult conversation. Other aspects to cover as you prepare for the beginning of the conversation include being clear on its purpose and the desired outcome, such as an improved relationship. Holding a clear intention is like setting the sat nav when you drive. Having the final destination in mind frees you up to 'course correct' as you go along and encounter unexpected turns.

As the old saying goes, 'hope for the best and prepare for the worst.' Think through the worst-case scenario and decide how to handle this, for example, 'I suggest we take a pause. Let's resume the conversation once we've had time to catch our breath.' It's better to take time out than completely derail.

Even if it seems a millions miles away, challenge yourself to think through the best-case scenario (see Exercise 12 – Generate a great outcome). Be like the great sportsmen and women, from basketball players to boxers, who have learned the power of using their imaginations to achieve results on the pitch while they're off the pitch.[9]

Exercise 12
Generate a great outcome

Often when faced with a difficult conversation, people get stuck on the problems and barriers they perceive are getting in their way, depleting their energy and motivation. If you're stuck in this way, you may find it useful to complete the exercise below, which has been inspired by the 'solution-focused' approach, which has its roots in therapy and which coaches are now using.[10] The exercise invites you to 'dream' your desired future.

Set aside ten minutes (or more) for this exercise. Find a place where you won't be interrupted. Take a couple of deeper breaths. Be as relaxed as you can.

Imagine that you went to bed last night having had the difficult conversation. You've woken up this morning with a clear sense that your issue has been resolved (e.g. your relationship is stronger, the air has been cleared, your frustration is settled). The conversation has an outcome that was better than you expected. Notice how the conversation has left you feeling today. ➤

In your mind's eye, see yourself having the conversation. Picture the other person and the place you were in. Notice any sensations you have. Ask yourself these questions:

1. What strikes you the most about the conversation?
2. What did you do that generated such a positive result?
3. What was your opening line?
4. What other words or phrases did you use?
5. If it got difficult, how did you handle this?
6. How did the conversation come to an end?
7. What's the first sign that tells you things have changed?

Take your time to capture any notes that will help you to 'call in' a great outcome.

Express yourself

For the middle of the conversation, there are several aspects to think through, which will strengthen how you express yourself. Inspired by *Nonviolent Communication*, these are to:

- **Share your observations.** Ask yourself what's enriching and not enriching about the other person's behaviour. Make your observations as specific and impartial as possible. Think about what a video camera might have recorded. Instead of saying, 'You're always late', better to say, 'When you arrived at our sales meeting last week 30 minutes after the start of the session . . . '. Draw on facts. Bring some neutrality.
- **Honestly 'voice' your feelings.** Not everyone is comfortable sharing their feelings but this part doesn't have to be touchy-feely. Some leaders fear triggering a stereotype ('I'm going to be seen as the angry, black woman'). Others say that speaking about their feelings makes them feel too vulnerable or 'we don't do feelings around here.' Remember that you don't need to say 'I feel' but

simply 'I'm irritated.' Beware of the phrase 'I feel that. . . ' as you're giving an opinion rather than a feeling (as in, 'I feel that you're not pulling your weight. . . '). Go for your primary feeling. For example, check if there's hurt underneath your anger or fear behind your frustration. See what needs of yours aren't being met. A good question to ask yourself is, 'When I am feeling angry/scared/disappointed, what am I really wanting?' (more on unmet needs below).

- **Speak about the impact.** Say what the tangible effect is on you, your team, clients or other stakeholders of the other person's behaviour. Follow 'When you. . . ' with 'it has the effect that. . . ', for example: 'When you don't complete the evaluation form at the end of a coaching session, it has the effect that the whole team misses out on valuable information. I'm concerned that we're missing seeing what really works and what doesn't work when we coach our clients.' Placing the conversation in a larger context will help you to be direct. Use a tone of voice that is kind but firm and clear.

- **Ask questions that 'open up' the conversation.** Asking supportive questions helps the other person to say what's really going on for them, as in, 'I see the report is behind schedule. Tell me about the challenges you're facing.' Tune into what's going on for the other person and reveal some of your own self to build an empathic connection. Instead of asking 'Why are you feeling like that?', it's more powerful to ask, 'Are you feeling frustrated because you'd have liked me to have shared the reasons for my decision earlier?' Making a wrong guess matters less than your attempt to attune to the other.

To leave the conversation with all parties feeling heard and better understood, here are two further considerations:

- **Explore needs.** Difficulties in communication often result from unmet needs. As Marshall B. Rosenberg points out, most of us have never been taught to think in terms of needs. Underneath troublesome feelings are needs we often don't know we've got. This could be for an acknowledgement, apology, acceptance or remedial action. In an intimate relationship, we might crave some appreciation, affection or a greater sense of connection. When we acknowledge our need, we take responsibility for our feelings. Examples from *Nonviolent Communication* include, 'I feel angry when you say that, because I am wanting respect and I hear your words as an insult' and 'I'm discouraged because I would have liked to have progressed further in my work by now.' Listen for the unexpressed needs of the other person and see if you can tease these out. When you sense into the other person, instead of asking 'What did I do that's triggered you?' you might ask, 'Are you reacting to how many times I've asked others to the senior team meeting?' Helping the other person to be aware of their need (in this case, to be included) makes the conversation more of a heart-to-heart.

- **Make a request.** Think back to the purpose of the conversation. In the light of this and how your conversation has unfolded, make a specific request. Elizabeth Stokoe, Professor of Psychological and Behavioural Science at the London School of Economics and Political Science, has found that people who had already responded negatively when asked if they would like to attend mediation seemed to change their minds when the mediator used the phrase, 'Would you be willing to come for a meeting?' Including the word 'willing' builds a bridge to future possibilities, as in, 'Would you be willing to consider my request for a pay rise?' If you get agreement, follow up with an email to say thank you and state the agreed action. Having it written down builds in accountability and makes it easier to follow up, if needed. If you receive a no, explore other options and suggest alternatives, such as 'Can we discuss it again before the end of the quarter?'

In bringing a conversation to a close, think 'needs' and aim to end on a positive note. As the poet Maya Angelo wisely observed, *'I've learned that people will forget what you said, people will forget what you did, but people will never forget how you made them feel.'*

Getting to breakthrough

Turning the clock forward nine years, Jegan and Mea are still together, managing a successful business and raising two 'beautiful boys' aged 4 and 8.

Mea and I had a recent email exchange where she shared that 'We both feel grateful and aware that even though there have always been difficult moments between us, which trigger our differences, we both keep working on ourselves and our relationship.'

I was delighted to hear this and not surprised. I'd been impressed by their willingness to deepen not only their self-awareness but their understanding of each other. Mea continued:

> **'We carry on finding ways to talk about the not-often-easy topics of our lives, including finances, business and now parenting issues with the ultimate challenge of having two children. Deep listening, real understanding and the decision to be unconditionally loving has helped us to choose the path of the heart in every moment. Thank you for being one of the inspirational diamonds on our path!'**

Mea's note moved me. It was a stirring reminder of how using the humble tool of dialogue can transform a business and a personal relationship. The precious gift of being heard and speaking candidly together is the real magic of a relationship and the key to bridge-building.

Summary

1 There are two key elements to 'building a bridge' in a difficult conversation so that you connect with, not disconnect from, the other person: deeper listening and authentic speaking.

2. Deeper listening builds a shared understanding. There are three 'allies'. These are to (1) Mirror back the essence of what the other person is saying; (2) Validate their perspective as making sense to them, even if you don't agree with it; and (3) Empathise by imagining how they're feeling or have felt.

3. When you're in a heated situation, it can help to take it in turns to be the speaker and the listener. As the listener, put your own 'stuff' to one side and focus on what the other person has to say. As the speaker, stand in your own shoes and be as real as you can about what is going on for you.

4. 'Voicing' is the practice of speaking authentically. You share what you see from your unique vantage point even if it feels risky. There are two allies: using collaborative, nonviolent language and structuring what you say so that you cover all the ground you need to.

5. To express yourself effectively, share your observations, honestly voice your feelings, and speak about the impact of the difficult situation. Ask questions that help the other person to 'open up' so you explore together what is at the heart of the issue.

6. Positive language includes replacing judgemental 'you' statements with 'I' statements where you take responsibility for your feelings. Eliminate using inflammatory words and 'blanket' statements with 'always', 'never' and so on.

7. Prepare for a difficult conversation by thinking through the beginning, middle and end. Have a general outline of what you want to cover without being too prescriptive. Be clear on the purpose and set a clear intention. Imagine the best-case scenario and be ready for the worst-case scenario.

8. During the course of the conversation, tune into what the unmet needs might be underneath troublesome feelings – yours and the other person's. These could be for an acknowledgement, apology, acceptance or remedial action. Ask questions to draw them out in an empathic way.

9. As you bring the conversation to a close, make a specific request if you have one. Send an email with the agreed action, if there

is one, so you can follow up if needed. End the conversation as constructively as you can. Aim to end with all parties leaving feeling as positive as possible about how the conversation went.

> **If you do only one thing now** . . . Put your own 'stuff' to one side so that you're available to listen to the other person. Before you say how it is for you, reflect back what you've heard them say. Remember that you don't have to agree with what they've said; what matters is that the other person feels understood.

Notes

1. Hendrix, H. (2005) *Getting the Love You Want: A guide for couples*, Simon & Schuster.
2. Donaldson-Feilder, E. (2023) 'What if we could practise being fully present during interactions with another as part of our meditation?', *The Psychologist*, October 2023.
3. Donald Walsch, N. (1997) *Conversations with God, Book 1: An uncommon dialogue*, Hodder and Stoughton.
4. Stone, D., Sheen, H. and Fisher, R. (2011) *Difficult Conversations: How to talk about what matters most*, Penguin.
5. Shakespeare, W. (1596) *The Merchant of Venice*.
6. Isaacs, W. (1999) *Dialogue and the Art of Thinking Together*, Currency Doubleday.
7. Collins, J. (2001) *Good to Great: Why some companies make the leap. . . and others don't*, Random House Business.
8. Rosenberg, M. B. (2003) *Nonviolent Communication: A language of life*, Puddle Dancer Press.
9. Block, N. (1981) *Imagery*, MIT Press.
10. Passmore, J. (2020) Solution-focused coaching in Passmore, J. (Ed), *The Coaches' Handbook: The complete practitioner guide for professional coaches*, Routledge.

chapter 7

Read the room

'You have come to the room to heal the room.
You have come to the space to heal the space.
There is no other reason for you to be here.'

Neale Donald Walsch

When working in teams or small groups, it is essential to notice what's happening if a conversation starts to derail, for you will then need to intervene and re-focus the conversation, provide what's missing or enable someone else to do so. Dealing effectively with negative team and group dynamics reduces the likelihood of 'group-think', polarisation and power struggles. Here deploying authentic dialogue fosters collaboration. It generates fresh thinking and enhances wellbeing. Before this can work, it is necessary to 'read the room'. Foundational to this 'reading the room' is sharpening your observational skills as well as raising your self-awareness and systemic awareness. We look at how to disrupt dysfunctional dynamics that threaten to keep a team stuck in frustration and explore what it takes to have a dialogue that will lift and shift their performance.

> 'The pressure is on', Marco said to me. 'We need to become a truly global team but everyone keeps looking at me as the leader to make all the moves. It's a lonely place to be. I need my people to come up with their own ideas to take us forward.'
>
> His voice was tight. His brow furrowed. His eyes downcast. Even on the screen, I could sense his agitation.
>
> Marco described how his team of 30, with diverse cultural backgrounds, worked in local operations teams in offices across the globe. While their goal was to provide excellent execution across multiple time zones, their overall performance was missing the mark. Even picking up the phone to resolve an issue was a day-to-day challenge, given the 11-hour time difference between some of the teams. Workloads were imbalanced across the different teams with some teams feeling more overloaded than others.
>
> 'We need a robust conversation about how we can take this team to the next level', Marco continued, 'But people don't speak up about what's bothering them. I make suggestions, which no one criticises but they don't act on them either. I'm not even sure that others notice that their lack of ideas is an

> issue. I really need to bring people with me on the journey to transform this team but I'm at a loss about what to do.'
>
> Listening to Marco's challenge reminded me of something I'd learned from the late David Kantor (1927–2021), an American family therapist, organisational consultant and author of *Reading the Room*.[1] 'Courteous compliance' is a common pattern in teams where the designated leader provides input and ideas and everyone else dutifully follows. It occurs in newly formed teams, which have yet to develop psychological safety, and, as I've discovered in the world of hybrid working, in teams that interact mostly on screen. The problem is twofold. The team lacks 'juice' with the low level of input, and so decisions unravel with 'covert opposition' blocking progress. People voice their objections in a closed-door bilateral rather than in a team conversation.
>
> We'll return to the story of Marco and his team later in the chapter. Developing the capacity to 'read the room' helps a leader, like Marco, make sense of what's going on and to intervene more skilfully.

There are many dynamics that scupper a group or team's ability to discuss what really matters. Going down rabbit holes, becoming side-tracked by personality clashes and being in the weeds are all potential saboteurs. These phenomena are inevitable on the corporate pitch. The question is not how do you get rid of them, but more effectively: How do you deal with them when they arise, particularly when they are so pervasive?

Research from the US shows that over two-thirds of meetings (71 per cent) are unproductive. Workers spend an average of 31 hours per month in unproductive meetings. Employees multitask in at least 41 per cent of meetings, mostly in remote meetings where they check their email or perform house chores. Nearly four out of ten employees have slept during a work meeting and at least 91 per cent of employees daydream during work meetings.[2]

These findings are unsurprising given that most meetings lack a 'container' (as we explored in Chapter 3). Instead of discussing what really matters, people multitask, speak past one another rather than with one another and the air feels clogged with what's left unsaid. Meeting culture is the butt of many jokes. As the old saying (that Jeremy Clarkson reinvigorated) goes, *'Never have a meeting on a Wednesday, as it ruins both weekends.'*

There are common dynamics that get in the way of people talking about what matters most. Psychologists articulated these patterns decades ago and they beset many groups and teams to this day:

- Groupthink – groups that are highly cohesive can become more concerned about protecting the convivial atmosphere than making optimal decisions (Janis, 1972).[3]
- The pressure to conform – groups can exert powerful pressures to conform to the majority position and stifle dissenting voices (Asch, 1956).[4]
- In-group/out-group dynamics – groups can become polarised by an 'us and them' attitude as sub-groups fail to identify with the other parties involved (Tajfel, 1978).[5]

All these dynamics play out whether it's in the board room, meeting room or on the shop floor. Little wonder that there's been a trend for culling meetings given that so many are unproductive. At Shopify, the Canadian retailer, Kaz Nejatian, its chief operating officer, started 2023 with the tweet: *'Meetings are a bug. Today, we shipped a fix to this bug at @Shopify. To start 2023, we're cancelling all Shopify meetings with more than two people. Let's give people back their maker time. Companies are for builders. Not managers.'*

The problem is, if you cull meetings of more than two individuals, people might feel excluded, and you risk missing out on brilliant ideas. Conversation is a powerful tool for accessing collective intelligence but only if a leader knows how to engage all concerned in dialogue and refocus the conversation when it gets stuck.

Without the leader's ability to 'read the room' and intervene when needed, team members often struggle to talk with one another about what really matters. Partnerships grind to a halt. Departments operate in silos. Teams are taken over by turf wars. However, even when the benefits of collaboration clearly outweigh the short-term advantages of maintaining isolation and avoiding discomfort, the alternative – talking together – can seem very daunting.

In my team coaching work over the years, I've observed that it's possible to have a difficult conversation even when there are 8, 28 or even 88 people in the room. In diverse contexts that included a team of financial planners in an energy company in London, a group of NGO founders in Dhaka, and the senior leadership team of a bank in Jaipur, I've learned that it's possible to generate great outcomes through dialogue. This chapter explores how.

Reading the room

'Reading the room' is an essential leadership skill. Developing this capacity enables a leader to deal with difficult dynamics and instead create thriving conversations. David Kantor defines it as:

> **'The ability to understand what's going on as people communicate in small groups, including how the leader himself or herself is participating, when the conversation is moving forward, when it may be just about to leave the rails, and possibly even how to guide it back on course.'**[6]

Developing this capacity calls for 'dual processing'. Some of your attention is on the content of the conversation and some of your awareness is on the process. When you are 'reading the room' you are noticing:

- Whether the interaction is a real conversation or a series of monologues, a fractious debate or a febrile discussion that's going round and round in circles
- Who's participating in the conversation and how typical this is of how this group or team interacts

- What 'actions' are happening in the conversation (more on the four core actions shortly) and, crucially, which actions are missing
- Whether individuals are moving fluidly between the 'actions' or getting stuck in a specific role.

When a leader is able to 'dual process', they shift from being an 'executor' to being a 'healer'. In his book *Leader as Healer* (which won the 2023 Business Book award), Nicholas Janni contrasts these two modes of leadership. He writes: *'The Healer can analyse and strategize every bit as well as the Executor but knows what it is to connect with themselves and others, to integrate being and doing, proactivity and receptivity, rationality and intuition.'*[7]

'Reading the room' is a natural capacity we all have to some degree. We can sense when the atmosphere is flat. We know when we walk into a room that an argument has just happened by the thickness in the air. We can see on people's faces when they're engaged or when they're holding back from saying what they're really thinking. Crossed arms, searching eyes and hunched shoulders tell us more than words can ever say.

To expand this 'reading' capacity, tools and frameworks are great allies. There are several layers to 'reading the room': (1) Being aware of your strengths and development areas in conversation; (2) Noticing when a conversation gets stuck and which actions are missing; and (3) Providing what's absent or enabling someone else to bring it in. We'll cover each of these in turn.

The Four-Player model

To sharpen your observational skills with regard to dialogue, a useful tool is the Four-Player model created by David Kantor, who called his body of work 'structural dynamics'. It's a model of how communication works and doesn't work in human systems. Taking an evidence-based approach, Kantor discovered through observing families and later teams that there are four basic 'actions' or 'speech acts' that can be made in any conversation (see Figure 7.1).

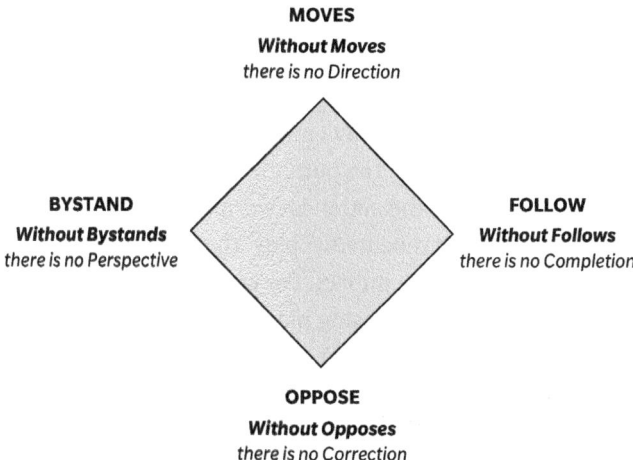

Figure 7.1 The four actions and their intentions
Source: Adapted from David Kantor (2011) *Reading the Room: Group Dynamics for Coaches and Leaders*

Kantor refers to this as the 'Four-Player' model which emphasises the dynamism that arises when all four actions are present.[8]
Each action carries a different intention and brings a distinct quality:

- A **'Move' brings direction** – by saying, for example, 'I suggest we talk about. . . ', 'I think our best option is. . . ', 'To move forward, we need to. . . '
- A **'Follow' brings completion** – by saying, for example, 'I agree that. . . ', 'It's a great idea that we. . . ', 'Let's do as Chris says and. . . '
- An **'Oppose' brings correction** – by saying, for example, 'I disagree that. . . ', 'I see things differently in that. . . ', 'I'd challenge that given. . . '
- A **'Bystand' brings perspective** – by saying, for example, 'I'm noticing that. . . ', 'There's a pattern here. . . ', 'What I'm observing is. . . '

In a productive dialogue, all four are present and there is an even flow. When a conversation becomes difficult, one or more of them are often missing. This can lead to repeated patterns among the speech acts that are present. When a conversation becomes rigid and draining, you can make it more dynamic by identifying which is missing and bringing it in. The absent action is like a 'missing vitamin'. When you include it, the conversation is more nourishing for everyone involved.

While each action has a positive intention, it doesn't always 'land' in this way. Figure 7.2 shows the potential quality of each action and the unintended impact if the action is overplayed or poorly executed. If we become 'stuck' and repeatedly 'play' the same action, we can unwittingly have a negative impact. For example, you might make a Bystand and say, 'There's a missing piece here' but if you repeatedly point out that there's an absence of data or shared assumptions, other people might see you as aloof or even blocking. It's not what you intend but it's the message you send.

The other issue that can arise is when people put a 'spin' on their action. For example, you really want to Oppose but you make a Bystand with a roll of the eyes, saying, 'We've tried that several times and it's never worked.' Other people don't hear you bringing a wider perspective; they pick up on your frustration and you can seem negative.

	Positive intention If done well, we bring to the conversation:	Unintended impact If overplayed, we may come across as being:
Move	• Direction • Focus • Purpose	• Pushy • Dictatorial • Impatient
Follow	• Completion • Harmony • Connection	• Placating • Compliant • Wishy-washy
Oppose	• Correction • Realignment • Challenge	• Critical • Objectionable • Attacking
Bystand	• Perspective • A wider context • Neutrality	• Disinterested • Withdrawn • Aloof

Figure 7.2 The gap between intention and impact
Source: Adapted from Kantor, D. (2012) *Reading the Room: Group Dynamics for Coaches and Leaders*. Jossey-Bass

The Four-Player model helps you to keep your communication 'clean'. If you want to Oppose, say it as it is. If you want to make a Move, be clear not fuzzy with your suggestion. If you want to Follow, show some enthusiasm; don't just sit there nodding or thinking 'good idea' in your head. If it's Bystand you want to bring in, do so without appearing disengaged.

Reading the room also makes you more understanding of others. When your colleague keeps on Opposing, for example, it pays to look for the positive intent: in what way might their point of view bring some valuable correction? Consider inviting them to make a Move: 'I hear your objections and I'm wondering if you can make a suggestion instead?'

See where you get stuck

To become more skilful at dialogue, it helps to become aware which of the four different actions you are most comfortable and least comfortable with. David Kantor has found that we typically have strengths in one or two of the actions and that we underplay at least one of them. When we are not using the full set, our dialogue is more likely to derail.

By contrast, playing to your strengths and also developing your capacity to bring in your least preferred action enables you to have an authentic dialogue. Without individuals developing this capacity, there is a risk that they stay in a pattern of serial monologues, oppositional debates or unproductive discussion.

There are several tools online that will help you to assess your preferences for Move, Follow, Oppose and Bystand. You might already have an intuitive understanding of your 'conversational profile'. If not, you can explore your preferences using this free online questionnaire developed by my colleague Dr Claus Springborg.[9] Exercise 13 – Your conversational profile (a little further on) will also help with reflection on your preferences for the four actions, including, most valuably, what happens to you when under pressure.

Understanding your 'conversational profile' enables you to be *responsive* rather than *reactive* when talking with someone or a team. A conversation is then something that you create rather than have. We saw in Chapter 4 how deepening your awareness of your 'reactive tendency' increases your capacity to stay in conversation. Here we explore how reactive tendency intersects with the four dialogic actions, so that you expand the space of possibilities when you talk, even when there are tough topics on the table.

'Awareness is curative', as Timothy Gallwey wrote in *The Inner Game*.[10] Being aware of your reactive tendency – a survival strategy developed in childhood to cope with stress and anxiety – helps to heal repeating patterns. When you go tense, your behaviour narrows. You are more likely to become 'stuck' and overplay an action, even though it would be more effective to bring in a different one. Here's how your ability to 'play' the four actions might narrow once your reactive tendency kicks in:

- **'Moving towards' or complying.** Given the need to be liked, loved and safe, individuals with this tendency are more likely to become stuck making Follows. In their search for approval, in a high-stakes conversation, they're less likely to raise contentious issues (Move) or disagree (Oppose).

- **'Moving away' or avoiding.** Given the need for independence and self-sufficiency, individuals with this way of operating are more likely to become stuck making Bystands. Rather than making Moves or Opposes that risk others asserting themselves or talking about feelings, it's safer to make more neutral comments.

- **'Moving against' or confronting.** Given the need to maintain control, individuals with this tendency can be at risk of becoming stuck making a Move or Oppose. They might lose their ability to see the bigger picture and therefore not make Bystands. Making a Follow could feel threatening given their desire to be in control.

Let's return to the story of Marco. When we explored this model together, he realised that under pressure, he would revert to making Moves.

'I feel so uncomfortable with an awkward pause. But I'm left with this awful sense of being out on a limb', he said. 'When no one responds or I sense some silent opposition, I make another move as if by compulsion.'

'So what could you do differently?', I asked. 'Given that your tendency is "move against" or confront others, what are your other options?'

'Well, I could pause and take a deeper breath. Before impulsively making another Move, I could ask myself whether it was wiser to make a Follow, Oppose or Bystand.'

'And what would that give you?'

'I'd no longer have a sense of 'I'll just wind my neck back in' or of tumbleweed.' Marco said. 'My conversations would be calmer. My team might get better at making decisions if they sense I'm not steamrolling them.'

Being aware that there are four actions to choose from makes you less likely of falling into the trap of only playing one. Exercise 13 – Your conversational profile – will help you to reflect on your own tendencies and the impact that these have.

Exercise 13
Your conversational profile

1 Think about the conversations you have with your team, manager and other colleagues. Look at the four actions in the earlier figure and ask yourself these questions:
   - Which action am I most comfortable with?
   - Which action am I least comfortable with?
2 Now recall some situations which are 'higher stakes'. The increase in pressure might involve talking with your boss about an important issue, delivering some bad news or dealing with an unhappy stakeholder. Now ask yourself:
   - What happens to me under pressure?
   - Which of the four actions do I tend to 'play' or even 'overplay'? ➤

You might find it helpful to think back to the three reactive tendencies (see Chapter 4). See if you can join the dots between your reactive tendency and which of the four actions you're most at risk of 'overplaying'.

3 Reflect on your answers to questions (1) and (2). What are the consequences of your conversational preferences? What's working for you? What's not working for you? How might you change your behaviour to have a more positive impact?

Notice what's missing

High-performing teams don't get stuck in talking tough, talking nice or not talking at all. They find their way through conflict and avoidance and have the conversations that matter.

Psychologists Losada and Heaphy studied 60 different teams of around eight people in the same organisation and found key behavioural differences between the teams.[11] Low-performing teams operated in a distrustful and cynical atmosphere. They fell into rigid and overly stable patterns in their interactions. Flourishing teams had a buoyant and trusting atmosphere. Their interactions were flexible and fluid. My read of that research is that all four actions were present in the conversation rather than some of them going 'offline'.

There are several types of 'mired meetings' where people get bogged down in difficult dynamics. Here are some of the most common:

- **The dominated meeting.** One or two strong personalities take up most of the airtime. Others struggle to get a word in and, when they do speak, it's often to agree with what the central 'mover' has proposed. Some team members switch off and stop listening; others stay silent and save their objections for informal catch-ups after the meeting has finished.
- **The off-topic meeting.** Discussion is vague, repetitive and goes nowhere. People keep going off at a tangent or don't take the

meeting content seriously. There's often no agenda or if there is, it's ignored. People talk for too long or in too much detail. No one 'owns' the meeting. There's a lack of agreement about what's important so the meeting doesn't move forward.

- **The conflicted meeting.** People disagree without respecting each other's point of view, even in front of a client. Colleagues have side conversations during the meeting. People type away on their device and don't respond to calls for input. The meeting is so off-putting that team members turn up late or don't turn up at all. Those who disagree with one another make things personal, rather than being objective about what the other person is thinking or proposing.

These meetings carry hidden costs to which many managers don't pay attention: decisions unravel afterwards, there's no fresh thinking, people lose momentum and morale drops. These interactions have a predictable pattern to them: one or more of the actions is missing.

Below are the missing speech acts from the three 'mired meetings' (spoiler alert: gather your own thoughts before reading further if you'd like an opportunity to 'read the room' right here, right now).

- **The dominated meeting.** One or two people make the Moves. Others tend to Follow. What's missing are Opposes and Bystands.
- **The off-topic meeting.** This is a series of monologues. People make Moves but without building on what others have said. A wider perspective is absent. What's missing are Follows and Bystands.
- **The conflicted meeting.** People Oppose one another without making proposals of their own. Others are absent and it's hard to know what they think. What's missing are Moves and Bystands.

Expand your repertoire

To have authentic dialogue, a leader needs not only to 'read the room' accurately but also to expand their repertoire so as to be in the room with more resourcefulness. They need to bring in the missing action, as appropriate, or to enable others to expand their repertoire in order to provide the speech act that's absent. As Michael A. Genovese observes in *The Future of Leadership* (2016):

> **'Great leaders have the ability to *style-flex*. They can adjust their dance to the music being played... They recognise when to push and when to back away, when to lead and when to follow, when to speak and when to remain quiet, when to force the action and when to refrain.'**[12]

In recent years, there's been less and less tolerance of 'command-and-control' leadership where leaders call the shots. Some leaders I've met declare their dislike of the directive style but still operate by issuing commands and trying to maintain control. Their comments either assert and cast the direction (Move) or challenge and pushback (Oppose). They expect others to agree (Follow). They overlook the wider perspective-taking (Bystand).

To lead during these testing times, a leader needs to develop their ability to bring in all four actions as appropriate. When there are not only Moves and Opposes but Follows, which provide agreement and support, and Bystands, which bring perspective and objectivity, the atmosphere is decidedly different, and so are the outcomes. This really matters now that we are living in an era where it is significantly harder to get decisions right.

To provide the action that's missing in a conversation, develop your ability to 'play' your least comfortable action. For example, if you hardly ever Oppose in a team meeting or when you do, it gets you into trouble, you need to find ways to disagree, challenge and fight your corner more skilfully. There are several strategies that you can draw on:

- **Practise in a safe environment.** You might, for example, say 'no' to a meeting that's been scheduled that you're not willing or able to make. Tune into the truth of this.
- **Think ahead about how to flex.** Anticipate a meeting where making an Oppose would be beneficial. Think through a reason you could give for your challenge.

- **Identify a great role model.** Look around at who embodies the action you want to develop. Observe their timing, words and tone of voice. Identify what you can apply.
- **Find language that works for you.** Use words that you're comfortable with. You might not want to say 'Playing devil's advocate' and prefer, 'I see things differently.'
- **Have a trusted ally in the room.** Be aware of others who hold a similar view. Realise that you're not a lone voice. Feel resourced by the presence of others who back you.
- **Ask for feedback.** Invite a trusted colleague to share their observations about your 'experiment'. Check in to see how it landed. Reflect on what you'd do another time.

The above are all strategies that enable you to disrupt without being disrespectful. You can adapt these approaches regardless of whether you ought to extend to make a Move, Follow, Oppose or Bystand. This expanded capacity will strengthen your leadership and enable a team to develop a strategy successfully or meet a challenge effectively.

Finally, as a leader, encourage your team to mature their inter-play. Instead of you and your team members being trapped enacting one of the four 'roles', create a shift in identity to promote a change in behaviour. Dr Peter Hawkins, Professor of Leadership at Henley Business School, makes the following four suggestions:[13]

- A **Mover** becomes a challenge framer. Rather than proposing solutions, take a step back, contextualise the challenge and invite others to address it. *'We have the following challenge and I need your help to work out how we address it.'*
- An **Opposer** becomes an inquirer. Instead of arguing against solutions, share concerns, ask questions and explore possible unintended consequences. *'What would a great outcome be if we managed to collectively address that challenge?'*
- A **Bystander** becomes a contributor. To replace sitting on the sidelines, share a pattern, name a dilemma or connect with the bigger picture. *'One pattern that I've noticed that's scuppered us in the past is. . .'*

- A **Follower** becomes an implementer. Rather than just agreeing, be willing to make change happen. Offer to take a lead with some follow-through on actions. '*How about we do Y by this time next month? I could provide an update on how Z has progressed.*'

'Change it up'

Coming back to the story at the start of this chapter, Marco decided that he needed to disrupt the repeating pattern of 'courteous compliance' in his team. His understanding of the Four-Player model increased both his self-awareness and his systemic awareness. Marco acknowledged that his comfort zone was Moving whereas Following was uncomfortable for him. His 'read of the room' was that he made the 'Moves' and everyone else fell in line with 'Follows'. Absent from the team's conversations were Opposes and Bystands. He needed to 'change it up' by finding a way to bring the missing speech acts into the room.

To lift and shift the team's performance, Marco invited them to an offsite and asked me to facilitate the session. When we discussed the design, I asked people to stand in different places in the room rather than remain seated in their chairs, so we could disrupt rigid dynamics and change the conversation. 'Maps' create movement. Physicality changes mentality.

To create the first map, we placed 11 sheets of paper on the floor to represent the 11 local offices. The layout reflected as closely as possible the global geography. It was striking how far apart the teams in Singapore and Argentina were from one another when people stood in their place in the system.

When I asked team members to describe the atmosphere in their local office, the range of responses was telling. Some teams were 'happy', 'noisy' and 'commercial' but others were 'silent', 'tense' and 'stressed'. The more isolated teams were geographically, the more they appeared to be struggling with their sense of belonging to the wider team.

'What do you make of this pattern?' I asked, inviting some wider observations.

'It's a real challenge to work across time zones.'

'We tend to engage in lengthy email exchanges rather than pick up the phone and talk.'

'We need to punch out of this vicious cycle', said the most recent joiner. 'We feel disconnected because we don't talk which makes it even harder to have a conversation.'

People stood in clusters looking thoughtful. Valuable though these Bystands were, I had a sense that more was needed.

Drawing on the work of John Katzenbach and Douglas Smith in *Harvard Business Review Classics*, I projected a definition of a high-performing team onto a large white screen at the front of the room:

'A team is a small number of people with complementary skills who are committed to a common purpose and set of performance goals and an approach for which they hold themselves mutually accountable.'[14]

It's not a snappy definition but it covers the essence of what makes a team different from a group of high-performing individuals.

'Now imagine that there's a "continuum line" stretching across the room', I said. 'On a scale of zero to ten, the screen represents ten. It's a team performing at the top of their game. Across the other side of the room where the door is, it's zero and the exact opposite. Where do you think the team is? Go and stand there.'

Some people walked briskly to a spot on the scale. Others shuffled into position. One person tried out various places until they found a position that felt right. It took a few minutes for the room to settle. Team members were stood across the spectrum from two to eight.

'I'd put us at four out of ten', a recent arrival to the team said. 'We have some great skills in the team but don't have a set of performance goals.'

'I disagree', said the next person who was stood at seven out of ten. 'We have a business plan where there are goals, you just need to read them!'

'I'd put us at eight out of ten' said one of the longest-standing team members. 'We've come a long way from a few years ago when we didn't even have our Asia and South America offices.'

'I agree', said Marco. 'A few years ago, we didn't have a common purpose. Now at least we have a shared desire to become a high-performing, flawlessly executing global team.'

Bingo! I thought. Now we've unlocked Opposes. Marco's even Following.

With people moving around the room, the conversation had become more dynamic. Standing on their feet, the team named how difficult it was to find a mutually convenient time to talk and aired their frustrations without any tense silence. They shared some success stories and patted one another on the back. Slowly, a sense of direction for the team started to emerge.

'We need to collaborate more', one person said. 'Get out of our silos and do some project work together.'

'We can be "one team" without everyone needing to be on everything', another person suggested. 'We could have a monthly "deep dive" into an issue for those who can make it.'

'I'd be happy to organise "drop-ins" for our key stakeholders' Marco's deputy said. 'Let me know who you'd like me to invite and I'll get the ball rolling.'

With team members making these Moves, the room was full of positive energy. By the end of the day, tricky business issues had been discussed and next steps had been agreed. The team had identified the windows of time when it would be possible to talk, they'd committed to a monthly meeting to discuss 'tactics' and a quarterly meeting to talk about emerging strategic issues. Given the size of the global operations this team managed and the amount that they invoiced clients each week, increasing their functioning through better dialogue could have a massive impact on the amount of working capital available.

In the closing round, one team member said how she felt 'touched' by how the whole team was working together to meet the problems that lay in their midst. There was a palpable sense of 'we're all in this together.' I looked across the room at Marco. His eyes were shining. The pressure was still on, but his team had risen to the challenge.

Exercise 14
Intervening in your team

---

1 What difficult dynamics or repetitive patterns operate in your team (or group that you regularly participate in)? If you look at these through the lens of the four dialogic actions (Move, Follow, Oppose, Bystand), what do you see?

2 Which actions are missing? How could you bring these into the room? What language would help you to make a Move, Follow, Oppose or Bystand?

3 How can you enable others to bring in the actions that they don't typically use? What 'maps' could you create in the room to encourage people to move around the room and take different positions? If you're working online, how could you disrupt the dynamics to engage people differently (e.g. you could still use a 1–10 'scaling question' and invite people to put their number in the 'chat').

Remember that if you're the most senior person in the room, you might have to go the extra mile to encourage others to take actions other than Follows. When team members make a Move, Oppose or Bystand, acknowledge their contribution even if you find it challenging. Remind yourself that it's better to have these actions in the room where you can respond than in closed-door conversations where you can't do anything about them.

A well-honed ability to read the room will give you an edge no matter with whom you are talking and whatever the setting. It's a key secret which leads to authentic, productive and healing conversations in which everyone engages. As Henry Ford said, *'If everyone is moving forward together, then success takes care of itself.'*

Summary

1. 'Reading the room' is an essential skill to develop in order to discuss what really matters. It enables a leader to spot difficult dynamics such as groupthink, power struggles and polarisation and then to intervene more skilfully.

2. Dual processing is key. Some of your attention is on the content of the conversation and some of your awareness is noticing how people, including yourself, are participating.

3. There are four dialogic 'actions' or 'speech acts' in a productive conversation. Each brings a positive intention: A 'Move' brings direction, a 'Follow' support, an 'Oppose' challenge and a 'Bystand' perspective. In dialogue, all four actions are present and there is a flow between them.

4. Developing your self-awareness enables you to play to your strengths and to notice where you get 'stuck' by overplaying an action. Being aware of your 'reactive tendency' and how this plays out in dialogue creates more choice about how you show up so that you can participate more effectively in conversation.

5. Cultivating your systemic awareness enables you to notice which action is missing. A skilful leader will then provide the speech act that's absent, invite others to do so and encourage more resourceful contributions through a shift in identity. Disrupting rigid dynamics makes authentic dialogue possible.

> **If you do only one thing now** . . . Stand back and observe. See what's happening and who is doing what. Track both the content of the conversation and the process. Pay attention to *how* people are talking as well as what they say. Notice who's contributing and who remains silent. Disrupt any stuck dynamics by encouraging the missing 'action' (Move, Follow, Oppose or Bystand) by bringing it in yourself or by inviting others to contribute.

Notes

1. Kantor, D. (2012) *Reading the Room: Group dynamics for coaches and leaders*, Jossey-Bass.
2. https://www.zippia.com/advice/meeting-statistics/.
3. Janis, I. (1972) *Victims of groupthink: A psychological study of foreign policy decisions and fiascos*, Houghton Mifflin.
4. Asch, S. (1956) Studies of independence and conformity: A minority of one against a unanimous majority, *Psychological Monographs: General and applied*, 70, pp. 1–70.
5. Tajfel, H. (Ed) (1978) *Differentiation between Social Groups: Studies in the social psychology of intergroup relations*, Academic Press.
6. Kantor, D. (2012) *Reading the Room: Group dynamics for coaches and leaders*, Jossey-Bass.
7. Janni, N. (2022) *Leader as Healer: A new paradigm for 21st century leadership*, LID Publishing.
8. Kantor, D. (2012) *Reading the Room: Group dynamics for coaches and leaders*, Jossey-Bass.
9. https://www.sensingmind.com/dialogical-preference-questionnaire/.
10. Gallwey, T. (2014) *The Inner Game of Tennis*, Pan Books.
11. Losada, M. and Heaphy, E. (2004) 'The role of positivity and connectivity in the performance of business teams: A nonlinear dynamics model', *American Behavioural Scientist*, Vol. 47, 6, pp. 740–765.
12. Genovese, M. A. (2015) *The Future of Leadership: Leveraging influence in an age of hyper-change (Leadership: Research and Practice)*, Routledge.
13. Transforming David Kantor's Four Player model of Team Roles.
14. Katzenbach, J. R. and Smith, D.K. (2009) *The Discipline of Teams*, Harvard Business Review Classics.

chapter 8

Hold space

'The role of a leader is not to come up with all the great ideas.

The role of a leader is to create an environment in which great ideas can happen.'

Simon Sinek[1]

When working with a group of stakeholders, it is vital that a leader 'holds space' rather than takes up space. These two stances have very different consequences. When a leader inflates, others deflate. As the group is usually then unable to move beyond politeness or breakdown, conflict festers. When, by contrast, a leader builds a container in which they 'hold space', they create an expansive emotional place where stakeholders respect their differences, develop fresh thinking and find a novel solution to a tough problem.

A skilful leader recognises that authentic dialogue moves through four 'fields' of conversation, each with its own distinct atmosphere. Understanding this sequence and sensing into each field enables a leader to navigate and harvest conflict. In what becomes a generative space, even with a diversity of perspectives, a group is able to talk about what matters most, resulting in better decision-making, problem solving and collective action.

Ade, the head teacher of a large primary school in the north of England, sounded stressed as he spoke. His voice was tight, his hands knotted.

'In the two years I've been at the school, the main challenge I've faced is not the 300 pupils or even the parents but the grumbling teachers.'

Oh, I thought, who's making the teachers grumble?
I decided it was best to 'bracket' this question. Ade, unaware of my 'left-hand column' asserting itself, carried on without taking a pause for breath.

'The school was performing, but now it's being held back by tensions among the staff. Some of the teachers and teaching assistants have worked here for more than 20 years. Others have been around for a much shorter time. We try and discuss making changes but it all grinds to a halt. You can sometimes cut the atmosphere with a knife in the staff room.'

I decided to stay in listening mode.

> 'Under the previous head, staff had become used to having their own way. With her "hands off" style, the teachers were left to their own devices. It was easy for them to blame her when things went wrong. When I arrived, I carried out a review of all the posts, which led to some of the staff being downgraded and having to accept a lower salary level. Feelings of resentment are still bubbling away for those who feel they've been unfairly treated.'
>
> 'What do you want to have happen?' I asked.
>
> 'I want to turn a good school into a great school', Ade said. 'I'd like more teamwork and better outcomes for the children.'
>
> 'That sounds like a "big win". What's getting in the way?'
>
> 'People jockeying for position and forming factions. I have moments when I wonder if we're even a good school.'
>
> Ade looked me dead in the eye.
>
> 'Trust is a must, but I'm stumped about how to build it.'

Why holding space is critical

Building trust involves a real conundrum. To surface a trust problem *requires* trust. If trust is lacking, how do you even get started? As Brené Brown's research has found the consequences of avoiding tough conversations include diminishing trust and engagement.[2] But while talking about trust when it is absent is tough, dialogue is essential to creating trust. It is risky and uncomfortable but, as therapists say: *The only way out is through*. Without voicing what's really going on, the walls that have gone up between people won't come down.

In his best-selling book, *The Five Dysfunctions of a Team*, Patrick Lencioni outlines the common pitfalls teams face when they work together.[3] The same psychology applies to groups of stakeholders. Lencioni uses a triangle with five layers to give a visual representation (see Figure 8.1).

Figure 8.1 The five dysfunctions of a team
Source: Adapted from Lencioni, P. (2002) *The Five Dysfunctions of a Team: A leadership fable.* John Wiley & Sons

At the base of the triangle sits lack of trust. All the other dysfunctions sit on top of this. Distrust leads to fear of conflict, which results in a lack of commitment as people haven't thrashed out their ideas. There is then avoidance of accountability as people haven't really bought in, and, finally, inattention to results.

By contrast, in a high-performing team or group, people trust one another and as a result, are able to engage in healthy conflict. Through robust dialogue, they arrive at commitment to plans of action, holding each other accountable and driving to achieve great results together.

For any group to go from good to great, they need to address the most fundamental dysfunction: lack of trust. Without this, a group will stay stuck in one of two places. They will either be 'interminably nice' to one another (as one client described it) and never get to the nub of the issue. Or disagreements will create divisions that escalate into a smash-up from which recovery seems impossible.

To talk constructively when there's a lack of trust between people, it is first necessary to create a different atmosphere in which the conversation takes place. A leader cannot command trust. They cannot mandate it. It is impossible to buy it in or roll it out. Holding court with a big brain (or a big ego) will never inspire others to step into unchartered territory. Another, more delicate, approach is needed, that of holding space.

What 'holding space' means

I learned about 'holding space' the hard way when I facilitated a session for a UK building society several years ago. It was on a Monday after I'd flown through the night on Saturday from the States. The red-eye flight had been a shocker with turbulence keeping me awake most of the journey.

By mid-morning on the Monday, I was puzzled. By this point in a session, a group would usually start to 'gather' but this group wasn't gelling. They were still talking past one another rather than with each other. Some participants were checking their smartphones for messages (despite my request not to). There were no ripples of humour, sustained eye contact or relaxed smiles.

'Darn!' It suddenly occurred to me why the usual signs indicating that the energy 'field' was becoming more coherent weren't there. In my jet-lagged state, I'd missed the most fundamental intervention of them all: holding a check-in (more on this shortly). By the end of the session, the group had started to talk together more easily but we never did arrive at 'hive mind'. Failing to hold a check-in cast a shadow over the whole meeting.

'Holding space' is not something that you analyse, it's something that you *feel*. When a room is 'gathered' with rapt attention, people look at one another rather than averting their gaze. The tight smiles of 'small talk' are replaced with bright, shining eyes. The next person to speak lets the previous one finish their sentence. When there's a misunderstanding, people slow down to unpack what's been said. When there's an unexpected moment of humour, laughter ripples around the room.

I've heard other consultants describe 'holding space' as a 'high art' of leadership. But what does this mean? It's an odd phrase. It might make you think of trying to nail jelly to a wall or hold water in a sieve. To make it real we need conceptual clarity and a model of practice.

Holding space includes and goes beyond simple 'psychological safety'. This refers to an environment in which team members sense they can take interpersonal risks without it being a career-limiting move; they are still respected and accepted. While it is always essential that people feel safe in order to be open and share their questions and concerns, as Professor Amy Edmonson's research has shown,[4] a difficult conversation calls for additional qualities.

Research in the nuclear industry has shown that even in the context of divergent and diverse opinions, it is possible to create the conditions for constructive and generative dialogue when five extra qualities are present. Through establishing a climate of inquiry, inclusion, spontaneity, possibility and freedom, people feel more connected, have a stronger sense of shared identity and agree to the better utilisation of resources.[5] We shall return to these qualities a little later in this chapter.

A space for a generative conversation needs to be both a 'crucible' and a 'sanctuary'. It is a place where we experience both the warmth of connection *and* the discomfort of truth-telling. It has creative 'fire' and yet the heat does not burn. This is how Robert Augustus Masters, an author and therapist, describes a healthy relationship.[6] We can let down our guard and be who we truly are while, at the same time, rising to the challenge of becoming a more compassionate human being through the demands of relating to another. Masters calls intimate relationship, ripe with the potential of awakening to a fuller version of ourselves, 'the ashram of the 21st century'. Authentic dialogue in teams is the corporate equivalent.

I define 'holding space' as the capacity to create an expansive emotional space where stakeholders respect their differences, navigate conflict and surface new possibilities. The 'new' that arises – whether it's a shared understanding, a compelling purpose or a set of aligned actions – serves the whole ecosystem and not simply the needs of the most senior person in the room. It emerges out of the 'mesh' of perspectives, not out of one person thinking out loud alone.

Changing the way people talk changes the way people act. Changing the way people act changes the outcomes that result. An excellent school, a thriving business, a top-class university and a successful not-for-profit are all networks of conversations. All the people in these entities have leaders and hold meetings. If their conversations are constructive, the organisation is likely to be productive. If their conversations are destructive, there's a real risk that the organisation flounders.

Holding space is both a subtle art and a critical skill that you can learn. There are three key enablers: (1) Build a 'container' which is a safe enough space for people to show up as themselves and feel valued; (2) Understand that dialogue moves through a predictable sequence of four conversational fields; and (3) Know how to cross the 'threshold' from one field to the next so that you don't get stuck in a field or exit the dialogue process prematurely or completely.

All this begins with sensing the space you're in and knowing how to navigate the currents that enter the room. Let's return to the story of the school and see how this plays out.

Build the 'container'

My colleague and I thought carefully about the challenge of creating more trust. Ade had invited us to facilitate an away day with all 42 staff. With the 'whole system in the room' – the teachers and teaching assistants, the caretakers and 'midday-ers' (who looked after the children at lunchtime), the admin staff and senior leadership team – it was an exciting opportunity to build a 'container' (see Chapter 3) for a conversation that could make a difference for the staff and the children they looked after.

As people filed into the school assembly hall, we asked them to sit with others that they knew less well. As trust builds on getting to know one other, we suggested that individuals sitting together found out something they had in common. It was an informal 'check-in': a way of bringing each person's voice into the room so that they had the chance to connect.

Some lively discussions followed. The hall, with its stacked up chairs and folded climbing frame, was cold on this crisp October morning. The small group discussions filled the hall with some much-needed warmth. As they talked, I noticed that some of the staff unfolded their arms and sat back in their seats, the chair legs scraping across the scratched, pale wooden floor. I invited each group to share something from their discussion.

'We're all right handed', one trio said.

'We've all worn glasses at some point', said another.

'We all wear pyjamas', said a group of women.

'We all have a piercing', another group revealed, 'or we've thought of having one!'

By the end of this round, their laughter had begun to thaw the atmosphere. The term 'ice breaker', which refers to an activity early on in a session that gets people to interact, is an accurate description. It's a way of settling the anxiety that lies beneath the surface of any group coming together. Will others like me? Will I be seen as competent? Is it safe to say what I really think? These questions gnaw away at us until we find our voice.

A 'check-in' process is a key tool for creating a space where people can 'land'. It changes the atmosphere in a room when you give people the opportunity to 'arrive' fully. People's presence – their undivided attention – is the most valuable resource in any organisation. Helping participants to let go of their journeys so as to arrive and put to one side distractions makes their speaking and thinking richer.

A 'check-in' also sets a pattern of roughly equal airtime. In an article originally published in *Science* in 2010, psychologists at the MIT Sloan School of Management in the US found that several factors we might expect to be associated with effective teams were not relevant. These included the average IQ of the group, the IQ of the smartest member and the size of the group. The groups that were more likely to perform well were the ones where conversational turn-taking took place. Groups with a more even pattern of participation outperformed groups where one or two individuals dominated, even in more seemingly 'intelligent' groups.

A simple way to establish a pattern of full participation is to start with a 'check-in'. For further reflection, see Exercise 15 – Hold a 'check-in'.

Exercise 15
Hold a 'check-in'

A check-in helps create a 'container', making it less likely that one or two people will dominate the airwaves. It is easier for those who struggle to find their voice to speak after they have spoken once. The mix of different voices creates 'psychological safety' when people feel able to speak truthfully from their unique perspective.

Think about a future meeting where it will be helpful to have full participation.

- What would be the benefits of starting to work in a more connected, human-centred way? What could be the challenges? What prep (in addition to this exercise) will help you to introduce a 'check-in' (e.g. talk it through with a trusted colleague who'll be at the meeting you have in mind).

- What 'check-in' question (or questions) can you use at the start of the session to hear something from each person? Think about the language. Asking 'how are you feeling?' might be off-putting. Asking, 'What's the energy you're stepping in with?' could be a better opener (see below for some more inspiration). Decide the tone you want to set and how informal or, if people will be dismissive of something 'touchy-feely', formal you want to be. You could do two rounds and cover both. What would be *your* response to the check-in?

- What process will you use? Will you (a) go round the table/circle/screen; (b) invite people to participate in a more random way by sensing when it's their turn; (c) ask the person who's spoken to 'pass the baton' and choose the next person (only the person holding the 'baton' speaks); or (d) do something else? If you're on a video call, you might invite people to speak in alphabetical order. With a global team, you could move from the southern hemisphere to the northern hemisphere or vice-versa (this geography 'test' might generate some much-needed mirth). ➤

- What practicalities do you need to consider? If you have a larger group in the room (over 12), think about how people can form smaller 'huddles' of 3 or 4 people so they can 'check-in' in this group. You can then hear back from each huddle or, if there are too many, a selection. See below for some other practical tips

Possible check-in questions

For a more informal approach (to encourage people to bring more of their 'whole self' into the conversation):

- How are you arriving? Use a colour to describe your state.
- What's a 'proud moment' you've had recently?
- What's raised a smile (whether at work or in your personal life)?
- If this organisation was a 'circus', what would your role be (plate spinner, juggler, clown, ring master. . .)?
- What have you given up to be here?

For a more formal approach (to stimulate curiosity and bring clarity to the purpose of the dialogue):

- What would be a great outcome from this session?
- What do you want to leave the room with?
- What's a question you're holding that would be good for us to explore?
- What would you want a stakeholder to say about this meeting's impact?
- What's a strength you bring to our exploration today?

Practical tips

Here are a few suggestions to make a check-in work, whether you're in person or online:

- **Be willing to go first.** As the leader, accept that you might need to 'break the ice' if others are reluctant to speak, for example, 'If I were to answer this question I'd say. . .'

- **Use prompts.** Put the question/s on a flip chart, on screen or in the 'chat box'. This will help people to stay on track when nerves are high at the start of a meeting.
- **Use a visual.** There are also some great resources available such as the 'blob tree', which shows figures with different expressions scattered around a tree. Variations include 'blob football' with figures on a pitch and 'blob beach' for a more leisurely scene. People sometimes find it easier to identify how they're feeling with images rather than words. One source where you can download images (including some for free) is https://www.pipwilson.com.

Set ground rules

Back in the school hall, after the check-in, Ade took the floor to set some context.

'I want today to be jolly but not *a* jolly', he said. 'There is work for us to do.'

He went on to read out his vision for the school that he'd included in his letter of application three years earlier. Part of his school development plan was that there would be robust relationships between teachers and pupils, parents and staff. This steady foundation would contribute to the development of the 'whole child' at the school.

Several of the staff gazed out of the window. Some fiddled with their phones. One person yawned. When Ade paused to catch his breath, the silence felt uneasy.

I took this as a good moment to introduce some 'ground rules'. Group agreements are invaluable for making dialogue authentic. For facilitators, contracting for confidentiality is SOP (standard operating procedure); less common is to put in place guiderails that help to build not only a safe space but an energising 'holding environment'.

In my experience there are five key ground rules. Each of these brings a different quality (drawing on the research I mentioned earlier about how dialogue worked in the context of the nuclear industry). They are:

1 **Use 'I' statements.** When people slip into using 'you' ("you get fed up when meetings start late") or 'we' ("we're terrible at making decisions"), dialogue loses juice. Invite people to speak from 'I' so that they 'own' what they say and bring their unique perspective ("I see X as our main priority"). This brings the quality of **possibility**.

2 **Welcome uncomfortable moments.** When teams talk about what matters, it's likely that people 'trigger' one another. Expanding tolerance for discomfort – even with this simple statement – makes room for curiosity. The deeper learning is often at the edge of our comfort zone. A climate of **inquiry** is invaluable.

3 **Be present and listen fully.** Dialogue cannot be scripted (unless it's for a play or a book). A real conversation is a co-creation. It emerges in the moment. Acknowledging this reality sets expectations and brings a sense of **spontaneity**.

4 **Share equal airtime.** Conversational turn-taking is vital for a productive dialogue. A group that tolerates egocentric, blabby individuals will never do its best work. If you allow others to be habitually silent, the whole group misses out on their wisdom. This brings the quality of **inclusion**.

5 **Nobody gets to be wrong.** Encourage whole-hearted participation by saying that everyone has a unique voice that others are to respect. Acknowledge the opportunity and challenge of having diverse perspectives in the room. If you get triggered by something someone else says, pause before you speak and consider the possibility that they're not wrong. This brings **freedom**.

'Is there anything else you want to put in place?', I asked.

'Yes', said one of the teaching assistants. 'Let's agree to disagree kindly.'

A murmur of approval echoed around the hall. I wrote it up on the flip chart along with the other ground rules. We now had our space marked out. As the poet Robert Frost says, '*Good fences make good neighbours.*' Putting agreements in place frees a dialogue to go where it needs to go.

A 'change in the discourse'

A little later in the morning, I shared some wise words from Stephen Covey about trust being the glue of life and the most essential ingredient in effective communication. I was describing the 'trust equation' when someone's hand shot up. I never got to finish saying, 'The higher the other person perceives your orientation toward yourself, the less they are going to trust you' as the teacher with the raised arm cut me off mid-sentence.

'It's a useful framework, but how do I decide if someone is trustworthy? Really?'

There was an edge of anger in his voice. The silence that descended this time was more charged. Several people sat up straighter. All eyes were on the front of the room. What happened next would be critical. A single comment can catalyse a change in the 'field'.

'Every day since I joined this school', Ade said slowly, 'I've asked myself, "How well am I helping to build trust?"'

He looked straight at the staff members. There was no shuffling or fidgeting. The shift in atmosphere felt like a 'change in the discourse'. Bill Isaacs uses this phrase to describe what happens when someone takes a risk to show up as 'real'. The dialogue becomes less abstract and more grounded; less intellectual and more authentic. It creates a 'human' moment. Communication becomes difficult when we stop seeing the humanness in others. Dialogue becomes easier when we're more 'contactful' without it being contrived.

'I have an idea', I said. 'An experiment if you're willing? You'll all need to be out of your seat and on your feet.'

People looked relieved and intrigued as they stood up. I've learned that when we move our bodies, our minds move too. Our physicality influences our psychology.

'Please stand on this imaginary continuum line', I said. 'At this end of the hall by the doors, it's for people who feel willing and able to open up. The other end – over there by the piano – is for those who feel unwilling to take this risk. There's no right or wrong place to be. It's just where feels 'true' for you right now.'

As people distributed themselves along the line, some watched carefully to see where others stood. We had a few people at each end but the biggest clump of people was in the middle towards the 'low-trust' side.

'OK, thank you', I said. 'Now, may I ask you a question?' I turned to one of the staff who had nodded. 'Why didn't you give us a lower number?' This question is, as David Taylor, author of *The Naked Leader* says, 'genius'.[7] It draws on three decades of research by Dr Pantalon (a clinical psychologist, research scientist and motivation expert).[8]

The person you are with expects you to ask the more typical, question: 'Why didn't you give me a higher number?' The problem is that it opens a discussion about why they lack trust. The question 'Why didn't you give me a lower number?' leads to a discussion about why they do indeed have some trust. A single word can fork a dialogue down a different path.

The woman looked at me with a puzzled gaze. She'd clearly been expecting the other question. After a thoughtful pause, she said, 'Well, I know deep down I can trust at least some of my colleagues. There are days when I wouldn't have coped had I not been able to talk things through. . . .'

On the back of her sharing, others made their observations. As their comments 'popped', it felt like the whole room was learning about where trust was present and absent. It's powerful and healing when people listen to understand rather than to speak and 're-load'.

I then asked people to take one small step – physically – up the line towards the 'greater trust' end. Trust isn't binary; it exists and grows in degrees.

'What would it now take', I asked, 'for you to be willing therefore to make yourself slightly more vulnerable?'

'I'd have to be able to be honest', one person said, 'without being afraid that what I say will be used against me.'

'I'd have to get to know my colleagues better', said another, 'and be willing to ask for help.'

'I'd have to find a way to look someone in the eyes', said a third, 'and say no sometimes.'

'I'd need more confidence to speak up', said the woman at the far end of the line.

'Done!' I said and she smiled.

When people returned to their seats from the trust continuum exercise, any hint of hostility had disappeared. We were off to the races.

Sensing the four fields

Understanding that dialogue moves through a sequence of four conversational 'fields' enables a group to think and act in new ways. When a leader is attentive to this unfolding, a more transformative dialogue becomes possible. When a leader fails to recognise this pattern, there's a much greater risk that the group stays stuck in politeness or breakdown.

There is, of course, a risk that this model makes a dialogue seem more linear than it is. Conversation, particularly in a group, is messy, circular and, to some extent, unpredictable, beyond the broad sequence I describe below. Even though the 'map' is not the territory, yet having a guide is a great support for a difficult conversation when there are many stakeholders with divergent points of view.

Sensing the Four Fields expands your capacity – individually and collectively – to 'sit in the fire'. This is how Arnold Mindell, co-founder of Process Work, describes the experience of working with power and 'rank' in order to build sustainable communities.[9] When conflict sparks, it's vital that a leader 'holds space' rather than collapses the 'field'. If a leader is able to feel the tension without 'acting out', a deeper dialogue becomes possible.

A 'field' is a space *'in which there is a particular quality of energy and exchange'*, according to Isaacs in *Dialogue and the Art of Thinking Together*. Each conversational field has distinct characteristics, patterns and pressures. A field transforms to the next in the sequence when a group passes over a threshold by drawing on a particular resource (more on this shortly).

The Four Fields is the creation of global thought leader and author, Otto Scharmer.[10] I included this model in my previous book, *Powered by Purpose*, as I observed that teams went through this process when talking about their 'why'. Articulating a compelling organisational purpose often involves resetting a company's relationship with, for example, profit, making it an uncomfortable conversation. If profit is no longer primary, some stakeholders find this threatening while others find it liberating. Discussing purpose is not a 'cosy chat'; it often involves conflict as various elements of the business model will need to be looked at (more on this in Chapter 10).

The Four Fields frames disagreement as being both essential and transitional for authentic dialogue to occur. The sequence of the Four Fields has echoes of other models of team development such as Tuckman's group stages of Forming, Storming, Norming, Performing and Mourning. Scott Peck's model of community evolution has a similar shape: Pseudo Community, Chaos, Emptying/Discovery and Community. In each of these 'maps', a group has to pass through a perturbation in order to mature. Growth through grit.

Scharmer's model is valuable because it captures several dimensions of dialogue: (1) Each of the four fields has a distinct atmosphere; the 'felt sense' is decidedly different. (2) There is a characteristic pattern of the four dialogic actions (Move, Follow, Oppose, Bystand) that marks out each field. (3) The experience of silence changes across the four conversational spaces. As Mark Cole and John Higgins write in *The Great Unheard at Work* (2023), we often overlook silence in organisations and yet it is so telling.[11] As you'll see below, silence is a valuable 'barometer' for tracking the sequence of dialogue.

The Four Fields are given in Figure 8.2:

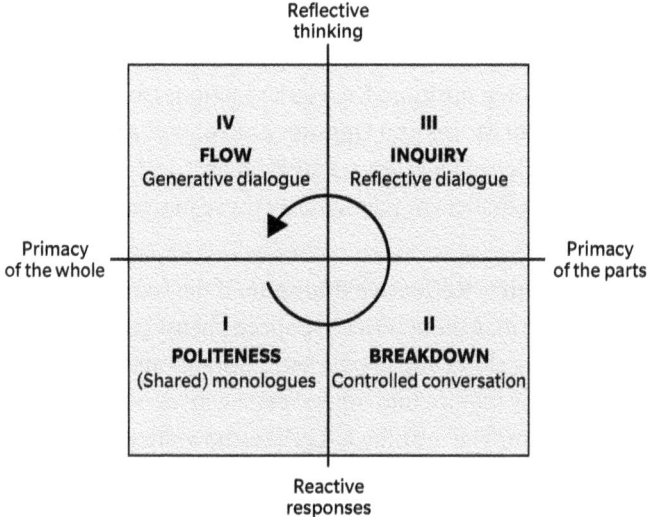

Figure 8.2 Four fields of conversation
Source: Adapted from Scharmer's model of the Four Fields appears in Isaacs W. (1999) Dialogue and the Art of Thinking Together. Bantam Doubleday Dell Publishing Group

The four fields are as follows:

- **Field I – Politeness/(Shared) monologues.** People say what they think they're expected to say according to social 'rules' (hence the 'primacy of the whole'). The ritualised chatter creates social 'glue'. Because people don't know one another, talking is superficial and full of pleasantries. The atmosphere is stiff. As there's no sense of a container to absorb or hold intensity and pressure, discussion about differences seldom happens. This field is more a series of individual monologues than a dialogue. With regard to the four actions, there are sequences of Moves and Follows, but no Opposes or Bystands. Silence, if it arises at all, feels awkward.

- **Field II – Breakdown/Controlled conversation.** People start to say what they really think (hence the 'primacy of the parts'). Differences of opinion are expressed as people begin to say what's on their minds. The atmosphere intensifies. It might feel scratchy, jagged or scary. As people become more reactive and take dug-in positions, some might try to 'win' or have their point of view prevail. Others might then look for holes in their argument and get dug into their own position. Kneejerk reactions can occur. There are sequences of Moves and Opposes but Follows and Bystands are missing. Silence feels tense and even hostile. Some people bite their lip and 'self-silence', particularly those in more subordinate positions.

- **Field III – Inquiry/Reflective dialogue.** If the spirit of curiosity can be brought in, a more reflective space opens. Listening deepens. The talking slows and people ask questions and don't just make assertions. They inquire into others' perspectives when they don't agree with them. The attitude is 'Let's see how this disagreement works.' There are Moves, Follows, Opposes and Bystands. Silence is thoughtful. There's a sense that pauses are naturally occurring, part of the ebb-and-flow of the dialogue. There's no sense that silence is being imposed or being used as a manipulative device. Out of this space, a new shared meaning can start to unfold.
- **Field IV – Flow/Generative dialogue.** This field is the rarest. People start to think together in creative ways. New insights arise that integrate different perspectives (the 'whole' becomes primary once more). The atmosphere is spacious enough to hold radically different points of view. The atmosphere is enlivening. The dialogue generative. Synchronicities occur. Silence might even feel sacred. Moments of stillness signal what a group really needs to pay attention to. As a flow of collective intelligence moves through, a sense of shared endeavour replaces the individualistic focus of the previous two fields. The 'hive mind', arising out of the shared understanding, often leaves people feeling 'wordless' as it's difficult to describe the experience.

With this 'map' of the Four Fields, it becomes easier to 'locate' where you are in the dialogue process. When a disturbance occurs, as it did with the teacher's question, the conversation stands or falls on this moment. A pointed question moves a group out of the pleasant yet uninspired first field of politeness. The 'rock' that someone throws (or even the tiny pebble) is a gift even if does not feel like a gift. It takes the group out of superficiality and into a more authentic, if uncomfortable, space.

How a leader handles the intensity of this high-energy moment is critical. Many groups cycle back into niceness and never get beyond this point. If a leader becomes defensive, others retreat or battle it out by taking more entrenched positions. This second field can provide the '*fuel for change*' (Isaacs) but only if there's the capacity to hold the fire of disagreement.

Without a strong container, the conversation turns toxic as the conflict becomes tightly managed. The leader often imposes their agenda, so others then hold their tongue and the group swings back into courteous conformity. People withhold saying what they really think. Unresolved issues are pushed under the table to fester.

With a strong 'container', conflict becomes the catalyst for transformation. The move from field two (Breakdown) to field three (Inquiry) is a 'threshold' to cross. It can feel risky as a former way of talking is being challenged. There are, in fact, three thresholds to cross as a dialogue moves through the Four Fields. Each requires a different resource or 'quality' to create a space that's more generative. I describe these 'resources at the threshold' next.

1 The threshold of presence

It is no surprise that the move from Field I (Politeness) to II (Breakdown) is a place where many teams struggle. If they have stayed too long being nice without being candid, the pent-up energy can be expressed in angry outbursts, edgy questions or sarcastic comments.

People lashing out can be tricky but it makes oppositions clear. Rather than see a provocative comment as a 'revolt', the challenge for a leader is to accept it as a catalyst for creating more depth in the dialogue. We can only do this if we are fully present in the room, breathing deeply, and feeling grounded.

Containing reactivity is vital. A great ally is what the poet David Whyte calls 'robust vulnerability'. When you're willing to self-disclose authentically (as Ade did), it inspires others to show up with more of their 'whole self' too. In Brené Brown's work, the only way to live a meaningful life is through making genuine contact with others. This means embracing vulnerability as this makes honesty, empathy and compassion possible.

It's counterintuitive in the Western culture that strength comes from making yourself vulnerable. Admitting a mistake, making an apology, or stating that you're uncertain does, however, keep a conversation going rather than shut it down. We've all messed up and when we admit this, it makes us more 'real'. Others can then relate to us more easily.

In the face of robust challenge, a leader needs to be 'larger than the biggest disturbance in the room'. Bill Isaacs shared these words of counsel when I was on his faculty for the *Leadership for Collective Intelligence* programme at Dialogos. When someone challenges us, it's understandable to feel defensive, resentful or embarrassed. Less common is to stay present to the discomfort and absorb its impact so that your reaction doesn't undermine the dialogic process. Saying thank you to a naysayer and then seeing what others think moves a discussion forward.

Welcoming dissent is a real act of leadership. To solve problems effectively, a team needs diverse points of view. Airing differences of opinion creates discomfort but this is necessary to have a robust discussion. It is more effective to acknowledge differences of opinion than to try and sweep them under the table. 'You're saying fundamentally different things' is more honest than a fudge, 'I think we're all saying the same thing here.' Clarity brings kindness. Follow this up with, 'Are there others who feel less strongly who can bring a different perspective?' and you will be well on your way through the field of disturbance. We realise that cultivating presence is helpful at every stage of the dialogue process and essential at moments when dissenting voices come into the room.

2 The threshold of curiosity

To break out of the pervasive pattern of moving from 'breakdown' back into 'politeness', expanding your capacity to tolerate conflict is essential. We need to be willing to 'meet' others who think differently to us without becoming defensive. Leaders who can 'hold space' in this field reframe 'breakdown' as transitional. Otherwise, it's just business-as-usual and the same old complaints keep coming up but never go anywhere.

The move from Field II (Breakdown) to Field III (Inquiry) happens when we stop giving opinions and stay curious. We inquire into what's really happening by asking others how they're feeling or what assumptions they're making. We express a desire to understand more where another person is coming from. We acknowledge someone's feelings and invite them to say more. Asking questions with genuine curiosity and no judgement is our best ally when a disturbance enters the room.

Bill Isaacs taught me the power of asking two specific questions at a critical juncture in a dialogue. I used these questions when working with the World Bank and International Finance Corporation on a project in Jaipur, India to rebalance its portfolio towards low-income states. Given this new strategic direction, some staff had expressed concerns about the way the strategy was to be operationalised. The dialogue session I co-led was to provide a safe space to explore the risks that staff perceived and to agree a way forward.

The questions are: (1) What's at risk if we make this change? (2) What's at risk if we don't? This line of inquiry provided an opportunity for staff to share concerns and identify risks as well as for management to voice how they would give support if things went wrong. At the start of the two-day session, the tension in the room was palpable. At the end of the second day, the group of 80 participants had co-created an action plan for implementation, but only because voices of dissent had been welcomed, heard and respected.

3 The threshold of emergence

Moving into generative dialogue from inquiry is rare but building a 'pool' of shared understanding does happen. For Field III (Inquiry) to transform into Field IV (Flow), a group needs to think together to create a common understanding, which might give a glimpse of a better future horizon. The field feels charged with creativity. Dialogue is effortless. Change happens without anyone trying to make it happen.

When there are multiple stakeholders, competing agendas and difficult emotions, real dialogue rarely happens but it's priceless when it does. The emergence of a 'generative image' (Bushe) is a powerful signal that a group has landed in the fourth field. This might be captured in a turn of phrase, metaphor or even a new acronym. Let's return to the story of the school to explore how to navigate the third and fourth fields: Inquiry followed by Flow.

Turning a corner

After everyone returned to their seats, the atmosphere felt more settled.

'We'd like you to consider two questions', my co-facilitator said. 'What's one thing you'd like to keep about the school? What's one thing you'd really like to change?'

After some time to think and scribble on brightly coloured, large sticky notes, people put up their suggestions on a board where everyone could all see them. Getting the collective issues aired in the room rather than in the corridor enables a team to talk about what really matters and create more trusting relationships.

There were several themes that emerged from the things that staff wanted to keep. These included staff social events, caring for the wellbeing of the pupils and 'chatty children'. When it came to what to change, there was a clear convergence on having quality time to talk, building stronger staff relationships, and more openness and honesty to resolve issues.

With this understanding in mind, I was keen to support the staff at the school in restoring trust. While there hadn't been any big betrayals, there were some feelings of bitterness going back to the time of the restructure. Even if only one or two staff members feel resentful and unappreciated, it can be enough to affect the atmosphere in the whole room.

We asked people to regroup so that the foundation years' teachers sat together as did the leadership team, the support staff and so on. We asked them to identify another team and to come up with two things: (1) something that they could offer by way of help and (2) a change in behaviour they'd like to request in order to build stronger relationships.

'Be specific and write it down', we said.

To get into Flow, it helps to give smaller groups time to think and talk together. It's often easier to have a conversation in a smaller group first, which can then feed into a whole group dialogue. Most of us learned to talk in families of six people or fewer, at least in the northern hemisphere. Finding our voice is easier in this setting rather than trying to have a conversation straight away in a room of 20, 40 or 80 plus participants.

Dialogue is possible in much larger groups but there is an art to it. David Bohm wrote in his book, *On Dialogue*, how he had learned from an anthropologist who'd lived for a long while with a North American tribe of about 50 people. From time to time the tribe met in a circle where *'They just talked and talked and talked... And everybody could participate.'* There was an interplay between the whole group and smaller groups. *'The meeting went on, until it finally seemed to stop for no reason at all and the group dispersed. Yet after that, everybody seemed to know what to do, because they understood each other so well. Then they could get together in smaller groups and do something or decide things.'*

Moving between smaller subgroups and the whole group makes dialogue easier. To apply the wisdom of this, see Exercise 16 – Change the choreography.

Exercise 16
Change the choreography

Think of a meeting where you want multiple stakeholders, with different perspectives, to think together. Reflect on the questions below to prepare for the meeting. Remember that authentic ➤

dialogue is not only being in 'Flow', it includes moving through the Fields of Politeness, Breakdown and Inquiry.

The 'choreography' you use – how you set up the room and invite people to interact – shapes the dialogue from the beginning. Aim for a strong start and a strong close. This exercise is a direct follow-on from the previous exercise (Hold a 'check-in').

1 How can you set up the room so that people move beyond Politeness as soon as possible? For example, instead of rows of chairs, form 'horseshoes' of five chairs so that people can easily get into huddles for a check-in.

2 What conflicts or breakdowns are likely to arise? What Opposes can you anticipate, from whom, or even invite? How can you stay grounded and present when these voices of dissent arise (e.g. take a deeper breath, put your feet flat on the ground, sit up straighter in your seat)?

3 What open questions could you ask to move into the Field of Inquiry (e.g. 'How might we...?'. 'What makes you say that...?', 'What are our options here...?')? What 'Bystands' could you bring or invite others to make? Think about ways you can get people out of their seats and onto their feet, for example by inviting people to stand on a 'continuum line' (see page 164).

4 To move into the field of Flow, how could you change the way people interact so that they do some thinking together? For example, you might, before a whole group dialogue:

   a. Invite people to go into 'similar type' groups and ask them to express an appreciation and make a request of another group in the room.

   b. Invite people to form trios with one 'issue holder' who wants to explore a key challenge, one 'supporter' and one 'opposer' who asks questions.

   c. Invite each person to voice what they're thinking in response to a key issue. Once everyone has spoken, open the dialogue to be free-flowing.

5 To draw the session to a close, what 'check-out' question could you use? It might be a simple as, 'What's one thing you've appreciated about this dialogue?' or 'What's one takeaway you'd like to share from this meeting?'

After they'd formed some 'pods', we heard back from each group in turn. The foundation teachers started.

'We want to thank the teaching assistants for all their help and flexibility', their spokesperson said. 'We don't often say how grateful we are and we need to do more of that, starting right now!'

The teaching assistants' eyes shone with the acknowledgement.

'And what we'd like to request', she continued, 'is your help with our lessons plans. You have great ideas and we're missing out on them. We suggest a regular weekly meeting to put our heads together, beginning next Monday.'

This is exactly what we were after: specific, tangible actions that would help to create a stronger sense of community among the staff. Trust emerges out of all the interactions between people. Each time we meet someone's gaze, send an encouraging text or ask how someone's feeling – and listen to their response – we create trust. Every time we talk someone down, ignore an important email or withhold information best shared, we violate it. Trust is the feedstock of a healthy team and a thriving organisation.

The other groups followed, outlining their offers of help and making respectful requests of each other. The midday-ers asked the leadership team to spend more time with the children at lunchtime. The teachers asked the midday-ers to ring the bell twice at the start of the afternoon to encourage the children back into class more promptly. Ade took it on the chin when he was told that he didn't spend enough time in the staff room and pledged to be there for at least one of the breaks during the school day.

'Now we're talking.' The voice of a teacher on the back row rang out across the hall.

I smiled. The words of Thomas Jefferson came to mind: *'If you want something you never had, you must be willing to do something you have never done'*. While trust is intangible, the actions that contribute to or detract from it are concrete.

Close with a check-out

As the afternoon rolled on, the 'pods' aired grievances, made requests and suggested ideas for moving forward. The conversation among the 42 staff had as much ease as if it had been four or five people chatting.

To bring the meeting to a close, we ended the session with a 'check-out'. We invited people to say whatever they needed to voice in order to feel complete. We were short of time so only a few people spoke but it felt like they were speaking for the whole.

'I feel quite overwhelmed', said one of the teachers, 'with all the love in the room!'

With that, I knew that trust was beginning to build, and the grumbles were starting to disappear. Later, as I lifted my bags into the boot of my car, I had a sense that my work there was done. I trusted that the learning and insights from the dialogue in the 'holding environment' we'd created would enable the team to build a 'great school'.

Talking together is important – but dialogue becomes much deeper in the context of whole team collaboration. Words are good, but actions are better – especially actions that build trust and bring people together to solve problems that affect everybody.

Summary

1 For a group to discuss what really matters, it is critical that a leader 'holds space' rather than takes up space. This means creating an expansive emotional space where people can air their differences without this undermining the group's cohesion and sense of a shared endeavour.

2 Psychological safety is necessary but insufficient for generative dialogue to occur. Other qualities are needed: inquiry, inclusion, spontaneity, possibility and freedom. Setting ground rules that tap into these qualities creates an environment that is conducive for conversation.

3 A 'container' is both sanctuary and crucible. It has the warmth of human connection and the edge of truth-telling. A 'check-in' process helps to build a container by helping people to 'land' in the here-and-now and find their unique voice.

4 Dialogue moves through a sequence of the four conversational fields: Politeness, Breakdown, Inquiry and Flow. Each has its own feel, energy and patterns. Many groups are unable to hold the discomfort of Breakdown and go back into Politeness.

5 There's a threshold to cross to move into the next field. At each of these thresholds there's a key 'resource' to bring into the room. These are Presence, Curiosity and Emergence.

6 A disturbance to the field of Politeness creates the possibility of change but requires a deepening of presence. A leader needs to stay grounded and present.

7 To move beyond Breakdown and into Inquiry, a spirit of curiosity is needed to stop conflict turning toxic.

8 To move out of Inquiry and into Flow, a deeper sense of thinking together needs to emerge. Changing the choreography helps, such as moving into smaller groups before having a whole group dialogue.

> **If you do only one thing now** . . . Observe your starting place carefully. Pay attention to the atmosphere in which your conversation is taking place. If there's too much politeness, be willing to show up more authentically. Share a concern, name a pattern or voice a risk. Consider using 'Here's what I'm thinking and here's how I got here' to take the dialogue to a deeper place.

Notes

1. Sinek, S. (2009) *Start with Why: How great leaders inspire everyone to take action*, NY Portfolio.
2. Brown, B. (2018) *Dare to Lead: Brave work, tough conversations, whole hearts*, Random House.
3. Lencioni, P. (2002) *The Five Dysfunctions of a Team: A leadership fable*, John Wiley & Sons.
4. Edmonson, A. C. (2012) *Teaming: How organisations learn, innovate and compete in the knowledge economy*, Jossey-Bass.
5. Ferdig, M.A. and Ludema, J.D. (2005) Transformative interactions: Qualities of conversation that heighten the vitality of self-organizing change, In *Research in Organizational Change and Development* (pp. 169–205), Emerald Group Publishing Limited.
6. Masters, R. A. (2012) *Transformation Through Intimacy, Revised Edition: The journey toward awakened monogamy*, North Atlantic Books, US.
7. Taylor, D. (2023) *Naked Leader Week 1021 newsletter*, 1 May 2023.
8. Pantalon, M. (2011) *Instant Influence: How to get anyone to do anything — Fast*, Little, Brown Spark.
9. Mindell, A. (2014) *Sitting in the Fire: Large group transformation using conflict and diversity*, Deep Democracy Exchange.
10. Scharmer's model of the Four Fields appears in Isaacs, W. (1999) *Dialogue and the Art of Thinking Together*, Bantam Doubleday Dell Publishing Group.
11. Cole, M. and Higgins, J. (2023) *The Great Unheard at Work: Understanding voice and silence in organisations*, Routledge.

part 3

Dialogic leadership in action

chapter 9

Lead change through dialogue

'The sinkhole of change is communication and motivation.

It's where change projects go to die.'

Nancy Rothbard

Open communication is motivating for groups who need to innovate. To stimulate this, leaders in these disruptive times need a communication competence that engages hearts, not just minds, turns activists into allies and imparts a bold vision without being domineering. The skill called for is that of building a culture of dialogue, starting with how a senior leadership team or board talk about what they want to create together.

With this approach, transformational change becomes possible. Leading change through dialogue is challenging, but not nearly as hard as trying to promote change without this.

Authentic dialogue among multiple stakeholders is an art. The leader is less in control of the outcome, which makes dynamics more alive but trickier. Perceptions of winners and losers mean some take fixed positions and block change from happening. Hidden agendas, whether real or perceived, scupper decision-making and coordinated action.

To cut through these obstacles, understanding the four key principles of a dialogic process – Potential, Participation, Coherence and Awareness – is a great resource. Applying this knowledge (along with attentive listening, candid speaking, reading the room and holding space) enables a leader to shift their sense of identity from controller to co-visionary, convenor, catalyst and coach, making sustainable change possible.

Naz, CEO of a large healthcare organisation, was sitting in her kitchen when we spoke on video call.

'It's been a stressful time', she said. 'Coming out of the pandemic, it feels like a really rocky period.'

Her brow furrowed.

'We want to do the right thing for the people of this community as an independent provider, but we need to increase our ambition. We've won the contract with the hospital, but we don't want them to railroad us. We're proud of our track record even if we're not great at celebrating success.

The "Covid gap" means that there's been less interaction among the Board members and staff at a time when the wider system wants to deliver £100m worth of savings. It feels like the perfect storm.'

During the five years I'd coached the Exec team, I'd been impressed by their willingness to invest in developing their dialogue capacity and be the very best at helping people to live healthier lives. In 2019 the Care Quality Commission (CQC) had awarded the organisation a rating of 'good' overall with two units receiving a rating of 'outstanding'.

'So, what will be a great outcome from the next Board meeting?', I asked, aware that the session was only two weeks away. It was a rare opportunity to have a different kind of dialogue. It was the second time I'd work with both the Executives and the Non-Executives, and the first time had been three years ago prior to the pandemic with a different CEO and Chair. They'd agreed to put aside two days to have the conversations that mattered most.

'It's not just about refreshing our business plan', Naz said, looking thoughtful. 'We need to develop our strategic direction.'

'What will it take for you to do that?' I asked.

'If we build more trust, we'll make decisions and get on with things. There's a risk we talk and talk and talk but go round and round in circles. We need to agree how to best position ourselves so that we become a valued partner. We have to get beyond our nerves so we're not suspicious of the hospital and create the kind of partnership we want.'

It made sense to me. I added Naz's 'take' to my own musings about the design of the session. With another ten calls lined up with the rest of the Board, I was curious what others had to say about the ground they needed to cover. I trusted that these conversations would give me a greater sense of the 'nut to crack' at the Board meeting.

Over the next week, I heard a mix of responses to my question about what would be a great outcome. Comments from the Execs included:

1. 'We need to challenge one another effectively without falling out. We need to be a strong and unified Board so that we're not easy pickings and get taken over.'
2. 'Let's have some real conversations about what our unique contribution is as an organisation and what we want to achieve this year.'
3. 'More trust so that we make decisions and develop a shared understanding about what a good Board is. We need a discussion about what accountability really means.'
4. 'We need to become stronger as a team and integrate the two new Execs. The NEDs can have conflicting views and we can all get lost in the weeds.'

The 'great outcomes' of the NEDs (Non-Executive Directors) included:

5. 'Articulating a clear purpose for the Board, to help us to become bigger and better collectively. We need more open and honest conversations so that we're not seen as a subcontractor by another organisation that could be predatory.'
6. 'Agreeing what our growth ambition is. We're not all in the same place in terms of how we see the organisation and how it sits in the wider system. The Execs are extremely busy and we all need to look outwards more.'
7. 'Stronger relationships and clarity about what information we need to share to make the right decisions. Some people think this organisation is on the way out and we need to challenge them.'
8. 'Speaking openly as a team about the contract negotiation process so we that stand as one team rather than as two teams. We need to work out how to best position ourselves so that we speak with 'one voice' in our discussions with the hospital.'

Activating change through dialogue makes me think of how multiple dimensions of reality really exist. In my worst moments, it's easy to feel confused and overwhelmed by the different versions. But then I recall what Alain de Botton (author and philosopher) has to say: *'Work is most fulfilling when you're at the comfortable, exciting edge of not quite knowing what you're doing.'*

In my best moments, I trust that the dialogue will arise from the 'mesh' of different perspectives. This emergence is important. If Board members perceive that an agenda is being imposed from the outside, it won't be a real dialogue.

To aid the process of prioritising topics for the Board meeting, I asked each member to do some prep before coming to the session. I asked them to think about the critical conversations that the Board could have which would add most value (for example about strategy, vision, growth, ways of working or any other relevant topic) and complete the Critical Conversations Grid (see Figure 9.1), developed in collaboration with my colleague Dr Andrew White.

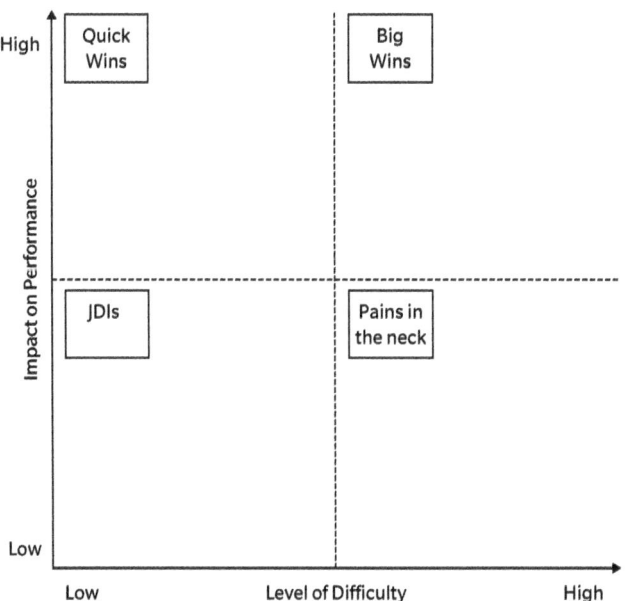

Figure 9.1 The critical conversations grid
Source: Co-created by Dr Andrew White and Sarah Rozenthuler, 2022

To complete the Grid, I asked Board members to identify three or more topics and place them on the Grid in the appropriate place and bring their annotated version to the meeting.

The critical conversations tool invites reflection in two ways: (1) The impact that having a conversation could have on performance and (2) The perceived level of difficulty that the conversation entails. This helps differentiate four types of conversation as follows:

- **'Big wins.'** These are conversations that are both impactful and difficult. Examples include discussions around a unified vision, workforce strategy, risk appetite and relationships among Board members. When a Board stops avoiding having these discussions, the benefits are legion. They resolve issues, make decisions and identify actions to take forward. Critical dialogue skills are also developed (speaking authentically, challenging effectively, listening deeply and suspending judgement), which are then transferable to other contexts.

- **'Quick wins.'** These are conversations that are impactful but less difficult. Examples include communicating a signed-off strategy, making investment decisions against established criteria, and agreeing a business planning process. These conversations move issues forward but, because they are more straightforward, participants do not develop transferable skills that would enable them to discuss what matters in other situations.

- **'Pains in the neck.'** These are conversations that have less impact and yet are difficult. Examples include establishing performance metrics, deciding how to conduct a 'townhall' or large-group meeting and agreeing what a Board Pack contains. These conversations are necessary but because people find it harder to see the payoff, they are often perceived as a drag.

- **'Just Do Its.'** (JDIs) These are conversations that are less impactful and less difficult. Examples include agreeing changes to a standard operating process, deciding on small spends and addressing missed deadlines. Once a group identifies these conversations, this often creates the momentum to have the discussion.

The Critical Conversations tool is a useful and oblique way in to discussing what matters most. Dialogue is not 'mere talk', as Isaacs has said.[1] Dialogue is pivotal to effective decision-making, which in turn generates aligned action. Without dialogue, a Board risks going round and round in circles as the discussion goes nowhere. With dialogue, people have the conversations that matter, sparking the change process.

It is widely accepted that in organisations change initiatives fail more often than they succeed. The popular belief in the '70 per cent change failure rate' has been questioned in recent times although the belief still lives on.[2] What can be reliably said is that change is more complex, nuanced and ambiguous than many leaders acknowledge, and that leaders have a crucial role to play in supporting cultural change. Leadership behaviours are clearly correlated to business performance.[3] For a change project to deliver rather than die, dialogue has a central part to play.

According to Professor Keith Grint at Warwick Business School, the pervasive problem of the 'change maze' confronts leaders everywhere. A good starting point for leading change is to pay attention to how we frame a challenge. We can either galvanise collective action or cut it off at the pass. It helps to differentiate between Rittell and Webber's classic (1973) typology of 'tame' vs. 'wicked' problems:

- Tame problems might be complicated but they are ultimately resolvable through applying existing knowhow, expert insight or standard operating procedures. Examples include building a hospital, timetabling the railways, or handling a wage negotiation.

- Wicked problems, on the other hand, are complex, intractable and require an innovative response to a novel situation. Developing a healthcare partnership, solving knife crime, or developing an industrial relations strategy are all examples of wicked problems. They involve longer timeframes and a more strategic focus.

Wicked problems also have what Grint calls no 'stopping' points. They do not end at the boundaries of a single organisation; they reside at the interface between different organisations or across the divisions of the same organisation. Consequently, wicked problems have no easy solutions. As leaders are typically more comfortable having to face tame or more technical problems, Grint comments:

> 'The irony of leadership is that it is often avoided where it might seem the most necessary.'

In a similar vein, in their landmark *Harvard Business Review* article published in 1997, Ron Heifetz and Donald Laurie state:

> 'Many efforts to transform organizations through mergers and acquisitions, restructuring, reengineering, and strategy falter because managers fail to grasp the requirements of adaptive work. They make the classic error of treating adaptive challenges like technical problems that can be solved by tough-minded senior executives.'

The issue facing Naz and her Board was an adaptive challenge with no ready answer. There was no manual, rulebook or clear-cut path to follow. Getting to grips with forming the right kind of partnership with the hospital was something that they would have to grapple with rather than trying to pull levers in the right sequence. Adaptive challenges do not call for elegance, but for a messier type of engagement where discussion, debate, experimentation, uncertainty and dialogue all have their place. To explore further, see Exercise 17 – Identify your most critical conversation.

Exercise 17
Identify your most critical conversation

If you're working in a team or on a Board that wants to lead change, ask each team member to complete the following before your next meeting:

1 Think about the critical conversations that this team/Board could have that would add most value. These could be conversations

about strategy, vision, growth, ways of working or any other relevant topic.

2 Take a look at the Critical conversations grid and:
   - Identify three or more topics and place them on the grid in the appropriate place
   - Reflect on what gets in the way of us having these critical conversations
   - Reflect on what it would take for us to have these conversations.

3 Bring a copy of your completed Grid and notes with you to the meeting.

A tale of two changes

A common oversight in leading change is focusing too much on the 'what' of change (a new strategy, operating model or organisational structure) and not enough on the 'how' (such as having a shared vision and getting the right people to have the right conversation at the right time). Here are two examples of change done well and change done badly, and the pivotal role that dialogue – and the lack of dialogue – played in the change process.

Story 1: Finding Eden in Cornwall

The Eden Project is a visitor attraction in southwest England, located in a reclaimed pit where for 160 years the land had been used for china clay extraction. Tim Smit, a Dutch-born British businessman and Jonathan Ball, a Cornish architect, co-founded the project which the Guardian has called a 'mind-boggling feat of both architecture and biological engineering'.

After work began in 1995, the centre opened in 2001 on a mission to create a 'living theatre of plants and people' and a 'refuge for the world's endangered species'. It has become famous for its two huge greenhouses known as 'biomes', which grow a vast array of plants including massive banana trees in a temperature-controlled environment. It's an impressive achievement given the wet and chilly Cornish climate. A scar on the landscape has been transformed into a place of beauty and inspiration that attracts over 1 million visitors a year. Smit has claimed that the Eden has contributed over £1 billion to the Cornish economy.

In 2006, the project entered a new phase of work with the construction of an education centre. When I visited the building in 2008 to run a wellbeing workshop, I found the light-filled, spacious rooms with their lawn-green carpet tiles highly conducive to having great conversations. My 'A New You' workshop was all about giving people back a sense of worth through an expansive dialogue about our true nature and the rooms really sustained our work together.

The intention for Eden was to become recognised as an 'exemplar of sustainability' and mobilise the organisation towards more ecologically sustainable ways of operating. Donna Ladkin, a professor of inclusive leadership at Birmingham University, has written a case study about this phase of the work in her book *Rethinking Leadership*.[4] She attended meetings on-site, interviewed people involved in the construction and spoke with two key personnel. Her book includes many verbatim quotes including one from the project manager, Andy Cook, who said:

> **'I've never been involved in a project where you just had to keep talking and talking and talking so much... It became clear that no one person had the answer to how to be an exemplar of sustainability. We had to talk together to figure out what it might mean. It was kind of like a puzzle, everyone had a piece of it. I began to see my job as just getting the right people in the room together with the right knowledge so that we could figure it out together.'**

The two project leaders reflected on how their role was to help connect people from different professions and departments. They explored how their jobs contributed to the big picture purpose and were open to their answers. They were sensitive to the need for 'glue' to motivate people to continue to engage. They tapped into feelings of pride, excitement and enthusiasm for the project, generating goodwill and a willingness to work together.

They asked people a recurring question: What does it *mean* to be an exemplar of sustainability? It was a contested concept; the 'lived' meaning had to emerge as people debated decisions, took action and evaluated impact. Some broad agreements gradually emerged, such as not using PVC in any of the buildings, engaging local contractors and aiming to produce zero waste. Asking the 'right' question was not easy but doing so distinguished authentic dialogue – which actively pursues difference – from inauthentic dialogue – which constantly narrows and restricts possible meanings.

The creation of meaning is a dialogic endeavour. It emerges from conversations between leaders, team members and other stakeholders. Ladkin asks: *'Can a vision be heartily adopted if the ranks serve only as recipients of the vision? What if they don't believe in the vision?'* She reflects that constructing meaning through dialogue might often be more appropriate than unilaterally uttering declarations. The leader 'holds the purpose' but the 'lived meaning' is co-created between those participating in a creative dialogue. Staying in dialogue enabled people to tune into 'right action'; actions that were coherent with the organisation's purpose.

Only through dialogue can a 'fusion of horizons' emerge. Ladkin concludes that the role of a leader is not to pronounce the way forward but to provide a safe and stimulating space where 'inquiring conversations' can occur. This is a messier type of engagement than a heroic leader who 'shows the way' with their preconceived and rarefied vision, which they then try to get others to buy into. Here leading change successfully involves letting go of control and inviting others to contribute, in a spirit of openness, inclusion and curiosity.

Story 2: The 'Sheffield Chainsaw massacre'

When I moved to Sheffield in 1998, I heard locals refer to the city as 'an ugly picture in a beautiful frame'. Surrounded by the expansive moorland of the Peak District with its rounded hills, green valleys and limestone gorges, the city attracts ramblers, rock climbers and walkers. A saving grace of the city is being able to walk from densely populated residential districts into the heart of the Peak District through tree-lined, leafy streets.

Sheffield's streets are home to 35,000 lime, ash, sycamore, cherry and rowan trees. Their large canopies create green corridors between rows of terraced houses flanking the pot-holed roads. Their sturdy trunks sprout leaves that brush against parked cars and pushchairs.

In 2012 Sheffield City Council decided to remove half of the trees and replace them with saplings. The reasons were unclear but pointed to making road maintenance easier and, as the old saying goes, getting rid of old wood. Many of the trees dated back to Victorian times and some had been deemed unhealthy.

The first tree was felled by the contractor in 2012, sparking a sense of outrage among locals. Given the lack of dialogue, activists organised demonstrations, launched petitions and collected signatures. Their umbrella group, Sheffield Tree Activist Group (Stag), set up a 'flying squad' of volunteers to stand under trees and obstruct works. Between 2016 and 2018 the police attended 40 tree protests and arrested 41 people. In 2018 Stag made an application for a judicial review, which was rejected.

Following this, both sides dug in. The protestors used nonviolent direct action but still two pensioners in their 70s were arrested. The contractor started work at 5 am, waking up residents and asking them to move their cars.

The story hit the national headlines. MPs such as Michael Gove and celebrities including Jarvis Cocker condemned the council's behaviour. Eventually an independent inquiry was carried out and published its results in March 2023. By this time, 5600 mature trees had been removed and replaced by a similar number of saplings. Their conclusions included that the council:

1. Had a 'flawed' approach and that its decision to remove trees was 'misjudged'

2 Was 'deluded' and had misled the public
3 Had developed a 'bunker mentality' and eroded public trust
4 Showed a 'serious and sustained failure of strategic leadership'.

The report wrote 'The council had united almost everyone against them.' It had pursued protestors for claims for damages, which, if successful, would have made them bankrupt. It had caused high levels of stress among council staff and contractors, damaged its reputation and taken away the beauty of thousands of much-loved trees. In 2017, the council had taken Alison Teal, a former Green councillor, to court for allegedly breaking an injunction that was enforced to stop protesters from protecting the trees from chainsaws. She was later found not guilty and said that the council pursuing her for participating in a peaceful protest was 'frightening for democracy'.[5]

Sheffield Council eventually issued a lengthy, open apology in June 2023 for misleading the public, media and courts in the dispute, accepting that many of the trees they felled were healthy.[6,7] Although the roads, pavements and lighting ended up in better shape, it came at a very high cost. The report called it a 'dark episode' in Sheffield's recent history.

Four principles of dialogue

Embedded in these two stories are four principles related to generating change through dialogue. Isaacs, inspired by the thinking of Bohm, articulated these core principles, and I have applied and adapted them in my own work.[8] When a leader acts in line with these principles, the change process is inspiring, inclusive, incisive and intelligent. When a leader violates these principles, change is resisted, blocked, stalled and appears stupid to others. A leadership system, such as a city council, that fails to apply these principles hampers its ability to create a sustainable impact from the get-go.

Each principle invites a distinct set of questions, which I outline below (see Figure 9.2).

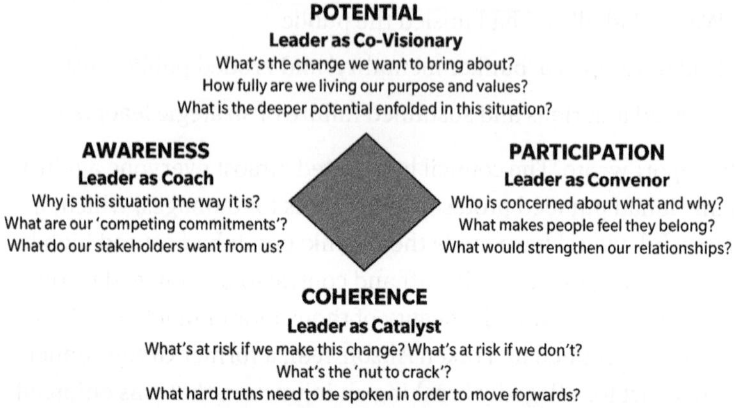

POTENTIAL
Leader as Co-Visionary
What's the change we want to bring about?
How fully are we living our purpose and values?
What is the deeper potential enfolded in this situation?

AWARENESS
Leader as Coach
Why is this situation the way it is?
What are our 'competing commitments'?
What do our stakeholders want from us?

PARTICIPATION
Leader as Convenor
Who is concerned about what and why?
What makes people feel they belong?
What would strengthen our relationships?

COHERENCE
Leader as Catalyst
What's at risk if we make this change? What's at risk if we don't?
What's the 'nut to crack'?
What hard truths need to be spoken in order to move forwards?

Figure 9.2 Four principles of dialogic change
Source: Inspired by Bohm (1996), Issacs (1999) and Dialogue Associates

These questions are not an exhaustive list. The energy of them is more important than the content. The questions act as 'seeds' for generating change through dialogue. When a leader, team or group grapples with these questions, their conversation creates change that sticks. I'll return to the story of Naz and her team later in the chapter to illustrate this.

All four principles call on a leader to re-imagine their sense of identity. As Bob Anderson writes in his 2017 whitepaper, *The Spirit of Leadership*, transformational change efforts call on leaders to expand their sense of who they are. There are two challenges, depending on how a leader has organised their sense of identity to date, and each has a different remedy:

- If someone derives their sense of value from being the one who's in charge, makes decisions or provides expert input, they need to shift from being 'the one' to become 'one among many'. This is a huge change in self-image and one that many managers never make. Even when managers have been trained to be coaches, they often slip into being a mentor and giving advice as the 'imprint' to be heroic is so strong. Such managers need to ask themselves the question, 'Who am I if I am not my ability to take command and be the one who makes the right decision?'

- If, on the other hand, someone has shunned power by playing small, staying loyal and being a hardworking follower, their challenge is to step up, risk being more visible and take on greater responsibility. They need to let go of the comfort of hiding by not 'rocking the boat'. Seeking approval, wanting protection and feeling valued by seniors can also be a trap that's hard to exit. Changing this sense of self can shake a manager to the core. They need to ask, 'How do I remain worthy and stay safe if I risk both failure and the displeasure of those above me?'

Much of what we term 'resistance to change' is, below the surface, the struggle that managers experience when trying to make these inner shifts. It is also why many change efforts fail; they are 'over the heads' of managers implementing them (to borrow the title of Kegan's book about this) if their mental model is 'I'm the boss' or 'I'm not up to this.'

The overall shift is from being a manager who deals with certainty and control (or the *illusion* of certainty and control) to being a leader who values the potency of uncertainty, and the collective. When a leader sees themselves not as a commander-in-chief but as a convenor, catalyst, coach and co-visionary, real change becomes possible. Their shift of identity creates the ground upon which an authentic dialogue can take place.

Potential

When new possibilities flow into a meeting room, this energises people. They experience a degree of liberation. A compelling purpose, and the potential enfolded within it, 'pulls' people in a new direction by creating a shared sense of endeavour. Without a sense of potential, people perish. As Eleanor Roosevelt said, *'The future belongs to those who believe in the beauty of their dreams.'*

We saw in the 'Sheffield Chainsaw Massacre' story the impact of the city council having no inspiring vision combined with the lack of dialogue with residents. The local people railed against their decision to fell trees as it felt like an unnecessary and unwise imposition.

The reason for chopping down the trees was unclear as was the council's purpose.

In a similar case, Plymouth City Council was taken to task after it felled 110 trees on Amanda Way in the city centre as part of the council's decision to invest in a £12.7m regeneration scheme. Nearly 12,000 people signed a petition against the plan and The Woodland Trust declared it was 'appalled'. Hundreds of people turned up at Amanda Way to pay tribute to the trees by leaving messages, laying flowers, and tying coloured ribbons to the trees. In March 2023, the Conservative council leader, Richard Bingley, who had signed the agreement, unexpectedly resigned. No purpose, no 'pull' into the future.

By contrast, at the Eden Project, the founding purpose of the organisation (to be a 'living theatre for plants and people') was a 'lodestar' that cast a direction for evolution of the whole organisation. The co-founders were attuned to the deeper potential of the disused clay pit and the possibility of being a 'beacon of sustainability' for others. The project managers used dialogue to explore what made people feel excited, energised and proud to work for Eden. They tuned into the untapped wisdom of people, understanding that ideas lie dormant in unexpected corners. It's the leader's job to uncover them.

Re-imagining the role of the leader is at the heart of a thriving organisation that unleashes sustainable, inclusive growth. Harvard Business School leadership scholar Linda Hill, with her co-authors of *Collective Genius: The Art and Practice of Leading Innovation* (2014), carried out extensive research to discover what makes organisations such as Pixar, Google and eBay highly innovative and hugely successful. They found that leadership in these progressive organisations was markedly different from the more common 'command-and-control' approach.

Leaders of innovation do not act as heroes, experts or solo visionaries as this approach would be flawed from the start. If a team or organisation is to generate something truly original – whether this is a partnership, film or a new product – a leader cannot know in advance the direction of the creative path. The leader who outlines their vision and then corrals others to follow it limits the possibility of truly motivating a community.

Change leaders create an environment where people are willing and able to contribute. They see themselves not as a commander-in-chief but as a 'co-visionary'. They combine individual 'slices of genius' into a single work of collective genius. They unleash and harness people's creativity to produce a shared vision that radiates inspiration to others. There are now new Edens in Lancashire, Dundee, China, Colombia, Costa Rica and Australia.

Only when leaders see themselves as 'social architects' (to borrow a phrase from Linda Hill) will they create real value by forming creative partnerships with suppliers, competitors, service users and the local community and by leading in a more open, fluid, adaptable way.

To activate the principle of potential, questions to explore include:

- What's the change we want to bring about?
- How fully are we living our purpose and values?
- What's the deeper potential enfolded in this situation?

Participation

When people feel 'done to', change becomes much harder. In *The Influence Agenda*, Mike Clayton writes: '*Projects and change would be easy if it were not for the people involved.*' Different stakeholders bring their own needs, agendas and priorities. If they feel railroaded, they are likely to resist whether overtly or covertly, as we saw with the Sheffield Stag group and the people of Plymouth.

Change through being directive is simpler and faster but it's an illusion. When a heroic leader (or city council) 'shows the way', it often unravels through a failure to get buy-in. The need to manage resistance and enforce compliance drains valuable resources. Dealing with the fall-out of a 'roll out' takes much longer than a participatory change process, even if this latter approach seems slower to start with.

Change that sticks is a co-creation. It arises out of people making meaning together. At Eden, people talked time and time again about what it meant to be a 'beacon of sustainability' and how this would manifest in tangible actions, such as replacing PVC or engaging local suppliers. It took time but the time taken is what made it work.

Change through dialogue is an iterative process of exploring an essential question together. It takes time to build a shared understanding, but the investment pays dividends. People are bought into change by being part of the co-creation. This makes even difficult change, such as buying in a more expensive sustainable material, digestible.

The job of the leader is to be not a controller but a **convenor**. Creating change is about getting the 'right' people in the room at the right time. This means involving not just the potential champions of the change but the naysayers, know-it-alls and sceptics. An insightful dialogue emerges when there are distinct voices that propose, support, challenge and reflect (remember the four dialogic actions of Move, Follow, Oppose and Bystand in Chapter 7, Read the room?). You need the skill of all four 'actions' to make positive change happen. When participants in a dialogue form deep, authentic relationships with one another over time, they share a degree of honesty and safety that is transformative in itself.

In the 'new psychology of leadership', there is more 'we' than 'me'. While we often associate heroism with leadership (think Elizabeth I, Churchill, Mandela), it is misguided. The leader is not 'the special one' but the one who makes others feel special, according to Professor Alex Haslam, a professor of psychology at the University of Queensland. Haslam points out that when José Mourinho, former Chelsea Football Club manager, styled himself as 'the special one', it was the beginning of his decline. Recent commentators have attributed the rise of psychedelic drugs in Silicon Valley to the desire people have to stand out, be extraordinary and have 'edge'. Superiority is sexier and more seductive than participation; it is also a massive roadblock on the path to dialogue.

When leaders take themselves to be a director not a connector, it compromises performance and organisational effectiveness. Warren Bennis, an American scholar, author and pioneer of leadership studies, repeated many times that a leader is only ever as effective as their ability to engage followers. A core task of the leader is not to impose their vision on their followers but to invite them to participate in a conversation where they shape a desired future together. Leaders 'crafting a common voice' rather than talking about themselves is how Haslam describes this orientation. Real leadership is not about individual heroics; it is a group process.

To activate the principle of participation, questions to explore include:

- Who is concerned about what and why?
- What makes people feel they belong?
- What would strengthen our relationships?

Coherence

Dialogue produces change when it leads to people taking 'right action'. By this I mean, people take action that is in alignment with the organisation's purpose and which benefits the whole rather than just themselves. It takes time to surface 'right action' as this arises out of a shared understanding of what the issue is.

Bohm saw all knowledge as imperfect 'because it is an abstraction of the whole'. Looking for incoherence between our intentions and our results points to where knowledge is defective. For example, a CEO might say that they want challenge but if they become defensive when someone disagrees with them, they end up silencing dissent ('He says he welcomes challenge, but when we do, he puts us on the naughty step' as one of his directors said). The gap between the CEO's intention and the unintended impact points to his incomplete knowledge about how effective challenge works.

Decades of research has uncovered many different biases that lead to poor decisions and incoherent actions. When these biases remain unexamined, making change sustainable becomes much harder. For example:

- Confirmation bias, where people value more highly information that's consistent with a favoured belief and discount information that contradicts it, skews a dialogue away from objectivity and towards groupthink.

- Overconfidence bias makes a team more at risk of listening to a leader who inflates their ability to predict an outcome and overlooks the role of chance (particularly if this is a 'hippo', the highest-paid person's opinion). This leads to a cascade of misinformation across the organisation.
- Controllability bias where people favour courses of action that appear to be less risky. In the absence of evidence or data, some people veer towards outcomes that can be controlled, making change less likely to happen.

Dialogue with a diverse range of stakeholders has been shown to make decisions more coherent through a better understanding of both the problem and the issues of implementation.[9]

Instead of enrolling others into their way of thinking, an effective change leader sees themselves as 'the keeper of a context where dialogue can happen' (Bob Anderson). They bring a focus on learning, shared understanding and sense-making. A leader acts as a **catalyst** who addresses fixed mindsets and expands other people's thinking. They are open to change, willing to be challenged themselves and ask clarifying questions such as:

- What's at risk if we make this change? What's at risk if we don't?
- What's the 'nut to crack' or central causative issue to address?
- What hard truths need to be spoken in order to move forwards?

Ladkin points out that asking questions and listening to the answers you hear is an important way that we learn about our prejudices. When someone says something that does not make sense to us, we are 'pulled up short'. This 'jolt' can help to reveal a prejudice we were carrying that we weren't previously aware of. Such moments also make it clear that actions need to be jointly negotiated. Each person holds a piece of the puzzle and no one person holds the whole puzzle.

Awareness

Dialogue becomes a tool for transformation when people talk about what matters most. As people share the truth of their experience and listen to the experience of others, they are more willing to discuss risks, share fears and name the 'undiscussables'. The more real the conversation becomes, the more possible it is that the assumptions and beliefs that shape collective reality surface. Becoming aware of these underlying beliefs means that people can examine them and even upgrade them, making outer change possible.

In their classic *Harvard Business Review* paper, 'The real reason people won't change', Kegan and Lahey highlight a key psychological dynamic that makes people 'change resistant'. They call this a 'competing commitment.' It is often unconscious and yet has a powerful influence. For example, the ongoing struggle someone is having about talking with their boss about their resignation might be due to a fear of upsetting their relationship and losing connection. They might develop an 'outdated loyalty' to their boss, which reflects their relationship with their mother or father, whom they also didn't want to disappoint. The direct report might be unaware of this repeating pattern even though it means that they carry on living in the shadow of not being able to talk. They perceive the conversation as being just too difficult due to this 'competing commitment'.

Hidden loyalties cast a long shadow over our experience unless we become aware of them, particularly in a collective context. A Board of a start-up might say that they want to lead a world-class organisation but staying with a more random, entrepreneurial way of operating that many are still bought into will make it hard to shift away from the pattern of 'going where the energy is'. Unless a 'competing commitment' is aired, shared and discussed, it will run the show from behind the scenes.

To activate the principle of awareness, it calls on the leader to be a *coach*. Instead of asserting the way forward, they become curious and ask questions:

- Why is this situation the way it is?
- What are our 'competing commitments'?
- What do our stakeholders want from us?

As the dialogue deepens, the group consciousness expands. As the 'field' starts to include what was previously undiscussable or out of awareness, a group can enter a state of flow. It is palpable when this happens. People feel connected. There is a heightened sense of trust. As boundaries and limitations to thinking loosen, new insights and intuitive flashes appear. The group harvests the wisdom and newness in the room.

When people access a deeper level of awareness, this remains available after the dialogue has ended. Dialogue leaves people feeling like they're a bigger version of themselves, both individually and collectively. As a result, a disparate group of individuals starts to operate as a whole.

To explore further, see Exercise 18 – Activate the four principles of dialogue.

Exercise 18
Activate the four principles of dialogue

1. Identify a 'wicked' problem that your leadership team/Board is facing. For example, formulating a new strategy for a systemic problem or developing a partnership across organisational boundaries.
2. Think about how to create some momentum with this 'wicked' problem. Review the four shifts in identity and dialogic principles that this could entail you embodying as a leader:
   a) A **Co-visionary** who senses the deeper **Potential** in the problem situation
   b) A **Convenor** who invites **Participation** in the change and acknowledges concerns
   c) A **Catalyst** who brings **Coherence** by naming hard truths and looking at risks
   d) A **Coach** who increases **Awareness** about 'competing commitments' and stakeholder wishes
3. Rank (a), (b), (c) and (d) in order of importance. Focusing on the top priority, explore the relevant questions in the figure on the

four principles of dialogic change (Figure 9.2). For example, if you ranked being a Convenor as number one, ask yourself these questions:

- Who is concerned about what and why?
- What makes people feel they belong?
- What would strengthen our relationships?

4 Reflect on your answers to question (3). Identify what you could do to move forward with the 'wicked' problem you're facing.

On the up

Back to the story. Six months after the Board meeting, Paul, the deputy CEO, and I caught up on a video call. He was standing in for the CEO while she was on holiday.

'We've been working well together', Paul said. 'The new execs have settled in and the team's functioning well. We've had good, challenging conversations without falling out.'

I breathed a sigh of relief. There had been some tense moments at the Board meeting, including early on, when I'd shared an anonymised version of the 'great outcomes' people had said they'd wanted. The desire for 'more trust' had unsettled some. They'd interpreted it as meaning that there was a lack of trust, which they'd not felt; at least not until then.

The 'jolt' reminded me of Ladkin's point that the sensation of feeling 'pulled up short' is an effective way of bringing assumptions to the surface. Fortunately, we'd already agreed a ground rule of 'welcome uncomfortable moments' so we slowed down, listened to the questions and different perspectives. Diving into what trust meant and how much trust people felt there was brought a shared understanding to the dialogue that wouldn't have been present without the rupture.

'The session brought to a head a number of matters I hadn't anticipated', Paul said. 'Do you remember all the discussion about the integrated performance report?'

I did. After people had shared their completed Critical Conversations Grid, the report had emerged in the 'Big Win' box in a collective version of the Grid that I'd produced using masking tape on the floor. As people debated in small groups which items to place in which box, there had been a buzz in the room that only happens when there's full **participation**.

Later in the session, two of the NEDs had spoken out about their discomfort around not having seen the report. When one of the NEDs used the word 'secret', the temperature in the room shot up. It was a classic Board dynamic: the NEDs suspecting that key information was being held back, making them ask questions about the detailed content, and the Execs feeling affronted. The 'nut to crack' had appeared.

'It was uncomfortable, but it flushed it out', Paul reflected. 'We, as the Execs, were able to say that the report was still in development. It's not that we were keeping it from them, it's just that it wasn't ready.'

As the dialogue continued, a way forward gradually emerged. The Execs, who'd worked hard over the past five years to build a culture of productive dialogue, agreed a date when the report would be complete and identified the person who would be responsible for sharing the report with the NEDs. As the CEO wrote the agreed actions up on the flip chart, it felt like everyone was breathing more easily, bringing a sense of **coherence** to the room.

'The NEDs were right', Paul continued. 'That report is important as it will give us the strategic view of all the key dials on performance – but they were wrong about our reasons for not having shared it.'

As I listened to Paul, I was reminded of the tension that many Boards experience between being strategic and operational. It's easy to look back and view a heated discussion about a report as a 'storm in a teacup' but it had been a critical part of the meeting. The 'outing' of the NEDs' suspicion had increased the Board's **awareness** of the fine balance between keeping a helicopter view and drilling down into detail when needed.

'We were able to share the report a month later' Paul added, 'and we were all happy with the detail. I think the discussion highlighted to us all that the NEDs add most value when they provide challenge at the right level. They're now doing more of that.'

'And what about the external environment?' I asked.

'We've had a concern about our reputation, as you know', Paul said. 'Especially as we've felt threatened by the hospital. But we're on the up. Naz is developing a trusting relationship with the CEO there. It's one of her strengths. Now that the Execs have a more trusting relationship with the NEDs, we're showing up with a united front which really helps build a productive partnership with the hospital.'

Bingo, I thought.

'The commissioners are regularly giving us positive feedback and asking us to do more and more. They see us as an example of good practice given that the CQC has rated us as the top performing organisation in the region. We're in the best position we've ever been in.'

I thought back to something that the CEO had expressed during our one-to-one conversation and at the Board meeting. She'd voiced her ambition for the organisation to be a system leader in the region and for it to inspire other providers to be like them. It was a clear statement of the untapped **potential** of the organisation, which had resonated for the rest of the Board. At the meeting, I'd taken them through a 'timeline' exercise, where they'd reviewed the last year and identified the key milestones, successes achieved and lessons learned. Looking backwards to go forwards helps bring a 'fusion of horizons' into the room.

'Thank you', said Paul, 'you've not only seen our culture; you've contributed to our culture as well. How are you fixed for another session in the autumn?'

'I'd be delighted', I said.

As I logged off, I was left with a real sense of how skilful, participative and authentic dialogue has a crucial and powerful part to play in leading change. Learning to talk, think and act together in honest and effective ways is essential for a true partnership.

Dialogue brings to the surface that which has been hidden in an organisation and allows a Board's intention to promote transformation to translate into cultural and systemic change for the benefit of all involved, including the staff, suppliers and wider community.

Summary

1. Re-imagining the role of the leader is at the heart of what it means to lead during these disruptive, unstable times. Shifting from manager or controller to convenor, catalyst, coach and co-visionary enables a different kind of dialogue to take place.

2. There are four key principles to a dialogic process that enable positive impact: Potential, Participation, Coherence and Awareness. By following these principles, sustainable change becomes possible. Violating them means change becomes stuck.

3. *Potential* emerges when a leader invites others into a dialogue about future possibilities. They do not impose their vision on the organisation; they act as a 'co-visionary' and create a 'fusion of horizons' through making meaning together.

4. *Participation* cuts through resistance to change. A leader as convenor focuses on getting the right people in the right conversation at the right time. People support change that they feel they've shaped, having been included in the conversation.

5. *Coherence* arises among stakeholders when they air differences and challenge respectfully. The leader as catalyst allows hard truths to be spoken, invites dissent and listens for 'right action' that serves the whole system not just themselves.

6. *Awareness* sheds light on unseen patterns, difficult dynamics and untapped potential. 'Competing commitments' and hidden loyalties no longer hamper change as the leader as coach asks questions, stays curious and sees the larger system.

> **If you do only one thing now** . . . See the deeper potential of the dialogue you want to have. Ask other participants 'what would be a great outcome from this conversation?' Allow their responses to shape how the dialogue goes. Focus on what you can change through coordinated action rather than getting stuck talking about what you can't.

Notes

1 https://spectrum.mit.edu/winter-2001/the-art-of-dialogue/.
2 Hughes, M. (2011) 'Do 70 per cent of all organizational change initiatives really fail?', *Journal of Change Management*, *11*(4), pp. 451–464.
3 Cameron, E. and Green, M. (2015) *Making Sense of Change Management*, Fourth Edition, Kogan Page.
4 Ladkin, D. (2020) *Rethinking Leadership: A new look at old questions*, Second Edition, Edward Elgar Publishing Ltd.
5 https://www.theguardian.com/environment/2017/oct/27/sheffield-councillor-cleared-of-breaching-tree-felling-order.
6 https://www.sheffield.gov.uk/sites/default/files/2023-06/an_open_apology_for_the_behaviour_of_sheffield_city_council_during_the_street_trees_dispute.pdf.
7 https://www.theguardian.com/uk-news/2023/jun/20/sheffield-council-issues-apology-over-tree-felling-scandal.
8 Isaacs, W. (1999) *Dialogue and the Art of Thinking Together*, Currency Doubleday.
9 Rousseau, D. (2018) Making evidence-based organisational decisions in an uncertain world, *Organisational Dynamics*, *47*(3), pp. 135–146.

chapter 10

Conversations about purpose

'The meaning of life is to find your gift.
The purpose of life is to give it away.'

Pablo Picasso

Purpose entails a conversation that really matters. Some managers, however, think purpose is a luxury and therefore a waste of valuable time. Others feel unsettled and think that they're not good enough to have a 'higher' purpose. Teams struggle to see the bigger picture of their purpose and want to stay in their comfort zone firefighting. Organisations find it difficult balancing the needs of different stakeholders to articulate (and then live) a purpose beyond making a profit or meeting metrics.

To overcome these challenges, it helps to have a safe and energising space to talk and think about purpose. Without an authentic dialogue that this allows, purpose remains elusive. With an authentic dialogue, individuals feel energised as day-to-day work becomes more meaningful; team members pull together and make effective decisions; and an organisation attracts and retains top talent, generating sustainable advantage. Purpose is therefore both a source of difficult conversations and a great resource for them.

> I was ready to relax and enjoy the evening. It had been a full day: I'd travelled by train from my home in Shrewsbury to Oxford and delivered a session about purpose at Saïd Business School on the 'Preparing for CEO' programme for leaders in the FE (Further Education) sector. Taking my seat at the long wooden dinner table, I pulled the dark green napkin out of the wine glass, and spread it across my lap. The smell of the Thai curry had wafted into the bar area where I'd been chatting earlier with participants and my taste buds were tingling.
>
> As I was now alone, before the group joined the dinner table, I pulled out my smartphone to check my inbox. The title of one email jumped out: 'Is this it?'
>
> It was from a client; someone I'd not heard from for a while. We'd done some executive coaching work together ten years earlier and had stayed in touch intermittently.

Hi Sarah,

I hope this email finds you well.

You might recall that when we first met and discussed the framework of how we were going to work together, we had numerous discussions. At one stage I mentioned to you my eternal question 'Is this it?'

Anyway, all of that is a long time ago and I don't expect you to fully remember. However, I wanted to share a recent 'light bulb moment' with you in relation to 'Is this it?'

To put this in context, I haven't been asking myself this question for a very long time and as a matter a fact I don't ask the question at all anymore. Still, thinking back I remembered having this 'burning' question and it suddenly came to me. . . . 'Is this it?' was always a rhetorical question. By virtue of asking the question, I was answering the question.

The answer was a solid NO. This 'wasn't it', by any stretch of the imagination. It was merely an expression suggestion, to myself; surely I can do more BUT HOW? The question, 'Is this it?' is, I now recognise, a trigger, a catalyst to suggest that as an individual I want more out of life and I shouldn't waste anymore time finding the answer to the question.

Reflecting, I now feel that – if I had understood the question better at the time – I would have left the job I was doing (it wasn't satisfying anymore) but I was TRAPPED – great salary, big title and responsibilities, part of an organisation etc. I didn't know any better which is why I was asking the question.

A clear image of Martin from years ago, sitting with his head in his hands and a sad look in his eyes, appeared in my mind. We'd had many conversations about his purpose – or lack of purpose – and his sense of frustration came flooding back. Suddenly, at the dining room table, a participant appeared and took the seat next to mine. I stopped reading and put my phone back in my pocket. The rest of the update would have to wait.

Perhaps you can relate to the 'Is this it?' question? Maybe it gnaws at you too. Many managers want a sense of purpose at work, and Martin had been no exception. Research by McKinsey has found that around seven out of ten employees say that their purpose is defined by their work; and executives are nearly three times more likely than others to say that they rely on work for purpose. Nine out of ten say they want purpose in their lives.[1]

When purpose is absent, there's often a real sense that something is missing. Motivation ebbs away. When purpose is present, people are more productive. They are also healthier, more resilient and more committed to stay with their organisation. People with a sense of purpose live longer, have higher levels of wellbeing, are less susceptible to stress, depression and substance abuse, and report higher levels of life satisfaction, emotional stability, optimism and self-esteem. The only 'catch' is that your purpose needs to be 'true' or authentic – one that's contributive and self-expansive – rather than extractive and self-absorbed, such as seeking only to grow your own wealth, status and success.[2]

Despite the well-documented benefits, some managers perceive purpose to be an irrelevance or even a danger. As a retired CEO said to me: 'I wouldn't have employed a consultant like you. Organisations want "more with less". I'd have felt I was losing control. Asking people to explore their purpose will be a distraction at best and a disturbance at worst.'

And it's true. People leave jobs, shun big salaries and drop the sexy job title when the 'pull' to do what is theirs to do becomes impossible to ignore. No wonder some people feel that the 'purpose conversation' should come with a red-light warning.

Reactivity around purpose is widespread. 'Consultant rubbish', one director said at a team coaching session when I introduced a new tool to focus their conversation onto purpose. He came round after this put-down, but his initial reaction was cynicism. Other managers perceive purpose to be 'do good-ery', fuzzy or flummery. Others get triggered into feeling that they're not good enough to have a 'higher' purpose. And some say that taking home a pay cheque *is* their purpose and want to leave it at that (which is fair enough).

The business case for purpose though has been growing over the last decade. Since my book *Powered by Purpose* was published in 2020, several other books have contributed to the evidence base for the benefits of purpose, including *Grow the Pie* by Professor Alex Edmans,[3] *Deep Purpose* by Professor Ranjay Gulati[4] and *Net Positive* by Paul Polman and Andrew Winston.[5] Paul Polman kindly contributed the foreword to *Powered by Purpose*, sharing that during the ten years he was CEO, Unilever's shareholder return was nearly 300 per cent, well ahead of the FTSE 100 index, which rose by around 70 per cent over this period. The strong financial results of purpose-driven companies, who out-perform their competitors, has won the attention of leaders, managers and investors the world over.

But how?

Organisations, particularly post-pandemic, increasingly understand they need to change and make work more meaningful for their people – but struggle with the 'how'. In the absence of some know-how, there's a risk that purpose is either neglected or becomes a tick-box exercise. While many books highlight the value of purpose, few offer practical steps for uncovering purpose using the most available tool of all: conversation.

Articulating and amplifying purpose – whether for an individual, team or organisation – is possible only when people are able to have a quality dialogue. Purpose is a highly personal topic; it taps into what we perceive is meaningful and what makes us unique. Listening deeply, speaking authentically, respecting differences and suspending judgement all help to create the psychological safety needed to dive into the deeper territory of purpose. Building on the four interventions already covered, leaders need a different set of questions to engage their people to think and talk together, so that they become aware of a flow of new possibilities through the exploration of purpose.

There are, as I wrote in *Powered by Purpose*, three territories to explore in dialogue. These are the 'bridges' of:

1 **Ambition** – An *organisation* moves away from being focused primarily on profit or metrics towards serving stakeholders and being a force for good in the world profitably.
2 **Alignment** – A *team* moves from being scattered to everyone pulling in the same direction, inspired by delivering a potent purpose that individuals could not achieve by working alone.
3 **Aliveness** – An *individual* connects their daily work with their purpose so instead of feeling disengaged, they feel fired up to do the work that is uniquely theirs to do and develop the resilience to keep going during tough times.

A strong 'container' for a productive dialogue at each of these three levels is essential. Perhaps 'vessel' is a better word as it communicates a sense of going on a journey and crossing the 'bridge' of purpose together. Below are seven practical steps for making happen one of the most important conversations you can have, not just as a leader or manager, but as a human being: the purpose conversation.

Carve out time

Purpose articulation often begins with the executive or senior leadership team grappling with the question of 'what is' purpose. There are, however, several obstacles that get in the way of an executive team being able to have a value-adding conversation about purpose, including:

- Lack of quality thinking time from staying in the operational mode
- Being out of touch with stakeholders and failing to understand fully all the ways the organisation can have a positive impact
- Seeing purpose discovery as an analytical exercise and overthinking it
- Lack of safety and willingness to challenge mediocracy
- A fear of looking foolish by declaring a purpose with passion.

To overcome these blocks, re-visit Figure 2.1 (Time spent on having dialogue vs. Time spent due to lack of dialogue in Chapter 2 about the time taken for dialogue – see page 26). You might also reflect on where you currently are as an organisation as a way of creating some momentum. See Exercise 19 – Organisational purpose reality check below.

Exercise 19
Organisational purpose reality check

1 In your executive or senior leadership team, invite team members to reflect on the following categories of organisation with regard to their purpose:[6]

- **'Prioritisers'** – the organisation has a clearly understood and articulated purpose.
- **'Developers'** – the organisation is working to develop a clear and well-understood purpose.
- **'Laggards'** – the organisation has not yet begun to develop or think about purpose.

2 Invite each person to state in which category they would place your organisation with a reason why. Encourage people to stay curious rather than make any one answer 'right' or 'wrong'. Then, go more deeply into your chosen category. Reflect together.

3 Have a conversation about what the benefits might be of clearly articulating your purpose and aligning your organisation around it. Research has shown that 'Prioritisers' experience three core benefits:

- They have higher growth rates, including an edge on revenue growth, as well as greater customer loyalty and brand gains.
- They are more successful at transformation and innovation initiatives, such as a new product launch or expanding into a new market. ➤

- They have more engaged employees who demonstrate more willingness to partner across functional and product boundaries.

Defining your organisation's purpose is not something a team can do in a one-hour meeting. Trying to 'shoehorn' a purpose discussion into an already packed agenda is a waste of time. Grappling with questions such as 'Why do we exist?' requires spaciousness.

With enough time, the dross falls away, insights percolate and a compelling purpose statement comes into view. Writing down a shared purpose brings several benefits, which include the executive team being able to:

- Be precise about how its reality can actually come about
- Hold itself accountable as they revisit the purpose
- Evolve the articulation of the purpose, when needed
- Engage stakeholders in meaningful dialogue about the purpose
- Create a basis for more effective decision-making and innovative thinking
- Build resilience during turbulent times by having a clear focus.

If there's unresolved conflict or ruthless competition among team members, no amount of discussion about purpose will solve these issues. As I wrote in *Powered by Purpose*, there's also a corporate version of a 'spiritual bypass'. Ignoring messy human dynamics by focusing on something more transcendent does not make the negativity go away; it instead increases cynicism.

Naming the obstacles – people working in silos, a turf war between departments or a stand-off between directors – is sometimes enough to clear the air. Other times you need to engage the issue and address these dynamics (if necessary, with the support of an external facilitator, mediator or coach) before turning to the question of purpose.

A supportive 'container' or 'vessel' is essential for having a conversation where people feel safe enough to discuss what really matters (see Chapter 3). I've worked with several teams where the founders have given me a clear brief to galvanise their values and purpose. When I've asked the rest of the team what a good outcome would be, some have been brave enough to say it would be to see a better relationship between the founders. Bringing this into the room in such a way that the founders could listen without being reactive has cleared the way for having a meaningful conversation about purpose. Without addressing this relational issue first, purpose will never have the heft people hope it will.

Make it clear and compelling

Start with focusing on your organisation's purpose. As a leader, it's the 'bridge' that's most within your sphere of control and making your 'why' authentic creates sustainable advantage. Research has shown that even in these challenging economic times, around 40 per cent of employees globally say they might leave their jobs in the near future.[7] The global pandemic has been an accelerator for the trend of 'conscious quitting' in this era known as the 'Great Resignation'.

Becoming purpose-driven is an ambitious journey for an organisation to take. Purpose articulation can be a difficult conversation given the existential questions it raises about profit, stakeholder primacy and lived contradictions, with which many stakeholders struggle. In the words often attributed to Peter Drucker, *'Profit for a company is like oxygen for a person. If you don't have enough of it, you're out of the game. But if you think your life is about breathing, you're really missing something.'*

Conversations about corporate purpose are also riddled with misunderstandings. A common confusion is to use *vision*, *mission* and *purpose* interchangeably. It brings clarity to differentiate. According to Dr Victoria Hurth and colleagues, vision is what an organisation is trying to achieve; mission is how an organisation goes about it, and purpose is an organisation's enduring and meaningful reason to exist.[8]

Take the case of Brompton Cycles. The folding bikes that people carry onto trains and tubes now make up one in five bikes on the road in London. They are a feat of British engineering. Under the leadership of Will Butler-Adams, CEO, Brompton has become a UK powerhouse. Their vision is to have more and more urban dwellers across the world riding foldable bikes. Their current mission is to grow the American market beyond the few stores they have across the country. Their purpose is to 'change the way people live in cities'.[9]

Purpose statements that pack a punch have a simplicity that takes time to nail. Landing a memorable set of words which resonate and that people can easily recall is worth the time it takes. Check out the succinctness of these statements:

- Re-imagine commerce in ways that build a more fulfilling and lasting world (Etsy)
- Unlocking the potential of those who advance the world (Boston Consulting Group)
- We make jeans. That's it (Hiut Demin Co.)

Alongside any work on purpose that a PR consultancy or branding agency performs, middle managers and frontline workers must be involved in the conversation, not just executives. This will help to reduce the risk of purpose being seen as a 'bolt-on' or of 'purpose wash' accusations. The intelligence needed to infuse day-to-day work with meaning is there in the organisation; the magic is to access it and bring it into action.

In *Powered by Purpose*, I shared the story of how Standard Chartered Bank uncovered its authentic purpose through dialogue. Senior leaders asked their people: What does the Bank stand for? If the Bank ceased to exist tomorrow, who would care, and why? They crowdsourced and analysed the responses of 70,000 people with the help of smart machine learning and defined the behaviours they most valued. From these conversations, the Bank defined its purpose: 'Driving commerce and prosperity through our unique diversity'. As a result, what differentiated the Bank – the diverse people that intimately understand the local clients and markets in which they work – was captured in their purpose statement.

A compelling purpose statement has five dimensions, which I summarise using the acronym 'MAGIC' (see Figure 10.1)

What makes a great organisational purpose?

Meaningful – It provides a sense of belonging for *all* employees who are excited by the *enduring* 'why' and want to give of their best

Authentic – It refers to what the organisation *commits* to, not just what it espouses to do, in terms of creating real value

Generative – It creates conversations that lead to better *decision-making* and new possibilities. The words are simple and repeatable

Implementable – It states what the organisation *stands for* in a way that can be practically applied

Collaborative – It creates a *flow of positive energy* in the whole system by unifying stakeholders to pull in the same direction

Figure 10.1 A MAGIC purpose statement

This 'MAGIC' tool gives a 'lens' with which to examine a draft purpose statement. Further refinements become possible. When I've used this framework with clients, the dialogue about their organisation's purpose has deepened. They've then left the meeting room with their purpose defined and aligned, and a palpable sense of satisfaction.

Find inspiration

Purpose is not a static entity. It is never fixed or final. As author and consultant Pete Burden says: '*Purpose develops out of conversation. It grows over time, as people talk together, bring in new ideas and get creative.*'[10] To uncover or evolve your purpose, find inspiration by looking backwards and outwards.

Most businesses started with a founding purpose beyond merely making money; and digging into this can be revealing. Unilever has successfully evolved its founding purpose of making hygiene commonplace. The development of Lifebuoy – now one of Unilever's most successful and profitable brands – goes back to the vision of William Hesketh Lever, who was concerned about cholera and other infectious diseases spreading through the slums of Liverpool. Lever created a bar of soap that would be available to the masses who were at risk of dying – a mission that is still consistent with how the soap is marketed in India today.

Paul Polman, when he became Unilever CEO, held the first meeting with his leadership team at Port Sunlight (a small village on the south bank of the Mersey where, in the 1880s, the founding Lever brothers built a community for the employees of their nearby soap factory). Having the conversation about what had made Unilever such a successful and sustainable organisation in this setting was a deliberate decision. The founding purpose provides insights into the uniqueness of an organisation. It is a source of competitive advantage, as the founding energy cannot be replicated. Unilever's current expression of its purpose – 'to make sustainable living commonplace' – is the next iteration of the organisation's DNA.

Looking at what other organisations are doing around purpose is also motivating. The highly successful US airline company, Southwest Airlines, which carries 120 million passengers a year, has been a source of inspiration for many business leaders. Southwest Airlines has turned a profit throughout its 48 years (while early competitors Pan Am and TWA no longer exist) by staying focused on its founding purpose. The video Southwest Airlines made about their purpose using a series of stories told by staff and customers shows how meaningful day-to-day interactions can be when they 'connect people with what's important in their lives through friendly, reliable and low-cost travel'.[11] When I've watched this video with teams in other companies, some have found it inspiring; others 'schmaltzy' so here's one more exemplar, this time from a UK not-for-profit.

Choice Support is a charitable Community Benefit Society that provides support to autistic people, people with learning disabilities and/or mental health needs. Senior leaders are clear that purpose is not a purpose statement (full disclosure: I've been coaching the executive team since 2019). At an offsite I facilitated for them, the directors discovered how a focus on purpose could bring clarity to decision-making, more collaboration and less turnover. Once they'd arrived at their purpose – 'to support people to find opportunities for creating their own happiness' – and values ('We care, we respect, we learn, we lead'), they acted on their desire to put these 'at the core of everything we do'. Sarah Maguire, CEO, produced a regular blog, the exec team created a video where they talked about purpose,[12] two project leaders ran a series of purpose engagement sessions and the Trustees were invited to explore what the organisation's purpose meant to them.

Other organisations expand their purpose statement with a clear set of strategic goals. At Kiwibank (a New Zealand state-owned bank and financial services provider), their purpose is built around three 'pillars': "Tamariki [children] are better off, Kiwi are better off, and Aotearoa [New Zealand] is better off." Each pillar has a clear goal: 'By 2030, we will support all tamariki (children) to have access to quality financial education.'

Their purpose-led approach has led to great results. Their annual sustainability report states the key progress made and the intended actions to keep the momentum going.[13] The purpose pillars drive everything Kiwibank does to ensure they're making a real difference. In 2023, their net profit after tax ($175m) increased 34 per cent on the previous year. They reduced their carbon emissions by 9 per cent and improved their company culture by 8 points, placing Kiwibank in the top 25 per cent of companies.

'We get performance through purpose', Steve Jurkovich, CEO, said to me when we caught up on a video call. 'Once we worked out what purpose really meant to us and what we truly cared about by talking it through with our team members, it became a win-win, not a trade-off.'

Kiwibank is also a certified B Corporation (along with 5697 other organisations in 85 countries). This means that their ethical, social and environmental practices are assessed and certified by independent monitors to meet the rigorous standards laid down by B Lab, a not-for-profit group in Pennsylvania, who make the results public. B Corps are required to have a social purpose and to commit legally to act in the interests of all stakeholders, not just shareholders.

Leaders see possibilities in the reality of what other organisations are doing. As one client said, 'Purpose is the potential energy that gets kinetic.' An authentic dialogue about purpose needs to be both inspired by future potential and grounded in the present, which is where we turn next.

Create alignment

The purpose of an organisation is the big-picture context that brings people together. There are two important conversations that help to align people around a purpose: an authentic dialogue around what makes people feel proud to work for the organisation and an authentic dialogue to explore contradictions that have arisen in relation to purpose.

Purpose is not something 'out there' to be achieved, it is something felt deep inside. It's the emotional connection that's important. You know you're living your purpose when you:

- Feel proud to work for your organisation
- Are engaged by your day-to-day work
- Keep going even when it gets tough as work feels like a meaningful challenge
- See potential collaborators rather than competitors in the field around you
- Are willing to take a stand on an issue and even make yourself unpopular
- Have a felt sense of rightness about what you're doing
- 'Get over yourself' more easily and have less 'imposter syndrome'/ inner critic interference.

A simple question that sparks a great conversation about purpose is: When have you felt proud working for this organisation? By 'proud' I don't mean puffed up; I mean healthy pride, the feeling you get when your heart glows. When I asked participants at the 'Preparing for CEO' session in Oxford, some spoke about their FE college winning an award, others talked about their team achieving a key goal, and others talked about the difference their coaching had made to a student or teacher. The room swelled with positivity.

This question casts a clear light on an organisation's purpose. Dr Victoria Hurth and colleagues define organisational purpose as an organisation's *'meaningful and enduring reason to exist that aligns with long-term financial performance, provides a clear context for decision making, and unifies and motivates relevant stakeholders. Purpose contributes to long-term wellbeing for all.'*[14]

Problems arise when the espoused purpose of an organisation fails to align with the lived purpose. Fine words written on a website lead to cynicism when they are spoken but not acted upon. Unlived purpose statements are virtue signalling at best and hypocritical at worst. To reduce these risks, it is important to discuss the trade-offs, dilemmas and difficult decisions that purpose entails.

In *Net Positive* Paul Polman and Andrew Winston write about the challenges that Unilever encountered along the way to become more purpose-driven. One of these was to get the 'right people on the bus'. This meant starting at the top so that the executives were enthusiastic about the organisation's purpose and cared about the state of the world. An external firm interviewed senior leaders, mapped skills to jobs and 'exposed some disturbing insights about the culture and capabilities', which included the assessments showing weaknesses in 'thinking systemically'. This exercise led to dramatic changes in personnel in the early months of Paul Polman's leadership with some executives self-assessing that purpose wasn't their thing. About 70 of the top 100 executives were 'refreshed' along with significant changes to the board. Finding purpose alignment can be a major challenge but is critical for purpose to power an organisation to greater impact.

A further 'rude awakening' came when Unilever received pointed attacks for their skin-whitening products in India. Senior leaders decided the message they were sending was a mismatch with their other purpose-led, body-positive brands like Dove. They removed the whitening ingredients from their face creams and re-branded from 'Fair and Lovely' to 'Glow and Lovely' but 'the brand damage was done'.[15]

Contradictions, left unaddressed, fester. Without an authentic dialogue, purpose stands on fragile ground. In a safe 'vessel', leaders can linger in the space of truth-telling, discomfort and ambiguity. To explore more, see Exercise 20 – Dialogue to unpack an organisation's purpose.

Exercise 20
Dialogue to unpack an organisation's purpose

A free-flowing, upbeat conversation is invaluable to create alignment around an organisation's purpose and includes questions such as:

1 When have you felt proud working for this organisation?
2 What's the most positive impact we have?
3 What do our customers/suppliers/wider community/others stakeholders love about us?
4 What would happen if this organisation didn't exist? What essential function do we fulfil? What would others miss?

Deepen the conversation with the following questions to explore areas of tension about your organisation's purpose:

5 Where have you seen our purpose come to life already?
6 What do you see as contradictions?
7 What are one or two things that you can start doing tomorrow to be more in alignment with the purpose?

If there's limited time, discuss the question that has most juice. It's often question (6) that receives the most attention.

Power teams with purpose

Teams that are powered by a common purpose are the most potent unit of change in an organisation. In the words often attributed to Margaret Mead (anthropologist and Recipient of the Planetary Citizen of the Year Award in 1978), *'Never doubt that a small group of thoughtful, committed citizens can change the world: indeed, it's the only thing that ever has.'*

For a small group of people to deliver excellence, they need to have a strong shared purpose. Without an inspiring 'why', a group of individuals remains a group; they do not become a team. In the absence of purpose, leaders get things done by control, command or coercion.

In a purpose-led team, people stop working in silos, start to resolve conflicts and change their way of working. Instead of operating as a 'Single fixed leader work group', team members start to become a 'Purpose-led collaborative team'. Rather than the leader being the centre of the action, the 'why' becomes the beating heart of the team (see Figure 10.2).

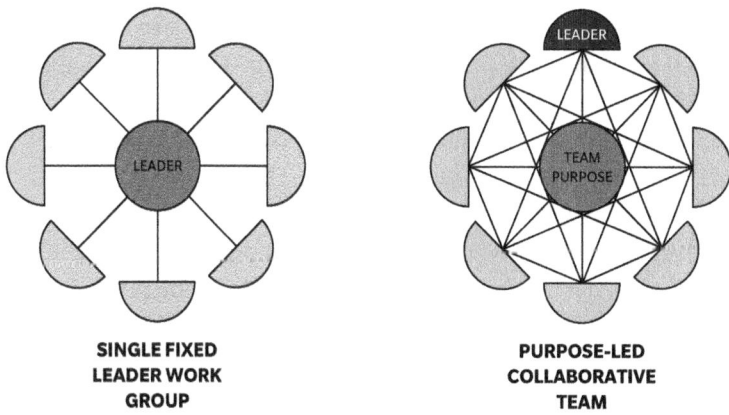

Figure 10.2 Single fixed leader work group vs. purpose-led collaborative team

Of the three 'bridges' of purpose, team purpose is the most often overlooked. This is a real oversight for several reasons. Firstly, a team will flourish only if everyone pulls in the same direction; a team purpose casts that direction.

Secondly, a focus on team purpose provides an opportunity for a conversation about purpose to extend beyond the executive or senior leadership team. Research shows that for organisational purpose to drive higher levels of financial performance two factors need to be present: clarity of organisational purpose and engagement of middle managers. The 'frozen middle', who are often caught between competing demands, is vital for cascading purpose to frontline staff.[16] While some middle managers might be 'squeamish' about exploring their personal purpose (for reasons I've already shared), exploring team purpose is an easier starting point and helps to bridge the communication gap between senior management and frontline staff that exists in so many organisations.

A valuable output from a conversation about team purpose is a purpose statement for the team. This can take the form of 'We do X for Y so that Z.' With one Board I worked with (which had 12 members), the Executive Directors and Non-Executive Directors mixed themselves up into three small groups of four members. Decades of research has shown that the ideal group size in which people can think productively together is four. There is enough richness of input and it's small enough to be highly cohesive.[17]

Each group of four produced a draft team purpose statement, which they shared with the whole Board. Three volunteers then crafted a team purpose statement which was a synthesis of all three. After the Board agreed this statement, they discussed the key actions needed to bring this purpose to life. Words are powerful but actions even more so.

It's important to make sure that the team purpose is authentic. Many teams have a 'commissioned' purpose along the lines of *'We make money to manage and grow the business.'* While this is the reason the team came into being (as mandated by their seniors), it's not truly motivating. *'We meet our KPIs and provide the Board with updates'* doesn't hit the mark either. One team told me that their purpose was *'To feed the beast by producing reports and making presentations'* which, while honest, wasn't an enduring and meaningful reason to exist. Much more like it is the team purpose statement that one Board produced: *'We lead and enable the delivery of outstanding health and social care services by providing strong and compassionate leadership so that more people can lead fulfilling lives.'*

Engage individuals

To overcome managers' resistance to talking about their personal purpose, give people an experience of the physiology purpose brings. Purpose buzzes us. It lights us up. Work no longer feels arduous. Individuals get this once they experience it.

An easy way in is to create a light-hearted atmosphere that's conducive to exploring purpose. At Saïd Business School, I took people through Exercise 21 below (Explore alternative roles) to start the conversation about purpose.

Exercise 21
Explore alternative roles

---

1 Invite each team member to spend a few minutes making some notes in response to these questions:
   - What's the informal role you play in the team?
   - What do others rely on you for?
   - What would others miss about you if you weren't there for two weeks?

2 Ask people to pair up and help one another identify an alternative job title that taps into what makes them 'tick'. Challenge one another to come up with an alternative role title that would make another team member smile.

3 Invite people to write down their name, official title and alternative title on a bright sticky note (in legible handwriting so that they can share it). Ask them to find a new partner with whom to share their sticky note. Repeat several times so that the learning spreads across the group.

Here are some examples that the participants from the FE sector came up with:

- Director of Finance and Estates – Chief Bubble Burster
- Deputy Principal – Battery Distributor
- Chief Financial Officer – Say It As It Is Guy
- Senior Leader Curriculum and Quality – Challenge Champion
- Director of Student Engagement and Partnerships – Circus Ringmaster
- Deputy CEO – Chief Signal Box Operator

Inspired by Dan Cable's book *Alive at Work*,[18] this activity quickly changes the atmosphere from ponderous to playful. Two minutes into the swapping of sticky notes, the laughter was so buoyant, it reminded me of a street circus show. Not a serious face or corporate mask in sight. According to Dan Cable, this exercise improves team performance because it leaves people with a keener sense of each other's roles as well as responsibilities. Understanding who the go-to person is for a team task and that person's unique contribution starts to generate a shared understanding of what the team is about and the 'place' each person inhabits. Research has also shown that inviting employees to identify a self-reflective job title reduces emotional exhaustion, perhaps because it encourages people to reflect on the value that they bring to their work and what they find meaningful.[19]

Doing this exercise with frontline managers and frontline staff also helps to close the 'purpose hierarchy gap' I mentioned in the introduction (see page xxx). Research shows that executives and senior management are eight times more likely to experience living their purpose at work than frontline managers and staff.[20] For an organisation to be powered by purpose at scale, all team members need to be brought into the conversation, not just the elite few.

Call up your courage

We have seen throughout this book how dialogue is a different kind of interaction that involves people learning together as they talk, think and explore together.

Dialogue is also about shifting the relationship of power in an organisation. As Isaacs writes:

> **'We must suspend our differences to gain access to new information and action, so the professor can learn from the student and the boss from the employee. All good bosses know that when you're really leading well, it's not clear who's leading and it doesn't matter. If I see you as a partner, rather than an employee, suddenly the possibilities for creativity are present.'**[21]

Purpose has a pivotal part to play in levelling out power differences between people and making conversation more creative. We each have a purpose, whether we know it or not. We are all capable of feeling our heart sink when something is not ours to do. We all have the capacity to feel a 'pull' towards what *is* ours to do by the sense of exuberant excitement or quiet acceptance that this 'whisper of the future' brings. These can be subtle 'currents' so little wonder that we sometimes miss them, particularly in the cut and thrust of corporate life. By slowing down and taking time to reflect on what really matters, our purpose path comes more clearly into view.

There are many ways to catch a glimpse of your purpose through dialogue. I covered several tools in the last chapter of *Powered by Purpose*. Just as an organisation benefits from evolving its purpose to reflect the current marketplace, an individual benefits from evolving their 'inherited' purpose (the expectations that their family of origin, particularly their parents, placed on them) into a more expansive version. Reflecting on key moments in your life brings the 'thread' you're following more clearly into focus. These include the following:

- **'Crucible moments'** are times that have tested you by putting you in the 'fire' so you see your essence.[22]
- **'Transmission moments'** are the times when you have a strong sense of who you are and experience a vibrant sense of 'This is me! This is who I really am!'

- **'Synchro moments'** are meaningful co-incidences that occur, which give you a sense that you're on your 'right' path. The great Swiss psychologist Carl Jung coined the term 'synchronicity' to refer to unexpected and energising events that feel significant. These moments might seem like mundane occurrences but they are not to be underestimated when they resonate with the undercurrents inside us. Conversations are great examples, such as someone mentioning just the thing you needed to hear or asking you an unexpected question that led to a key insight.

Since then, I've had several other insights about how to make individual purpose come to life through conversation and here's where I discovered them. During lockdown, fellow purpose pioneers, Chris Blackwell, Alberto Gonzalez-Otero, and I started to build an online global community of people interested in purpose. Three years later, we'd connected with over 3000 people from the UK, Netherlands, Sweden, USA, Turkey, Israel, India, Singapore, Australia, Namibia and many more countries and run over 50 free sessions. We called ourselves the Purpose Collective and mused on how we felt like a 'band' when we worked as a trio alongside our solo 'gigs'.

When Alberto, Chris and I finally met in person in the Hague (where Alberto lives) in May 2022, we couldn't believe how much ground we'd covered virtually. Given that we were each offering similar services to organisations, we could have been competitors, but we'd become collaborators. Our shared belief that purpose is a practical tool to drive business transformation had enabled us to transcend any rivalry and find strength in synthesis.

At several Purpose Collective sessions, Alberto introduced a question that led to many people having ah-ha moments. Inspired by the best-selling book, *Ikigai*,[23] it helps people to think beyond the prestige of their job title or the security of their monthly salary (just as Martin did in our coaching conversations). The Japanese word *ikigai* (pronounced ick-ee-guy) roughly translates to 'life purpose' where 'iki' refers to 'life' and 'kai' to 'the realisation of what you expect and hope for'. You could see it as the reason you get up in the morning with a spring in your step. The catalytic question is:

'If you knew you couldn't fail, what would you do?'

The answers that flow from this question always move me. They include 'start my own business', 'write a book', 'take up piano', 'make a film' and 'work three days a week'. It has brought home the reality that when we're in touch with what we really want – and give voice to this, witnessed by others – it strengthens our resolve to move in that direction.

The importance of being true to yourself is highlighted in the best-selling book *The Top Five Regrets of the Dying*. Bronnie Ware, an Australian, spent many years working in palliative care. Originally an article that resonated with millions of people around the world, her book draws together the wisdom of people in the last 3 to 12 weeks of their lives. The most common regret of the dying is: 'I wish I'd had the courage to live a life true to myself, not the life others expected of me.' The *'If you knew you couldn't fail'* question is powerful because it reduces the risk of feeling this remorse later in life.

Finally, conversations about purpose also provide stimulus for crafting a personal purpose statement. Like an organisational purpose statement, this is a simple set of words that says what you're about. Examples from our Purpose Collective sessions include:

- Help people become more open minded through travel
- Support women to feel less lonely so that they can achieve their full potential
- Create unique moments that bring empathy and compassion between people
- Create an ecosystem where people can educate themselves to achieve career stability.

My own seven-word purpose statement – energise people to do great work together – has been a real asset. It has sharpened my decision-making and enabled me to say 'no' and 'yes' more clearly. I no longer do leadership assessments using psychometric tests (it doesn't energise). When a potential client asked me to coach the executive team of a gambling company, I turned it down (I couldn't see what was 'great' about their work). When I felt that I could no longer work with a former colleague (there was more tension than 'togetherness'), I took my leave. However, when Steve Mostyn, Associate Fellow and programme director at Saïd Business School, asked me to run the purpose session, I jumped at it.

Taking your time to put words to your 'why' has an additional benefit for small business owners and sole traders. As their individual purpose is often the same as their organisation's purpose, this doubles the return on crystallising it. An individual purpose statement can, like a team's or organisation's, take the form of 'We do X for Y so that Z'. A good starting point is to ask yourself the resonant questions from Exercise 20 (Dialogue to unpack an organisation's purpose), where the 'unit of analysis' is you, as a sole trader or small business.

Just as we saw with an organisation the size of Unilever, walking your purpose path involves taking risks, but the regret of living a life that's not 'you' is far larger. Letting go of a job, saying 'no' to a high status but burdensome project, leaving behind a cherished set of colleagues to go in search of more fulfilling work are not easy thresholds to cross. These losses and endings become easier through the warmth of a conversation and the fire in your belly that being in touch with your purpose provides.

This is it

Back to Martin. His note was a real reminder how change begins with acknowledging what is. Many people stay in jobs they don't enjoy because they're in denial of what's going on. To change something, you must become aware of what's working and what isn't. Getting in touch with his frustration hadn't been comfortable for Martin but agreeing to reality as it is, rather than trying to push it away, creates the possibility of changing it. Here's the rest of his note:

> 'The stronger and louder the 'Is this it?' question sounded, the more the answer was clear, I needed to get out, but the pay cheque and prestige were pulling me back.
>
> All of that is many years ago. We now live in Cyprus, where our girls are going to International School, and I can run my business from here. My motto is 'enjoyment fuels success' so it is all good.
>
> My wife recently said, 'you are a late bloomer.' I rolled into the 'entrepreneur' type of approach later in life and I am playing catch up and trying to do lots of different things. The notion that I have nothing to lose or 'what is the worst that can happen?' are directing my actions as opposed to money and status. It is liberating.
>
> What is even more freeing is the fact that I now understand that the question 'Is this it?' is actually a trigger to take life and your destiny in your own hands and you shouldn't waste time trying to answer the question.
>
> Anyway, I know we haven't been in touch for a long time (although I receive your newsletters). However, I wanted to share this with you as you have been part of my journey.
>
> Sarah, I hope all is well in work and life and I do hope we have the chance to catch up again at some stage.'
>
> With best wishes,
>
> Martin

Martin's story shows it's never too late to find more satisfaction in your work. As Henry David Thoreau writes in his classic book Waldo: *'The mass of men lead lives of quiet desperation.'* Working and worrying is what many of us experience in our day-to-day life, but it doesn't have to be this way. Some companionship makes all the difference. Talking together generates insights that you'd never have just on your own, galvanises you to take a next step, and reduces the risk of us *'going to the grave with our song still in us'*, as Oliver Wendell Holmes pointed out. A real catalyst for making positive change happen – and one that is often overlooked – is the humble yet magic tool of an open and honest conversation.

Summary

1 Talking about purpose is both tricky and transformative. Confusion about purpose abounds. Resistance is rife. Cynicism is common. 'But how?' is front of mind. Some know-how for conversations about purpose makes all the difference.

2 There are three territories to cover (or 'bridges' to cross): Purpose at an individual, team and organisational level. Clarity of purpose brings aliveness to an individual, alignment to a team and ambition to an organisation.

3 Having the conversation about organisational purpose reduces the risk of 'purpose wash', creates alignment, reduces cynicism and engages team members who make meaning together. Before talking about purpose, it is sometimes necessary to resolve messy human dynamics.

4 Purpose is not a purpose statement. Even a compelling organisational purpose needs to be brought alive through day-to-day behaviours. Amplify the impact of purpose with a set of strategic goals (or purpose 'pillars') that bring purpose to life in thoughts, words and actions.

5 Articulating a shared team purpose calls for an unhurried, quality dialogue. This needn't be sober; playfulness brings the physiology of purpose into the room.

6 Uncovering your personal purpose sharpens decision-making, makes it easier to say 'no' and enables you to call up your courage to do what is yours to do.

7 Purpose isn't static; it evolves. Authentic dialogue in a safe 'vessel' generates insights about how to develop your purpose to meet the needs of a rapidly changing world. Purpose is one of the most important conversations you, your team and organisation can have.

> **If you do only one thing now** . . . Ask people when they've felt proud of the impact they've had. Then ask what this feeling does for their personal growth. From this energised place, it's easier to see the essence of purpose, whether the focus is on personal, team or organisational purpose.

Notes

1 https://www.mckinsey.com/capabilities/people-and-organizational-performance/our-insights/help-your-employees-find-purpose-or-watch-them-leave.

2 Taylor, S. (2016) A model of purpose: From survival to transpersonal purpose, *Transpersonal Psychology Review*, Vol. 18, No. 1, Spring.

3 Edmans, A. (2021) *Grow the Pie: How great companies deliver both purpose and profit*, Cambridge University Press.

4 Gulati, R. (2022) *The Heart and Soul of High-Performance Companies*, Penguin Business.

5 Polman, P. and Winston, A. (2021) *Net Positive: How courageous companies thrive by giving more than they take*, Harvard Business Review Press.

6. EY Beacon Institute and Harvard Business Review Analytic Services (2015) *The Business Case for Purpose*, https://assets.ey.com/content/dam/ey-sites/ey-com/en_gl/topics/digital/ey-the-business-case-for-purpose.pdf.

7. https://www.mckinsey.com/capabilities/people-and-organizational-performance/our-insights/the-great-attrition-is-making-hiring-harder-are-you-searching-the-right-talent-pools.

8. Ebert, C., Hurth, V. and Prabhu, J. (2018) *The What, the Why and the How of Purpose: A guide for leaders*, Chartered Management Institute and Blueprint for Better Business White Paper, https://www.managers.org.uk/~/media/Files/Reports/Guide-for-Leaders-White-Paper.pdf.

9. Pete Samson MAY 20, 2022, Brompton Bike CEO Shares His Vision For Cleaner, Happier Cities, Mr Feelgood.

10. https://www.hrzone.com/lead/strategy/systemic-dialogue-a-gateway-to-purpose-led-leadership.

11. https://www.youtube.com/watch?v=eGxMf88I5g4.

12. https://www.youtube.com/watch?v=2K_hMGIJG1w.

13. https://media.kiwibank.co.nz/media/documents/Kiwibank_sustainability_report_2022.pdf.

14. Ebert, C., Hurth, V. and Prabhu, P., (2018) *The What, the Why and the How of Purpose: A guide for leaders*, Chartered Management Institute and Blueprint for Better Business White Paper, https://www.managers.org.uk/~/media/Files/Reports/Guide-for-Leaders-White-Paper.pdf.

15. Polman, P. and Winston, A. (2021) *Net Positive: How courageous companies thrive by giving more than they take*, Harvard Business Review Press.

16. Gartenberg, C. Prat, A. and Serafeim, G. (2019) Corporate Purpose and Financial Performance, *Organization Science* 30, no. 1, pp. 1–18, Harvard Business School.

17. https://www.psychologytoday.com/us/blog/out-the-ooze/201707/what-is-the-right-size-group-conversation.

18 Cable, D. (2019) *Alive at Work: The neuroscience of helping your people love what they do*, Harvard Business Review Press.

19 Grant, A. M., Berg, J. M. and Cable, D. M. (2013) 'Job Titles as Identity Badges: How self-reflective titles can reduce emotional exhaustion', *Academy of Management Journal*, Vol. 57, No. 4.

20 https://www.mckinsey.com/capabilities/people-and-organizational-performance/our-insights/help-your-employees-find-purpose-or-watch-them-leave.

21 Isaacs (1999), Dialogue: The Art of Thinking together, Doubleday.

22 Craig, N. George, B. and Nook, S. (2015) *The Discover Your True North Fieldbook: A personal guide to finding your authentic leadership*, Wiley.

23 Garcia, H. and Miralles, F. (2017) *Ikigai: The Japanese secret to a long and happy Life*, Penguin Life.

Afterword

Whatever gnarly situation you're facing where a difficult conversation is called for, may you feel more confident, competent and courageous after reading this book. I trust that knowing about building a container and applying the four secrets enables you to unlock any block that's been in the way so you're able to talk and thrive.

This book itself very nearly didn't make it. When Eloise Cook, the editor at Pearson, first got in touch to say that she was 'mulling over' commissioning a book on difficult conversations, I said it wasn't for me. I'd already written extensively about dialogue, as noted in the introduction, and wondered what else I could say.

A few weeks later, I went on holiday to Cornwall to spend time with friends, walk the coastal path and step out of my hurried, busy days. It was March 2022 and as I pottered around the holiday cottage, the radio in the background gave updates from Ukraine about the Russian invasion. The loss of life on both sides, the distress of the people, the evacuation of the Ukrainians from their homes to Poland and beyond. What a devastating scene. Why for decades had Western leaders failed to talk properly with each other about Putin's Russia. There's so much we don't understand about how to talk with each other, particularly when there are crucial, far-reaching matters to discuss.

With a jolt, I suddenly realised that the time was ripe to share the knowledge, skills and tools I have acquired over the years working as a dialogue coach. With a complete change of mind and fire in my belly, I said Yes to the writing. In the words of Mahatma Gandhi, *'Be the change you wish to see in the world.'*

History is littered with the catastrophic consequences of failed dialogues. In the First World War, the disaster of the Nivelle offensive in 1917, which was part of the Battle of Arras, was partly due to difficulties in conversation. According to Sir Edward Spears (the chief liaison officer between the British and French armies), the French politicians and generals were reluctant to express their grave doubts about his plan to General Robert Nivelle, who was in command of the entire Allied force in France. The General's supreme confidence of success, and the subsequent lack of dialogue, led to a greater number of British causalities than on the Battle of the Somme.[1] Jeremy Clarke in *The Spectator* gives losses of 187,000 men for an attack that failed completely.[2] For the want of a nail . . . the battle is lost, as the old proverb goes (there have been numerous versions of this saying over several centuries, reminding us that seemingly unimportant acts or omissions can have grave and unforeseen consequences[3]).

Contrast that failure with Gorbachev's account of the turning point in the Cold War. The crucial moment came at the 1986 summit in Reykjavik with Reagan. This was the first time these two leaders were able to have a dialogue, where they shared their assumptions, values and aspirations. The understanding they built began, at that time, to turn around the nuclear arms race.[4]

Leaders really do need to keep talking to one another, even – or especially – when they're not on speaking terms to avoid conflict escalating into something more serious. Entering into and maintaining authentic dialogue isn't easy, but avoiding or botching it is much more costly. Even in everyday corporate life, recoiling from a colleague or leaving 'undiscussable' topics to fester in a team often just makes for a bigger mess for someone else to deal with.

We are at a *shock point* in humanity's history (to borrow a phrase from Gurdjieff[5]). Unless we harness our collective intelligence wisely, we risk destroying ourselves. The *polycrisis* – the interplay between multiple crises piling on top of one another – is leaving us feeling overwhelmed, unable to cope and unsure of the ground on which we stand. As Adam Tooze (the English historian who coined the term polycrisis) says, there's a real sense that the pressure will continue rising, not only for us, but for future generations. The complex, entangled problems we face – the climate emergency, accelerating weapons development, increasing political differences and migration issues – are much worse than they need to be because of failed political coordination. A house divided against itself cannot stand.[6]

We can't reverse the polycrisis quickly but we can learn how to discuss it. Sustained conversations, whether between experts in different domains, leaders in different countries or managers in different departments, are our best hope of living through these times of great change and challenge. One small thing we can each do is to put our own house in order. We can clear up the difficult conversations we need to have and hold an authentic dialogue instead. We then see this was actually a big step.

As Baraka Obama said,

> 'One voice can change a room, and if one voice can change a room, then it can change a city, and if it can change a city, it can change a state, and if it can change a state, it can change a nation, and if it can change a nation, it can change the world. Your voice can change the world.'[7]

And that is my wish for you, for us all, in agreeing to write this book.

Notes

1 Spears, E. L. (1939) *Prelude to Victory*, Cape.
2 Clarke, J. (2022) *The Spectator*, 15 October.
3 https://en.wikipedia.org/wiki/For_Want_of_a_Nail.

4. The Mind Gym (2006) *Give Me Time,* Time Warner Books.
5. https://gurdjiefflegacy.org/40articles/making_trilogy.htm.
6. https://think.ing.com/articles/were-in-a-polycrisis-and-this-is-what-it-means/#:~:text=The%20word%20of%20the%20moment,occurrence%20of%20several%20catastrophic%20events.
7. President Barack Obama, Remarks by the President at Rally on Health Insurance Reform, THE WHITE HOUSE September 12, 2009.

Index

'A New You' workshop 190

accidental managers 37
accountability, avoidance of 154
acting out 68
active listening 110, 111
alignment 214, 222–4
aliveness 214
allies 143
always and never 119–20
ambition 214
amygdala 69
Anderson, Bob 75, 200
 Spirit of Leadership, The 194
Angelo, Maya 124
anger 5, 35, 68
anxiety 46
Appeaser (moving towards) 75, 76, 77, 80, 82, 83, 138
Arcadia retail group 6
Argyris, Chris 93
artificial intelligence 4
atmosphere, quality of 46
attack 118

attentive listening 15
authentic dialogue 42
 definition 8–9
 getting to 38–40
 in teams 156
authentic leadership 7
authentic speaking 15
authenticity, importance of 7
automatic negative thoughts (ANTs) 96, 101
Avoider (moving away) 75, 76, 77, 78, 80, 82, 83, 138
Awareness, principle of 182, 200–2, 204, 206

B Lab 221
Ball, Jonathan 189
Bennis, Warren 198
biases 199–200
big wins 186
Bingley, Richard 196
Blackwell, Chris 230
Blatchford, Sir Ian 30
blob tree 161

Index

boardroom psychology 31
bodily sensations 90
body language 91
Bohm, David 13, 30, 193, 199
   'Dialogue – A Proposal' 29
   On Dialogue 38, 92, 173
Boston Consulting Group 218
Botton, Alain de 185
breaking the ice 160
breakthrough 125
bridge building 103–27
bridges of purpose 225
Brompton Cycles 217
Brown, Brené 153, 170
Brown, Byron: *Soul without Shame* 91
Burden, Pete 219
Butler-Adams, Will 218
'Bystand' 135, 137, 139, 142, 143, 148, 198

Cable, Dan: *Alive at Work* 228
Campbell, Alastair 15
change 144–7
   lead through dialogue 181–207
change maze 187
change resistance 201
chatbots 8
check-in process 155, 158, 159–61, 174, 177
check-out 176
Choice Support 220
Churchill, Winston 198
Clarke, Jeremy 240
Clarkson, Jeremy 132

Clayton, Mike: *Influence Agenda, The* 197
climate change 4
coach, leader as 201
Cocker, Jarvis 191
cognitive-behavioural approach 96
Coherence, principle of 182, 199–200, 204, 206
Cole, Mark and John Higgins: *Great Unheard at Work, The* 166
collaborative language 104, 118–20
collective leadership 6, 11
Collins, Jim: *From Good to Great* 117
command-and-control approach 6, 10, 11, 142, 196
commitment
   competing 201, 206
   lack of 154
competing commitment 201, 206
competitor 28
complying 138
concentration, lapses of 73
concussion 12
confidence for conducting dialogue 88
confidentiality 161
confirmation bias 199
conflict 35, 106
   fear of 34, 154
   in intimate relationships 108–9
   online 48
   reason for 107, 108–9
conflict resolution 37

conflicted meeting. 141
Confronter (moving against) 75, 76, 77, 78, 80, 82, 83, 138
conscious quitting 217
container 46, 49, 132, 177, 216
  building 59–60, 157–8
  creating 50–1
  critical for dialogue 51
  definition 52
containing relationship 52
contemporary leadership, definition 10
continuum line 164, 174
controllability bias 200
convenor, leader as 198
conversation
  questions that 'open up' 123
  difficult, beginning 99
  identifying most critical 188–9
conversation continuum 11–12, 14
conversational fields 157
conversational profile 137, 139–40
conversational turn-taking 162
Cook, Andy 190
corporate coaching culture 15
corporate culture, definition 15
corporate scandals 38
costs of meetings 32
courage 228–32
courteous compliance 131
Covey, Stephen 163
Covid-19 pandemic (2020) 4, 48, 183
CPP Inc 33

creative responses 78
creative self 66, 73–4
creativity 79–80
critical conversations grid 46, 185, 186, 187, 204
crucible moments 229
Culture Amp 33
culture of dialogue 15
customer complaints 33
cynicism 234

debate 12, 13
Deloitte 37
depression 68
developers 215
dialogic actions 148, 166, 198
Dialogos 49, 56
  Leadership for Collective Intelligence programme 170
dialogue
  definitions of 38
  vs discussion 13
dialogue of the deaf 15
difficult conversation, definition 24
difficult people 29, 42
  dealing with 27
discernment 91
discourse, change in 163–5
discussion 12, 13
distributed leadership 6
distrust 154
divorce 8
dominated meeting. 140, 141
Drucker, Peter 217
dual processing 133, 148

duplication of work 33
dynamic dialogue 13–14

eBay 196
Eden Project 189–91, 196, 198
Edmans, Alex: *Grow the Pie* 213
Edmonson, Amy 156
efforting 73
El Mago (American magician) 58
Eliot, George 21
Elizabeth I 198
emotional brain 70
emotional stability 212
empathising 104, 110, 114–16, 126
engagement of individuals 227–8
environment, safe 142
Environmental Social Governance 6
Estée Lauder 105
ethical compass 7
Etsy 218
exchange-traded fund (ETF) investors 37
executive functioning 92
expansive emotional space 62
expression 122–4
eye contact 37

Factor, Donald 29
fear 68
  of conflict 34, 154
feedback 143
feedback carousel process 29
fields, conversational 165–72
fight, flight or freeze reaction 70
finding your ground 89, 100

focus, redirecting 90
'Follow' 135, 137, 139, 142, 143, 144, 148, 198
Forming (group stage) 166
Forster, E.M.: 'Machine Stops, The' 16
Four Fields of conversation model (Scharmer) 166–72, 174, 177
  Field I – Politeness/(Shared) monologues 167, 174, 177
  Field II – Breakdown/ Controlled conversation 167–8, 174, 177
  Field III – Inquiry/Reflective dialogue 168, 174, 177
  Field IV – Flow/Generative dialogue 168, 174, 177
  threshold of presence 169–70, 177
  threshold of curiosity 170–1, 177
  threshold of emergence 171–2, 177
Four-Player model 134–7, 144
four principles of dialogue 193–5, 202–3, 206
freedom 162
Freire, Paulo 39
Frost, Robert 162
frustration among team members 33
Future Foundation 25

Gallwey, Timothy: *Inner Game of Tennis, The* 73, 138
Gandhi, Mahatma 240

Gap 33
Garrett, Peter 29, 56, 57
generative dialogue 13
generative image (Bushe) 172
Genovese, Michael A.: *Future of Leadership, The* 142
Gonzalez-Otero, Alberto 230
Google 196
Gorbachev, Mikhail 240
Gove, Michael 191
Great Resignation 217
Green, Miranda 34
Green, Sir Philip 6
Grint, Keith 10, 187, 188
ground rules, setting 161–3
group stages 166
groupthink 130, 132
Gulati, Ranjay: *Deep Purpose* 213
Gurdjieff 240

happiness 53
Harvard Negotiation Project 114
Harvard Study of Adult Development (HSAD) 53
Haslam, Alex 198, 199
Hawkins, Dr Peter 143
Heaphy, E. 55, 140
Heifetz, Ron 188
Hendrix, Harville 107, 109
  Getting the Love You Want 108
hidden loyalties 201, 206
Hill, Linda 197
  Collective Genius: The Art and Practice of Leading Innovation 196
Hiut Demin Co. 218
hive mind 168

holding environment 46, 47, 50
holding space 151–78
  critical 153–5
  definition 155–7
  see also container
Holmes, Oliver Wendell 234
Holt, Clare 10
honesty 62, 74, 122–3, 170, 172, 184, 198
hope 91
Horney, Karen 75
Horton, Simon: *Change Their Mind* 106
hostile debates 4
humility 39, 117
Hurth, Dr Victoria 217, 223
hybrid working 131

'I' statement 118, 126, 162
I'm-in-it-to-win-it approach 9
I'm-the-boss style of leadership 6
ice breaker 158
Ikigai 230
Imago dialogue 107, 109
immigration 4
impact 136
  speaking about 123
impulsive reactivity 16
inattention to results 154
inclusion 162
inflammatory words or phrases 120
information, gathering 98
in-group/out-group dynamics 132
inner dialogue, harnessing 89–92

Index

inner voice, harnessing 101
inquiry 162
inspiration 219–21
integrated performance report 203
intention 136
International Finance Corporation 171
interpersonal transparency 7
introspection 92
Isaacs, Bill 45, 49, 52, 56, 109, 117, 163, 170, 171, 187, 193, 229
  Dialogue and the Art of Thinking Together 38, 166

Janni, Nicholas: *Leader as Healer* 134
Jefferson, Thomas 176
Johnson, Boris 4
judge 28
judgement, unspoken voice of 91
Jung, Carl 230
Jurkovich, Steve 221
Just Do Its (JDIs) 186

Kantor, David 133, 134, 137
  Reading the Room 131
Katzenbach, John 145
Kegan 195, 201
Kiwibank 221
Klein: *Great Delusion Behind Twitter, The* 16
know-it-all 28
Kross, Ethan 92
  Chatter: The Voice in Our Head and How to Harness It 90

Ladkin, Donna 191, 200, 203
  Rethinking Leadership 190
laggards 215
Lahey 201
language 143
  body 91
  collaborative 104, 118–20
Laurie, Donald 188
Le Guin, Ursula K. 61
leader as catalyst 200
leader as coach 201
Leadership Circle 75, 77
leadership presence, cultivating 98
Left-Hand Column (LHC) exercise 93, 94
Lencioni, Patrick: *Five Dysfunctions of a Team, The* 34, 153
Lever, William Hesketh 219
life satisfaction 212
limbic system 69
LinkedIn 68
listening
  bridge-building and 106–9
  deepening 115–16
  deeper works 109–10
Losada, M. 55, 140
loyalties, hidden 201, 206

MAGIC tool 218–19
Maguire, Sarah 221
Mandela, Nelson 198
maps 144
Marcus Aurelius 77
Marr, Andrew 49
Masters, Robert Augustus 156

Mean, Margaret 225
meetings
  conflicted 141
  dominated 140, 141
  mired 140–1
  off-topic 140–1
  scheduling 98
  tangible costs of 32
Mindell, Arnold 165
mirroring 104, 110, 111–13, 116, 126
mission 217
monologue 10–12
  serial 4, 13
Mostyn, Steve 232
Mourinho, José 198
Mourning (group stage) 166
'Move' 135, 137, 139, 142, 143, 148, 198
moving against see Confronter
moving away see Avoider
moving towards see Appeaser
Musk, Elon 16
Myers-Briggs Assessment 33

NEDs 204
needs, exploration of 123
Neenan, Michael and Windy Dryden: *Life Coaching: A Cognitive-Behavioural Approach* 96
neighbours, good 163
Nejatian, Kaz 132
nervousness 73
Nestlé: Beneath the Surface campaign 6
Netflix 34

Nivelle, General Robert 240
no-holds-barred approach 89
non-verbal communication 37
Norming (group stage) 166
Norton, Richie 65

Obama, Barak 241
objectivity 91
observations, sharing 122
obstacles to conversation
  Obstacle 1: 'I don't have time' 25–6
  Obstacle 2: 'difficult people 27–9
  Obstacle 3: 'Nothing will change anyway' 29–30
  Obstacle 4: 'It's just too tricky' 30–2
  Obstacle 5: 'I'd rather not have *that* conversation' 33–4
  Obstacle 6: 'Better not rock the boat' 34–5
off topic meeting 140–1
online conflict 48
open questions 174
opening, finding 97–100
opening lines 98
openness 62
opportunity cost 32
'Oppose' 135, 137, 139, 142, 143, 148, 198
optimism 212
organisational purpose 215–16, 223
outcome 121–2
overconfidence bias 200

249

pains in the neck 186
Palmer, Parker 9
Pan Am 220
Pantalon, Dr 164
Participation, principle of 182, 197–9, 204, 206
Peck, Scott model of community evolution (Pseudo Community, Chaos, Emptying/Discovery and Community) 166
percussion 12
performance enhancing thoughts (PETs) 96, 101
Performing (group stage) 166
permacrisis 30, 42
physicality 144
Picasso, Pablo 209
Pixar 196
polarisation 42
policies, checking 98
politeness 9
Polman, Paul 220 (and Andrew Winston): *Net Positive* 213, 223
polycrisis 241
poor performance, tackling 33
possibility 91
Potential, principle of 182, 195–7, 205, 206
Power, Nina 49
prefrontal cortex 69
pressure to conform 132
Preston, Laura 8
Prioritisers 215
process work 165

psychological safety 177
psychology of leadership 198
public speaking 37
purpose 209–36
  Articulating and amplifying purpose 213
Purpose Collective 230, 231
purpose conversation 212
purpose hierarchy gap 228
purpose-led collaborative team 225
purpose pillars 234
purpose statements 218
purpose wash 234
Putin, Vladimir 239
PwC 37

quick wins 186
quietening self 76–7

radical candour 34
rage 68
ranting (to yourself) 90
reactive patterns 66
reactive self 66, 73–4
reactive tendencies 73, 75–6, 81, 82, 138, 148
reactivity 79–81
reading the room 148
Reagan, Ronald 240
Reflective dialogue 13
repertoire, expanding 141–4
request, making 124
resistance to change 195
respect 62
Rest is Politics, The (podcast) 15

Right Conversation, The 32
Rittell and Webber 187
robust vulnerability 169
Rock, David 69
Rogers, Carl 28, 38
role model 143
Roosevelt, Eleanor 195
Rosenberg, Marshall B. 123
   Nonviolent Communication 118, 122, 124
Roslansky, Ryan 68
Rothbard, Nancy 181
Rozenthuler, Sarah
   How to Have Meaningful Conversations 97
   Powered by Purpose 11, 98, 166, 213, 214, 216, 218, 229

sadness 68
Sanfacon, George 9
SCARF (Status, Certainty, Autonomy, Relatedness, Fairness) framework 69, 82, 88
Scharmer, Otto 17, 166
   Four Fields of conversation model 166–72, 174, 177
Schulz, Marc 55
self-absorption 92
self-awareness 7, 148
self-condemnation 73
self-defeating thoughts 89, 96–7
self-doubt 73
self-esteem 212
self-expression 122–4
self-reflection 92

self-talk, negative and positive 97
Senge, Peter 93
Shakespeare, William 116
shared leadership 6
Sheffield Chainsaw massacre 191–3
Sheffield Tree Activist Group (Stag) 191
SHL 25
silence 166
   as response to conflict 35
Sinek, Simon 151
single fixed leader work group 225
Situational Leadership 10
six-pointer 5
Smit, Tim 189
Smith, Douglas 145
social architects 197
social fitness 55
social media 16, 48
   see also X (Twitter)
Southwest Airlines 220
Spears, Sir Edward 240
speech acts 148
spiritual bypass 216
spontaneity 162
Springborg, Dr Claus 25, 137
Standard Chartered Bank 218
standard operating procedure (SOP) 161
Stewart, Rory 15
   Long History of Argument, A 48
Stokoe, Elizabeth 124
Stone, Douglas 114
   Difficult Conversations 114

Storming (group stage) 166
structural dynamics 134
stuckness 42
style-flex 142
Sunak, Rishi 48
superego 90–1
suspension of inner dialogue 92–3
Sutton, Robert 33
synchro moments 230
synchronicity 230
systemic awareness 148

taking stock 35–8
tame problems 187
Taylor, David: *Naked Leader, The* 164
Teal, Alison 193
Team Dialogue Indicator 32
team dysfunctions 153–4
team intervention 147
team purpose 225–6
thinking brain 70
Thomas, Dylan 89
Thomas-Kilmann Conflict Mode Instrument 33
Thoreau, Henry David: *Waldo* 233
time 214–15
   to talk 25–6
   wasted correcting mistakes 33
timeline exercise 205
tolerance for difference 7
tolerance for uncertainty 7
Tooze, Adam 241
Topshop 6
trans issues 4
transformation in action 61

transformation programmes 6
transmission moments 229
trigger culture 49
triggers 68–70
troublemaker 28
trust 163
   building 153
   lack of 34, 154
   in self 2 77–80
trust equation 163
truth-telling 7
Tuckman 166
TWA 220
Twain, Mark 87

uncomfortable moments 162
unconditional positive regard 28, 38
understanding 91
undivided attention 9
Unilever 219, 220, 223, 232
unresolved issues 33

Vaillant, George E.: *Triumphs of Experience* 54
validating 104, 110–114-16, 126
vanity 92
Veenman, Dik 32
vision 217
VitalSmarts 33
voice, tone of 62
voicing 116–17, 126
   feelings 122
   finding your flow 120–1
   using collaborative language 118–20

VUCA (volatile, uncertain, complex and ambiguous) 5
VW emissions cheating 38

Waldinger, Robert 54
  Good Life, The 55
Wallis and Burton 6
Walsch, Neale Donald 73, 114, 129
Ware, Bronnie: *Top Five Regrets of the Dying, The* 231
warm surround 53–4
Webber, Alan 3
Wheatley, Margaret 103

White, Dr Andrew 185
Whyte, David 169
wicked problems 187
Winfrey, Oprah 107
Woodland Trust 196
World Bank 171

X (Twitter) 16, 48, 49

Yeats, William Butler 96
'you' statements 126

Zeldin, Theodore 39